The politics of war reporting

MANCHESTER
1824

Manchester University Press

The politics of war reporting

Authority, authenticity and morality

Tim Markham

Manchester University Press

Manchester and New York

Distributed in the United States exclusively
by Palgrave Macmillan

Published by Manchester University Press
Oxford Road, Manchester M13 9NR, UK
and Room 400, 175 Fifth Avenue, New York, NY 10010, USA
www.manchesteruniversitypress.co.uk

Distributed in the United States exclusively by
Palgrave Macmillan, 175 Fifth Avenue, New York,
NY 10010, USA

Distributed in Canada exclusively by
UBC Press, University of British Columbia, 2029 West Mall,
Vancouver, BC, Canada V6T 1Z2

British Library Cataloguing-in-Publication Data
A catalogue record for this book is available from the British Library

Library of Congress Cataloging-in-Publication Data applied for

ISBN   978 0 7190 8528 4 hardback

First published 2011

The publisher has no responsibility for the persistence or accuracy of URLs for any external or third-party internet websites referred to in this book, and does not guarantee that any content on such websites is, or will remain, accurate or appropriate.

Typeset in ITC Charter and ITC Franklin Gothic
by Action Publishing Technology Ltd, Gloucester
Printed in Great Britain
by CPI Group (UK) Ltd, Croydon, CR0 4YY

Contents

1. Introduction: why use political phenomenology to analyse war reporting?   *page* 1
2. Theoretical preliminaries   24
3. Methodological issues   54
4. Practical mastery of authority, authenticity and disposition   74
5. Journalistic ethics and moral authority: being right, knowing better   94
6. How do audiences live journalism?   115
7. New developments in the field: brave new world or plus ça change?   134
8. Conclusion: implications for war reporting, journalism studies and political phenomenology   152

Appendix: interviewee profiles   182
Bibliography   184
Index   211

1

Introduction: why use political phenomenology to analyse war reporting?

that abominable, voluptuous act called 'reading the paper', whereby all the misfortunes and cataclysms suffered by the universe in the last twenty-four hours – battles which have cost the lives of fifty thousand men, murders, strikes, bankruptcies, fires, poisonings, suicides, divorces, the cruel emotions of statesman and actor, transmuted into a morning feast for our personal entertainment, make an excellent and particularly bracing accompaniment to a few mouthfuls of café au lait. (Proust, [1919] 1970: 200, cited in Bourdieu, 1984: 21)

Why is war reporting important and how should it be analysed? The obvious answer to the first question is that it is naturally significant in that it addresses itself to human suffering and conflict. This book, however, while in no way seeking to relativise or understate suffering, starts from the premise that instead of seeing its representation in deontological terms – that is, as something which makes sense in and of itself – we should unpack it in terms of its contexts, its contingencies and its effects. There are three broad approaches to this unpacking. First, it could be argued that there is nothing special about suffering and conflict that makes its media representation significant. Instead, these should be seen as subsets of the representation of humanity generally, which, after the work of Roger Silverstone (2007), is morally implicated insofar as it is obliged to commit to particular conceptions of relations between media subjects and their often distant others. This view rests on the proposition that morality is itself a natural object of analysis, and without being fatuous it bears emphasising that morality too can be unpacked in terms of its contexts, contingencies and effects. Second, it is arguable that conflict and suffering have significance in the contexts of particular cultures, that they emerge as meaningful objects in relation to the specific discourses by which we make sense of the world. This is not to resort to cultural relativism (Norris, 1992; Baudrillard, 1995; Wilcken,

1995) or suggest that there are contexts in which suffering is meaningless, but rather that the way journalists and their audiences care
about it is contingent upon particular ideas about power, aggression,
victimhood, human rights and so on which are sufficiently universalised in our everyday lives to appear natural but which are in fact
bounded by time and place.

Third, it is possible that the content of war reporting is not as
important as its function, either within the field in terms of relations
between journalists and news organisations, in terms of the relations
between journalism and other professions and spaces of cultural
production, or in terms of the way that audiences make use of their
media consumption (and increasingly production) in their relations
with colleagues, family and friends. What does this mean? With
regard to explaining the abilities of an individual journalist, it means
seeing authority not as innate but as relational. It means identifying
the practices which that journalist has mastered in order to be recognised (and to see herself) as authoritative, open to the possibility that
these practices may not emerge directly out of the 'stuff' of journalism
– the multifarious demands of doing journalistic work. If there is a
cultural romanticisation of the war correspondent as heroic and
ruggedly individualistic, we can see this not simply as the product of
doing a dangerous and difficult job well, but also as marking out a
particular position of power. Power too is relational rather than
something one simply has, and while it of course takes myriad forms
in the context of cultural production it is primarily a matter of status
relative to other cultural producers and in public life more generally,
and influence over the same (Lukes, 1973). Whether considering the
position of individual stars of war reporting or established myths of
the genre, there are political implications in that the contingent and
often misrecognised criteria by which these symbolic forms are established within the field and in the public imagination reproduce
structures of gatekeeping and hierarchy – making it a more natural or
unthinkable thing to embark on a career in journalism, depending on
one's social position, and to advance to a position of power once
inside. A pre-emptive disclaimer needs to be made that this is not
about reducing good war reporting to self-interest. Nor is it to call for
a radical opening up or democratisation of the field: indeed, it will be
seen that conflict journalism benefits greatly from its being a subfield
of relatively restricted production. But by detailing how categories
such as authority and communicative authenticity are not natural but
conditional on various structures and practices, some explicit and
others obscured, it becomes possible to discern trends in media and

culture more widely. In particular, it points to two parallel shifts: from the institution to the individual as the functional unit of authority, and from professional expertise to the authenticity of personal experience as the dominant form of that authority.

Living journalism

The phenomenological premise of this book is that conscious experience of the world is not pre-given but determined by the multiple contexts in which we are situated – material, economic, historical, social, cultural and mediated. None of these can be considered as discrete, nor should they be thought of topographically in layers: they are overlapping, mutually constitutive and sometimes in conflict. This does not mean that consciousness is false, nor that this book claims to know journalists better than they know themselves. However, the power relations of the journalistic field – what will be described in Bourdieusian terms as the 'structuredness' and 'structuringness' of cultures of journalistic practice – are embedded in everyday life. They in part determine and are entrenched and obscured by that which is experienced as common sense, instinct, nature and the sense of corporeality (the experience of living as a body in the physical world) and temporality (how time is experienced, particularly in terms of routines but also in the case of war reporting in terms of 'passing' and 'killing' time). So while conflict journalism is in many ways extraordinary and unpredictable, this research looks at the processes by which some things become normalised, such as the dominance of specific valorised qualities – symbolic capital, as it will be characterised[1] – and the practices by which they come to be embodied. It will be seen that these processes matter because they reproduce relations of power which have no teleological solidity or natural defensibility.

To be sure, there are hurdles to overcome in this approach. One is primarily methodological: a commitment to finding meaning in what is to interviewees the unremarkable and the obvious – that which is in specific contexts simply too insignificant to emerge to consciousness. Another is reflexivity: while both Bourdieusian and Foucauldian perspectives emphasise the implicatedness of processes of subjectification in unacknowledged and unacknowledgeable regimes of power, the interview data frequently throw up instances of acute insight and self-awareness. Both of these are superable through a combination of methodological pragmatism and a normative injunction on the limits of inquiry: simply put, there is a point beyond which to look for power structures and effects is counter-productive. But this book takes its cue from Husserl that the experience of the quotidian is determined and conditional, and from Merleau-Ponty, Goffman and Bourdieu that determination and conditionality are implicated in social structures and associated power relations (Bourdieu, 1977: 94; Schmidt, 1985: 86–9, 166; Crossley, 1994; Marcoulatos, 2001; Jenkins, 2008).[2] This does not equate to the claim (e.g. Baudrillard, 1995; Clark, 2005) that professional cultural producers inhabit a symbolic world which is entirely arbitrary and disconnected from another, more real, world. And yet there are a series of established commonplaces which underpin the experience of war reporting but whose unremarkable universality can be unsettled. Why is the world seen as facts to be gathered? Why are these facts encountered as things to be wrestled with and tamed? Why do conflict and suffering have more symbolic value than other aspects of the human condition? Why does inhabiting one of a limited range of dispositions, encompassing not only journalistic skills but character traits, equip one to be a 'natural' war reporter? By unpicking the symbolic economies in which these questions have decontested, obvious answers, it becomes possible to ask how different war reporting and journalism more broadly could be, rather than seeing the contemporary journalistic field as the product of either ongoing organic refinement or inevitable, immovable structures of power – and this is the meaning of the politics in this book's title. War reporting is traditionally conceived in terms of information retrieval and processing structured according to wider cultural values such as bearing witness, giving voice and holding power to account. Beyond these mechanical descriptions and characterisations of journalism's role in society, there are many ways to define what war reporting is: a profession, an economic enterprise, an institution, a culture, an ideological mechanism, a discourse, a deliberative space and so on. While all these are valid, this book aims to contribute to our understanding of journalism by focusing on how relations between reporters and the world they inhabit is ordered, and what it can tell us about the political aspect of our specific orientations towards information, authority, authenticity and professionalism in mediated culture more broadly.

Audiences of war reporting

While the overarching focus of this work is on professional journalists and others active in the field of war, audiences are not conceived as passive receivers of news but as social actors who have an active interest (or several interests) in consuming news about conflict.[3]

Likewise, while debates over ethics often regard audiences as innocents who need to be protected from both the visceral excesses of war and the unchecked behaviour of war correspondents, here journalists and audiences alike are seen as having a strategic interest in ethics. This does not cast news consumers as agents free to derive any meaning whatsoever they choose from news, or to use it as an unfettered resource in any aspect of their lives. But it does ask what cultures of practice news consumption is articulated with: that is, what audiences do with news (Schrøder and Phillips, 2007; Höijer, 2008). In particular this means looking at how audience consumption of war reporting contributes to two related sets of practice: subjectification and social positioning.

Recent developments in the field

It has been widely observed that the boundaries between media consumption and production, and between professional and non-professional journalism, are dissolving, and this is true in war reporting as for other specialisations. These trends are part of a larger debate about professionalism, democratisation and technology, but this book will focus in particular on how shifts in cultures of media production impact upon authority and authenticity, particularly in relation to the traditional individualisation of authority in war reporting relative to other fields, and the enduring value accorded to first-person witnessing, whether by war reporters or local non-professional eyes. Technology is a recurring theme, and illustrates above all else that war reporting, like war and like journalism, should not be thought of as static. That said, the research behind this book makes clear that technological development does not simply produce new cultures of journalistic practice. Indeed, it will be seen that the way war correspondents have adopted or reacted to technological innovations is determined less by the technology itself than by historic structures which are proving more durable than is often thought. For now, however, let us turn to the thinker whose work provides the theoretical backbone of this study.

Who is Bourdieu?

Pierre Bourdieu's corpus of work is strongly interdisciplinary, combining qualitative and quantitative research methodology with a theoretical framework that draws on sociology, anthropology, philosophy, political science and the history of ideas. This means that there are in effect many Bourdieus. But while there is considerable variation in his writing, perhaps to the point of inconsistency, it is possible to characterise the basic ethos of his work as an attempt to expose and explain the naturalised, everyday instantiation of the generative power structures which constitute the conditions of possibility of the experience of the world. Bourdieu rejects certain elements of the philosophical frameworks of Husserl, Schutz, Merleau-Ponty and Mauss, and indeed explicitly positions himself in opposition to them in certain regards (Bourdieu, 1977: 3),[4] but his emphasis on describing how phenomena come to be experienced as objects in the world means that he can be located in the phenomenological tradition. It will be seen in chapter 2 that there are divergences over the status of intention and reflexivity, but these approaches have in common the premise that the determinants of consciousness and everyday practices are mutually constitutive. In focusing on the preconditions of consciousness and the positing of conscious meaning by consciousness, Bourdieu is concerned in much of his work with that which is taken for granted, so naturalised as not to emerge to consciousness in normal situations – that is, without the epistemological 'double break' (Bourdieu, 1977: 3) central to Bourdieu's philosophy of social science.

Thus, like Husserl (1931; 1982), Goffman ([1959] 1971; 1972) and Berger and Luckmann (1966), Bourdieu's work aims analytically to reconstruct the determination of things like common sense, instinct and normalcy. This is a process in which all agents are engaged: there is a collectively embodied common sense or habitus by which individuals become self-aware and construct 'objective' realities. It is in this sense that the lifeworld[5] is not simply the context by which we make sense of the world; the lifeworld is itself actively constituted by collective subjective anticipation, interpretation, intention and action. In linguistics this is close to Austin's view of language as something which is spontaneously enacted as the situation demands, rather than carried with us as a continuous, solid interpretative matrix. This mutual constitution suggests a closed system of meaning production, but it is important at the outset to distinguish Bourdieu from traditional phenomenology which treats the lifeworld as self-contained and 'brackets out' what it sees as the irresolvable, chicken-and-egg question of the origin of consciousness. Bourdieu's genetic structures (Frère, 2004) and (to a lesser extent) Husserl's formal or 'eidetic' terms both aim to describe that space outside of or prior to meaning: that is, the metalevel at which categories easily regarded as universal or natural (such as meaning, explanation and subjectivity) are only a finite case of a wider set of possibilities. In reality we can always invoke outsides or origins which elude detection or logical reasoning, and limits to philosophical and empirical enquiry have to be set somewhere. For Bourdieu, this is the point beyond which the normative impetus of his work – showing how the experience of historical contingencies as universal and natural reproduces political inequity – is compromised.

What else is Bourdieu? Key concepts

Because Bourdieu is best known for work that dissects how the differentiated symbolic worlds of culture and education reproduce material differentiation between classes, he is often referred to as a Marxist or neo-Marxist (e.g. Eder, 1993: 63–4) in the mould of Weber's account of status, Althusser's model of ideological state apparatuses, Williams' reworking of base and superstructure or Adorno and Horkheimer's work on cultural production. There are similarities to be sure, but Bourdieu's focus on the structuring of practices at the microscopic level and his insistence that such structures are 'genetic' and actively brought into existence through these practices means that his conception of power is less monolithic than that of the Frankfurt School (Bourdieu, 1991a; Neveu, 2005). In interviews (Eagleton and Bourdieu, 1992) Bourdieu was either ambivalent or elusive when asked if he identified himself as a Marxist, though this is likely to have been a conscious strategy for avoiding the acrimonious tribalism of the left in France after 1968. If Bourdieu is a Marxist, it is because he takes as his philosophical starting point Marx's inversion of the relation of subject and object developed by Hegel in *The Phenomenology of Spirit*. Bourdieu criticises central structuralist theorist Ferdinand de Saussure for treating language as an autonomous object, separating internal and external linguistics (Bourdieu, 1991b: 107–15); for Bourdieu, language cannot be separated from its social situatedness and uses. However, insofar as Bourdieu develops Saussure's characterisation of the relation between linguistic and symbolic signifiers and signifieds as quasi-arbitrary,[6] it is fair to locate Bourdieu in the structuralist tradition – or, as will be seen in chapter 2, as one of several theorists who have sought to reconcile structuralism and phenomenology.[7] This draws on Cassirer's relationalism, moving from Saussure's assertion that words only make sense in relation to the whole set of concepts (what Foucault later called discourse) with which they are associated, rather than the object itself, to the characterisation of the entire symbolic worlds which effectively complete our subjective experience as similarly relational. As well as the phenomenological account of how structured logics or norms are embodied, Bourdieu is influenced by Bachelard's rationalism which emphasises that as professionals we spontaneously enact schemes of reasoning in everyday practice in ways which are quite different from how we might consciously reflect on how we make decisions and take actions. This in turn highlights Bourdieu's proximity to Wittgenstein's rule-following model (Bouveresse, 1999; Frère, 2004),[8] specifically as regards Bourdieu's conception of action as practically (rather than consciously) oriented by anticipation of likely outcomes.

The use of the term 'structure' in this book also warrants clarification. It does not refer to the material structure of Marxist theory, a set of power relations existing in the world which determine cultural forms and consciousness in a predictable or at least patterned fashion. We have seen that the generative structures which orient practice do not have a stable existence which precedes their enactment in practice. Their durability is a matter of hysteresis, of regularity occasioned by repeated, historical enactment. Hysteresis is the 'lag' which means that practices are structured not only by a situation as it presents itself, but by previously internalised anticipatory structures. Bourdieu summarises its broader significance of hysteresis thus:

> The hysteresis of habitus, which is inherent in the social conditions of the reproduction of the structures in habitus, is doubtless one of the foundations of the structural lag between opportunities and the dispositions to grasp them which is the cause of missed opportunities and, in particular, of the frequently observed incapacity to think historical crises in categories of perception and thought other than those of the past. (Bourdieu, 1977: 83)

Structures are above all methodological constructs, and it is the generative *logics*, determining the conditions of possibility of structural production, which are at the heuristic centre of Bourdieusian political thought. These logics are not just experienced but actively lived, through their shaping of increasingly naturalised dispositions to perceive and act. Habitus describes the set of dispositions,[9] both durable and adaptable, manifesting a particular case of possible dispositions emerging from generative power structures, and enacted in behaviour which is generally oriented towards the conservative reproduction of existing hierarchies and exclusions (Bourdieu, 1977: 72).[10] Habitus is not static, and over time will structure and be structured by practices which are aligned to varying degrees to the symbolic economies of the field in which it subsists. A 'perfect fit'

(Bourdieu, 1977: 166) indicates a set of perceptual practices ideally oriented towards the quasi-arbitrary 'rules' of a field: it means that we experience the motivation of our behaviour as being not an imperative to act correctly or appropriately, but simply that it seems the natural thing to do. Habitus is collective,[11] and the context in which it operates is never neutral: this is the Bourdieusian field, defined as a structured space of social positions in which the positions and their interrelations are determined by the distribution of different types of capital. This means that it is the positions individuals occupy rather than the individuals themselves which are important, an idea which has its roots in Durkheim's principle of nonconsciousness.[12]

That field positions are collectively misrecognised as character derives from Weber's model of symbolic economy, which rejects both the Marxist notion of specialised production and the structuralists' emphasis on texts.[13] In *Economy and Society*, Weber targets the producers of religious messages, the interests which motivate them and the strategies they deploy in pursuit of these interests (Bourdieu, 1998a: 57). Bourdieu extends the Weberian model by asserting that in order to apprehend the 'function, structure and genesis' (Bourdieu, 1994a: 16) of symbolic systems, one must apply (non-Weberian) structuralist analysis not only to the symbolic system and its various stances, but also to the agents who act as producers of symbolic goods or, rather, the positions they occupy. This is not to suggest that Bourdieu defends the psychoanalytic model of the repression of a truth by some part of an actor's psyche: this would imply an intentionality of consciousness at odds with Bourdieusian phenomenology (Bourdieu, 1998a: 97). Rather, by relying on the concept of acquired dispositions, the sociologist is able to interpret an action as oriented towards an objective without asserting that the objective was a conscious design. 'Strategy' is used in this book in a strictly Bourdieusian sense which has little to do with conscious calculation:

> The language of strategy, which one is forced to use in order to designate the sequences of actions objectively oriented towards an end that are observed in all fields, must not mislead us: the most effective strategies are those which, being the product of dispositions shaped by the immanent necessity of the field, tend to adjust themselves spontaneously to that necessity, without express intention or calculation. In other words, the agent is never completely the subject of his practices. (Bourdieu, 2000: 10).[14]

While it is often necessary to proceed as if conscious design were at work, it is the 'feel for the game' (Bourdieu, 1990a: 66–8), the capacity for spontaneous reaction without intention or reflection, which is salient. It is important to maintain the distinction between asserting that strategies for action in the long term and response mechanisms in the short are unconscious, and setting the exposure of these unconscious drives as a methodological goal. For Bourdieu, it is impossible to uncover what an agent is 'really' saying since the dialectical relation between the expressive drive and the structural constraints of the field 'prevents us from distinguishing in the opus operatum the form from the content' (Bourdieu, 1991b: 139). In short, the content of what is said or done in a field cannot be distinguished from the manner of saying it or, within the field, of hearing it. Thus, the key difference between Weber and Bourdieu here is that while the former believed that the recognition of legitimacy is a free individual act, for the latter it is always embedded in the pre-reflexive concurrence of cognitive structures and (unconscious) embodied structures (Bourdieu, 1993a: 38; 1998a: 56). Further, Bourdieu politicises Weber's symbolic economies as instruments of domination,[15] and it is through the phenomenal experience of fields as ahistorical and apolitical that dominatory power relations are sustained (Haugaard, 2008).[16]

Where does Bourdieu stand politically?

A glance at the political commentaries collected in *Acts of Resistance*, *Free Exchange* and *Political Interventions* gives a good indication of the sorts of phenomena Bourdieu opposed in contemporary Western society: neoliberalist capitalism, the exploitation of workers, the access of elites to tools of symbolic domination and the marginalisation of the disenfranchised.[17] Beneath these lie a worldview which is articulated fairly consistently across his written works, at the heart of which is the belief that life is primarily, inescapably, political. This means that all social spaces[18] are characterised first and foremost by struggle:

> When we speak of a *field* of position-takings, we are insisting that what can be constituted as a *system* for the sake of analysis is not the product of a coherence-seeking intention or an objective consensus (even if it presupposes unconscious agreement on common principles), but the product and prize of a permanent conflict; or, to put it another way, that the generative, unifying principle of this 'system' is the struggle, with all of the contradictions it engenders. (Bourdieu, 1993a: 34)

Bourdieu's principal concern is the unequal resources available to different groups in this struggle; the odds are stacked against those in a dominated position because society's dominant classes not only have the multifarious forms of symbolic capital at their disposal, but are also able to control what counts as dominant principles of differentiation. This is best illustrated by Bourdieu's contention in *Distinction*, echoing Durkheim, that if a member of the working class were to find himself suddenly wealthy, his lack of other forms of cultural and social capital – tastes, habits, manner of speaking – would prevent him from taking a place amongst the elite. Further, those who are dominated are complicit in their own domination: since their habitus are shared by members of a group – class habitus, in Bourdieu's words – to act in a manner which inflicts symbolic violence on themselves appears unproblematic.[19] Bourdieu's political philosophy will be set out in greater detail in subsequent chapters. For present purposes, however, let us turn to Bourdieu's stated views on journalism which, it will be seen, are not entirely concomitant with what we might distinguish as *Bourdieusian* theory.

Bourdieu on journalism

> 'Conforama is the Guy Lux of furniture,' says *Le Nouvel Observateur*, which will never tell you that the *Nouvel Obs* is the Club Méditerranée of culture. There is terrorism in all such remarks, flashes of self-interested lucidity sparked off by class hatred or contempt. (Bourdieu, 1984: 511)

Given that Bourdieu vocally decried the negative impact of the media on society, it is notable that he did not undertake systematic empirical research into the media as fields, logics or capital during his long career (Marlière, 2000: 199). *On Television and Journalism* (1998b) remains his most famous contribution to journalism studies, though he also published a limited amount through the research centre he headed at the Centre de Sociologie Européene and others working under him focused directly on this area. A lecture published in a posthumous edited collection (Bourdieu, 2005) sets out an interesting heuristic model for understanding the representation of politics in the media – in brief, he suggests that rather than thinking of political interviews as interactions between individuals, we should see them as encounters between positions in the political, journalistic and academic fields, and like all field interactions they entail a struggle between forces aiming to preserve or overthrow the status quo. Bourdieu also wrote newspaper and magazine articles on declining standards in journalism, detailing for instance how *Libération* succumbed to neoliberalist orthodoxy within 20 years of its founding (1994b). But this hardly amounts to a Bourdieusian approach to journalism or media studies. What explains this lacuna? It is certainly not that the field/habitus model is not adaptable to media contexts: Bourdieu makes it clear that his theoretical model and methodology are applicable to any symbolic system,[20] and scholars such as Couldry (2003a) have investigated precisely how the 'media field' may be constituted. It could be simply biographical, in that Bourdieu's interest in the media as an analytical object only crystallised in the final decade of his life. But while there are compelling arguments that Bourdieu's concepts are not applicable to fields of representation, this book takes the view that the world that media professionals inhabit, so long as it can be demonstrated to have a coherent nomos or internal logic, is comprehensible through the same conceptual lens as the fields of academia, education, religion and so on. This means seeing journalists not as discrete individuals but as position-takings (Bourdieu, 1993a: 30) in a competitive arena, the stakes of which they embody but of which they are not necessarily fully aware.[21] It also means that we can see both individual media personalities and institutions such as *Nouvel Obs* as situated configurations of symbolic capital whose constitution, recognition and concretisation all have real power effects. Before we turn to the possibilities of a Bourdieusian analysis of the journalistic field, however, let us look first to Bourdieu's own words on the subject.

Bourdieu on television

On Television and Journalism (1998b) was conceived as an intervention, delivered in two lectures on French national television in 1996 – thanks, Bourdieu concedes, to his own cultural capital as chair of the Collège de France and political experience as special adviser on culture to François Mitterrand. It is thus unsurprising that it takes the form of a political pamphlet, deploying a range of rhetorical devices to deliver its message in a deliberately polemical fashion (Neveu, 2005). This is perhaps the clearest example of what Bourdieu described as sociology's uses as a combat sport (Carles, 2001), with its emancipatory message of 'universalising the conditions of access to the universal' (Bourdieu, 1998b: 1), while simultaneously defending restricted production. The principal thesis of *On Television* is that the Western European journalistic field, that of the broadcast media particularly but also of the press, produces and imposes on the public a specific vision of the political field, one that is grounded in the structures of the journalistic field and the interests endemic to it. The depiction is not innovative (e.g. Debray and Macey, 1981). Bourdieu speaks of the increasing focus on political personalities and star journalists, the preference for sensation over rigorous argument, the promotion of conflict, cynicism, the tendency to conform to competitors' news output, and the obsession with scoops and the collective amnesia this brings (Bourdieu, 1998b: 6).[22] Time and space constraints result in issues being presented with reference to simplistic binaries (right/wrong, citizen/foreigner, business/unions) which are not only misleading (Sparks, 2000) but tend to conceal more complex and often more powerful hierarchies. Life is presented in the news as a series of 'disconnected flashes' with neither antecedents nor consequences; news is thus at once dehistoricised and dehistoricising, fragmented and fragmenting (Bourdieu, 1998b: 7). Bourdieu surmises that 'the journalistic field represents the world in terms of a philosophy that sees history as an absurd series of disasters which can be neither understood nor influenced', fostering disenchantment, disengagement and fatalism (Bourdieu, 1998b: 8).

If Bourdieu's political stance on the news media is not groundbreaking, his neo-Marxist account of the power relations which constitute the field is similarly fairly conventional. The journalistic field is increasingly subject to market forces. This subjection effects a powerful, often impalpable form of censorship (Bourdieu, 1991b: 19–22) by way of job insecurity (Accardo, 1998; cf. Gill and Pratt, 2008),[23] with increasing concentration of ownership the journalist does not have a large pool of potential employers, a loss of independence in more 'managerially' run media organisations (editors are more and more likely to interfere in journalists' work, a trend confirmed by four interviewees), and the ever-present time restrictions on journalistic practice.[24] While Bourdieu stresses the complicity of working journalists in these professional compromises, his framing of self-regulation in terms of 'symbolic violence' is not obviously different from theories of self-censorship which have been voiced for decades (e.g. Herman and Chomsky, 1988; Philo and McLaughlin, 1993). The most significant divergence is Bourdieu's insistence on the unconsciousness (or pre-reflexiveness) of actors' complicity (Bourdieu and Wacquant, 1992: 167). Systematic misrecognition instituted through the specific logics of practice of the field means that neither the victims nor beneficiaries of symbolic violence are cognisant even of a symbolic economy,[25] let alone their dominated or dominating position within it.[26] The obvious rejoinder is that agents are only too aware of the institutionalisation of exploitation, in line with Michael Mann's and E. P. Thompson's critiques of neo-Marxist class theory which argue that the working classes are fully conscious of their dominated-ness and that to speak of misrecognition is both misguided and patronising (Garnham and Williams, 1980; Garnham, 1993; Wacquant, 2000: 110–12).[27] In *On Television*, however, Bourdieu remains very much the determinist. He suggests that while journalists (and indeed any social actor, dominated or dominating) may be able to glean the effects of their organisation's position in the field's structure, they are necessarily unable to see the extent to which the relative weight of the institution for which they work weighs on them, that is, on their own place within the institution and their ability to affect it. It is only on this point that Bourdieu's analysis moves beyond the standard argument that market (and other) constraints limit jour-nalistic practice and do so in a way which prioritises a particular political position. He hints, briefly, at the processes by which such constraints are instituted in individual practice – namely the internal-isation and increasing naturalisation of conditional structural configurations as practical knowledge.[28] Otherwise, *On Television* contents itself with exposing the 'structuredness' of the field, leaving the mechanisms of its 'structuringness' underdeveloped.

L'Emprise du journalisme

The issue of *Actes de la recherche en sciences sociales* devoted to jour-nalism (no. 101–2, 1994) mainly concerns itself with the internal logic of the journalistic field only insofar as it impacts on other fields. Bourdieu disclaims the idea of journalism as a 'fourth power' (e.g. Hulteng and Nelson, 1971). He sets his sights instead on the influence which the mechanisms of a journalistic field more and more submis-sive to the demands of the market (readers and advertisers) exert first on journalists (and on journalist-intellectuals: see Pinto, 1994) and then, and partly through them, on the different fields of cultural production: the academic,[29] judicial, literary, artistic and scientific fields (Bourdieu, 1994c: 3). Journalists have historically occupied a dominated position both in the economic field and the field of cultural production. Dominatedness is characterised by a relative lack in the modes of symbolic capital recognised across the field as legitimate, as well as an inability to impose an alternative form of symbolic capital as dominant. In the cultural field academics, artists and writers have traditionally exercised a monopoly over dominant modes of capital, and over the authority to rule on what counts as such.[30] That said,

journalists also exercise a very particular form of domination insofar
as they establish the acceptable means of public expression and one's
ability to be recognised as a public figure. Journalists act as 'mystical
guardians' of concepts such as 'news value', carrying with them power
over the symbolic representation of other groups – 'mystical', because
professional practice is structured in such a way as to shelter the field
from social questioning of its own principles or conditions of possibility (Garnham, 1993: 185; Bourdieu, 1994c: 7).

Bourdieu defends the idea of esotericism in the cultural sphere.
There is, historically, an opposition between journalism and the more
rarefied fields of cultural production. Aside from economic
constraints, governmental and elite producers are in a position to
exercise the authority concomitant with a monopoly on legitimate
information (Bourdieu, 1991b: 152–5). Rhetorically, Bourdieu calls
this monopoly:

> a weapon in the struggle in which they (the scientific, juridical and
> academic fields) are opposed to journalists and in which they try to
> manipulate information or the agents charged with transmission whilst
> the press on its side tries to manipulate the holders of information in an
> attempt to obtain an assurance of exclusivity. (Bourdieu, 1994c: 4)[31]

Bourdieu regards the potential for journalists to wield power beyond
their own field as lamentable (Bourdieu, 2005: 41), because it poses
a threat to the structures of authority and legitimation endogenous to
specialised fields of cultural production.[32] If this implies that some
forms of elitism are legitimate (Blewitt, 1993: 367; Lane, 2000;
Marlière, 2000: 205–6; Verdès-Leroux, 2003; Garnham, 2005:
479–80), then Bourdieu would not entirely disagree (Bourdieu, 2005:
45).[33] As a general rule, those who exercise domination over cultural
capital operate at the pole of restricted production, the diametric
opposite of economically driven mass production. For Bourdieu, the
more a cultural producer is rich in the symbolic capital characteristic
of a given field such as art or literature, the greater the inclination to
resist market forces.[34] Conversely, mass market producers are more
likely to collaborate with the powers that be, not only the corporate
world but also the state, political parties, church and, more recently,
the mass media. Journalism's specific domination of the circulation of
the capital inherent in 'publicness',[35] and its increasing vulnerability to
market forces, introduce a specific principle of valorisation – that
defined according to profitability and popularity (Champagne, 2005a:
58) – to restricted fields of esoteric knowledge. And given that
resisting market forces is a *sine qua non* of Bourdieu's political agenda,

esotericism in the form of elite artistic exceptionalism and expert institutionalised knowledge should be both challenged in relation to its specific form and defended in principle.

This appears to leave several issues unresolved. Are quality newspapers benign insofar as they cleave to the same sorts of cultural capital as the political and literary fields, or are they complicit in the generalised exporting of journalism's logics? In practical terms this might boil down to the question of whether all media promotion of cultural products is essentially corrupting – a question taken up in several Bourdieusian studies, for example into the centrality of media profile to the status and influence of the Young British Artists of the 1990s (Cook, 2000). What are the implications for public broadcasters, especially those such as the BBC which are simultaneously involved in mass production and the consecration of high culture? And if elite cultural production depends on insulation from principles of publicity and popularity, how do we reconcile the role of the public intellectual of which Bourdieu was a prominent example (Swartz, 2003)? 'L'Emprise du journalisme' offers a response to this last question at least. Bourdieu's elitism at the point of cultural production is coupled with a call for the universalisation of access to the fruits of this restricted production. Public dissemination of expert knowledge is required, in other words, though only insofar as the expert retains control over the means of distribution of his cultural product. While this may appear to suggest that all popular or profitable culture is by definition degraded, Bourdieu's point is rather that there need to be spaces where popularity and profit are not indicators of merit. What most concerns Bourdieu is that popularity is easily conflated with democratic legitimacy (Debray and Macey, 1981; Fiske, 1992a; Johnson, 2007), and thus that a popularly legitimated market will thus pose in political terms what is in fact a problem of cultural production.[36]

The idea here is not that fields of cultural production should simply be left to their own devices. The dangers posed by the misrecognised internal logics of these fields are precisely the target of Bourdieu's research, especially insofar as they reproduce social hierarchies. Further, it does not mean that new political ideas can only emerge from within traditional politics, or that art cannot be challenged from outside an idealised, rarefied artistic world – only that to substitute populist for endogenous principles for ascribing value to symbolic objects carries no guarantee of improvement and risks destroying cultural and political forms which are of some benefit. Perhaps counter-intuitively for a political thinker firmly rooted in the French left, Bourdieu does not celebrate the decline of the elite's role as 'guardian of collective values' in the face of policy making by plebiscite or mediated populism. The political elite needs to be held to account, and it is important to challenge a system in which its principal function is not policy making but social reproduction – Bourdieu argues consistently that the political, cultural and educational elites systematically collude to preserve extant power structures. But while there is a need for transparency and exposure of vested interest, political decisions need to be taken free from the influence of what are essentially market principles.

A similar argument applies to the scientific field (Kuhn, 1962; Bourdieu, 1975; Gilbert and Mulkay, 1984; Lingard and Rawolle, 2004). There is much which is unjust about the way that power is distributed in science. In particular, Bourdieu detects an 'interest in disinterest' (Gaston, 2005) amongst scientists – an unacknowledged economy where the disavowal of interest in financial gain, embodied in the form of a noble pursuit of pure research, itself serves as a self-positioning aimed at the accrual of symbolic capital (and, ironically, economic capital as well). The upshot is that the status of a scientist may depend on her ability to play this game well and experience it as instinctive, rather her research outputs. However, Bourdieu's emphasis is on excavating such misrecognised economies which skew power relations, not insisting that the rules by which merit is accorded in science be opened up or democratised:

> There are economic and cultural conditions of access to a clear scientific judgement and one cannot ask universal suffrage (or a survey) to solve the problems of science ... without annihilating in the same blow those same conditions of scientific production, i.e. the barrier at the entry which protects the scientific (or artistic) city against the destructive irruption of external principles of production and evaluation, which are unsuited and misplaced. (Bourdieu, 1994c: 7)

Bourdieu characteristically attaches the caveat that access to the products of scientific work should be democratised. Journalism, by dint of the economic logic which increasingly pervades it, is complicit in the loosening of the monopoly of the instruments of diffusion upon which most advanced scientific research depends. It would be an exaggeration to suggest that scientific merit is ascribed according to popularity, but Bourdieu's reasoning can be seen as opposing, for example, policy decisions taken on the public perception of risk (Beck, 1992; Altheide, 2002; Furedi, 2003; Everitt and Mills, 2009) rather than scientific evaluation of the same. Chapter 4 explores the possibility of transposing this logic to the journalistic field.

In a 1997 interview originally published in the Brazilian newspaper *O Globo* Bourdieu was asked directly if he believed that media professionals are really blind to the mechanisms of their field. He answered in the negative, though quickly added, suggesting that the question was missing the point, that actors in the journalistic field have a 'dual consciousness' (Pires and Bourdieu, 1998: 70). This consciousness comprises 'a practical view which leads them to get as much as they can, sometimes cynically, sometimes without realising it, out of the possibilities offered by the media tool at their disposal', and 'a theoretical view, moralising and full of indulgence towards themselves, which leads them to deny publicly what they do to mask it and even mask it from themselves' (Bourdieu, 1998c: 70). In the interview Bourdieu offers a more caustic account of the multiple purposes of subjective reflection. He claims that dual consciousness allows the journalist to 'both condemn the objective description of their practice as a scandalous denunciation or a poisonous pamphlet, and say equivalent things out loud when speaking privately or even for the benefit of the sociologist who interviews them' (Bourdieu, 1998c: 71). This response owes more to Bourdieu's personal antipathy towards journalists (Marlière, 1998: 223; Bouveresse, 2004: 89–96) than to a thoroughgoing philosophical commitment to cynicism or self-delusion, though Bourdieu's well-known dismissiveness of agent reflexivity is difficult to reconcile with his normative political commitments. In truth Bourdieu was many things, and the following chapter aims to pin down what can defensibly be described as a Bourdieusian heuristic model. Chapter 3 tackles the sometimes knotty methodological issues that this model throws up, before we turn to the main findings of this Bourdieusian analysis of interviews with war reporters and their peers and rivals in chapter 4. Chapter 5 explores some of the broader themes that emerge from the interviews, in particular the question of morality and moral authority. In chapter 6 we look at what morality, authority and authenticity mean to audiences of conflict journalism, by surveying how news consumers present themselves in online discussion forums. Chapter 7 deals with recent developments in war reporting, including military media management, technology and the rise of citizen journalism, before the concluding chapter assesses the relative merits of a Bourdieusian perspective on journalism – and what it can tell us about some wider cultural trends.

Notes

1 Bourdieu (1986: 248) defines symbolic capital as 'the aggregate of the actual or potential resources which are linked to possession of a durable network of more or less institutionalised relationships of mutual acquaintance and recognition'.

2 The tensions between Bourdieu and Goffman are acknowledged, specifically Bourdieu's (2000: 241; see also Gouldner, 1971) claim that Goffman neglects the broader power structures within which individuals are situated and implicated. Jenkins (2008) offers an effective counterargument, detailing the implicit centrality of power to the Goffmanian model.

3 Bourdieu has been criticised (e.g. Berard, 1999: 143) for focusing on cultural producers to the exclusion of media audiences and content.

4 Wacquant, Bourdieu's student at the Collège de France (and later translator), writes that 'Bourdieu feels that phenomenology is mistaken in its view of society as an emergent product "of decisions, actions, and cognitions of conscious, alert individuals to whom the world is given as immediately familiar and meaningful"' (Throop and Murphy, 2002: 190).

5 'Lifeworld' (*Lebenswelt*) is used in the Husserlian sense of a taken-for-granted stream of everyday routines, interactions and events that constitute individual and social experience, rather than Habermas's conception of shared understandings and values which develop over time through face-to-face communication in a social group.

6 'Quasi-arbitrary' in this book denotes cultural forms which are a particular case of the possible; that is, reasonable but not inferable manifestations of material conditions. See, for instance, Reckwitz (2002: 202).

7 In the modern era, this can be traced to Hegel's *Phenomenology of Spirit* and Marx's problematisation of the relationship at that work's core between the ideal and the material, and between subjectivism and objectivism. Recent contributions to the debate include Roger Silverstone's (1994) 'double articulation' and calls (e.g. Jones and Collins, 2006) for the rematerialisation of social scientific methodology after the linguistic turn. See also Jung (1988); Merquior (1986).

8 In characterising rule following as embodied practice, Wittgenstein writes that one necessarily reaches a point where, in justifying rule following, one will inevitably say, 'This is simply what I do' (Taylor, 1999: 47–51).

9 Wacquant (1996: xvii) writes that practice for Bourdieu, then, is 'engendered in the *mutual solicitation of position and disposition*, in the now-harmonious, now-discordant encounter between "social structures and mental structures", history "objectified" as fields and history "embodied in the form of this socially patterned matrix of preferences and propensities that constitute habitus"'. On Husserlian origins of 'disposition', see Smith and Smith (1995: 204–8).

10 Shilling (2004: 474) labels Bourdieu's approach 'reproductionalism',

capturing not only the pervasiveness of determinism in Bourdieu's work but its dynamic, active constitution in practice. See also Jenkins (1982).

11 'Since the history of the individual is never anything other than a certain specification of the collective history of his class or group, each individual system of dispositions may be seen as a structural variant of all other group or class habitus, expressing the difference between the trajectories and positions inside or outside the class. "Personal" style, the particular stamp marking all products of the same habitus, whether practices or works, is never more than a deviation in relation to the style of a period or class' (Bourdieu, 1977: 86). See also Bourdieu (1985).

12 Durkheim asserts that the social must be explained not by the conceptions of its participants, but by the structural causes which elude awareness but which necessitate the phenomena observed by the social scientist. In Bourdieu's words (cited in Vandenberghe, 1999: 42), 'It is the structure of relations which constitute the space of the field, which commands the form which the visible relations of interaction and the content itself which agents have of it take on.'

13 See especially 'The economy of symbolic goods' in Bourdieu (1993a: 112–46).

14 Elsewhere Bourdieu (1998a: 76) writes that individuals 'may conduct themselves in such a way that, starting with a rational evaluation of their chances of success, it seems that they were right in doing what they did, without one being justified in saying that a rational calculation of chances was at the origin of the choices they made'. Methodologically, the sociologist runs the risk of 'describing as cynical calculation an act which claims to be disinterested' and as such any analysis must be able to deal with both levels of the inevitable 'double-truth' of practice. Introducing the symbolic economy method, Bourdieu argues that 'this duality of practice is rendered viable by a sort of self-deception or self-mystification; but this individual self-deception is sustained by a collective self-deception, a veritable misrecognition inscribed in objective structures and in mental structures, excluding the possibility of thinking or acting otherwise' (Bourdieu, 1998a: 93–8). See also Alexander (2004) on the usefulness of 'strategy' and 'ritual' in conceptualising social practices.

15 '[D]omination arises in and through that *particular relation of im-mediate and infraconscious "fit" between structure and agent* that obtains whenever individuals construct the social world through principles of *vision* that, having emerged from that world, are patterned after its objective *divisions*' (Wacquant, 1996: xvi).

16 Bourdieu defines language, for example, as 'an economic exchange which is established within a particular symbolic relation of power between a producer, endowed with a certain linguistic capital, and a consumer (or a market), and which is capable of producing a certain material or symbolic profit' (cited in Robbins, 2000: 179).

17 The lineage of Bourdieu's politics is the subject of much debate. Kauppi

(1996: 51), for one, identifies Bourdieu with French republicanism. See also Vincent (2004: 135–7).

18 For Bourdieu, 'space' refers to anything which is topographically constructed as a relational structure of differences generated by a principle that discloses and constitutes a region of reality. This conception of topography is closer to the Aristotelian sense of vertical mediation of subjectivity and objectivity than Marxist topographical metaphors or Adorno's reinterpretation thereof (Curry, 2002; Karakayali, 2004).

19 Symbolic violence, a key Bourdieusian term, refers to that which extorts submission without being perceived as such, based as it is on collective expectations or socially inculcated beliefs. The term is Sartrean in origin, and is used by Wittig in a similar fashion (Bourdieu, 1998a: 94–5).

20 A symbolic system is a network of connected, mutually referential social symbols which determine the conscious experience of the lifeworld. For Bourdieu (1977: 97), such systems are always characterised by hierarchies and oppositions, misrecognised as such since they are prior to – and legitimated by – habitus.

21 'The "I" that practically comprehends the physical space and social space (though the subject of the verb to comprehend is not necessarily a "subject" in the sense of the philosophies of mind, but rather a habitus, a system of dispositions) is comprehended, in quite a different sense, encompassed, inscribed, implicated in that space. It occupies a position there which (from statistical analyses of empirical correlations) we know is regularly associated with position-takings' (Bourdieu, 2000: 130).

22 Similar arguments are put forward by Schudson (1995: 169–88), Tunstall (1996: 155–255) and McNair (2000: 1–13).

23 Bourdieu's account of cultural production emphasises the importance of individual insecurity or impermanence. Cultural producers such as journalists do not simply define what counts as valuable, but act so as to 'shore up' their insecure position in the relations of cultural capital. Wright (2005) argues that it is necessary to view the relation between cultural production and reception not as immediate, but rather as mediated by a complex set of factors which operate beyond instrumental strategy.

24 It is these rationalising processes that underpin the commodification of news in the post-1968 period, as Bourdieu (1994b: 39) summarises in a commentary on the twentieth anniversary of *Libération*.

25 Poupeau (2000: 80) surmises that since for Bourdieu the value of words and other symbols is not determined with recourse to some external standards of rationality, the explanation of their recognition in a field is to be located in the 'institutionalised circle of misrecognition which is the foundation of the belief in the value of a given discourse'. Voirol (2004) argues that Bourdieu's account of symbolic misrecognition, and its institution of symbolic violence, is overly economistic. Fengler and Ruß-Mohl (2008) offer a defence of economistic analysis of the journalistic field in particular.

26 The complicity which characterises symbolic violence is comparable to Gramsci's account of the manufacture of consent (Garnham, 1993: 184). Bourdieu both extends and in part refutes Gramsci's ideological approach by locating complicity in domination at a more embodied level.

27 Giddens (1979: 5) writes: 'As a leading theorem of the theory of structuration, I advance the following: every social actor knows a great deal about the conditions of reproduction of the society of which he or she is a member'.

28 Garnham (1993: 185) notes the similarity between Bourdieu's account of naturalisation and Durkheim's 'logical conformity'.

29 Pinto (1994: 25–38) writes in the same journal issue about the rise of the journalist-intellectual in France, as well as the countervailing trend towards philosophical legitimacy being conferred by celebrity status.

30 Van Dijk (1997: 29–30) presents an account of journalistic discourse which is characteristic of the discourse analysis approach. Its broad conclusions are not expressed in vastly different terms from Bourdieusian analysis, but its scope is predominantly *ideological*: that is, there is no account of individuation or practical strategy. Van Dijk casts ideology as 'social cognition', which 'forms the basis of knowledge, attitudes and other more specific beliefs shared by a group'. He concludes that journalists as a group 'acquire and use an ideology that consists of a self-schema that self-servingly defines them as people with special abilities, who professionally produce news and background articles in order to inform the public, by value standards such as objectivity, reliability and fairness, while being positioned independently between the public and the elites, and having special access to the resource of information'.

31 The increasingly strident tone of Bourdieu's writing during the last decade of his life is noted by several scholars. See, for instance, Schinkel (2003: 70–4).

32 In Bourdieu's (1998b: 70) words: 'The journalistic field tends to reinforce the "commercial" elements at the core of all fields to the detriment of the "pure". It favours those cultural producers most susceptible to the seduction of economic and political powers, at the expense of those intent on defending the principles and values of their professions.'

33 For a discussion of the defensibility of elitism from the political science literature, see Bachrach (1969).

34 Bourdieu (1994c: 5) goes so far as to say that fields of cultural production risk becoming alienated, in the Marxist sense of the term, because of the transformation of cultural production towards the commodification of culture. This alienation suggests alienation *from* some essence or ideal – unBourdieusian as the notion is – and in *Contre-feux* (the published output of the 'Raisons d'agir' activist group) this essence is the field's 'inalienable ideals', to which field members retain a strong commitment through the durability of the habitus. However, this space for resistance extends only so far as members of the artistic and intellectual communi-

ties resisting the rise of journalism. Journalists are implied to have 'capit-ulated' so completely as to have lost all identification with any 'noble' role for the profession.

35 Both in the sense of publicity and the elevated status of public knowledge, the latter denoting not only information which is widely accessible but that which normatively should be known. See also Nolan (2008); Zandberg (2010).

36 Champagne's (1994; 2005) opposition to opinion polling and referen-dums is discussed in chapter 5, but warrants mention here as it emanates from the same line of argument and illustrates well the thinking behind Bourdieu's qualified elitism. Each is an apparently democratic process which establishes a purportedly direct relationship with the public (though in the context of journalist–audience relations it will be seen that such immediacy is a functional myth), doing away with the individuals politically or culturally mandated to propose solutions to social questions, whether they be politicians or newspaper editors. But while the political and journalistic fields (or their convergence in the Westminster bubble) may be self-serving and corrupt, their internal logics are uniquely capable of producing answers appropriate to the questions faced – that is, political or cultural.

2

Theoretical preliminaries

My entire scientific enterprise is indeed based on the belief that the deepest logic of the social world can be grasped only if one plunges into the particularity of an empirical reality, historically located and dated, but with the objective of constructing it as a 'special case of what is possible', as Bachelard puts it, i.e. as an exemplary case in a finite world of possible configurations. (Bourdieu, 1998a: 2)

Introduction

Bourdieu's work spans a vast array of subjects, disciplines and agendas, and there is a formidable industry devoted to interpreting, critiquing and re-assessing it. Since the mid 1970s Bourdieusian theory has been appropriated and modified so as to support post-structuralist feminist theory (Weedon, 1987; Butler, 1990; Moi, 1991), to undermine other feminisms (Lovell, 2000: 27–48), to demonstrate both the strengths and weaknesses of Habermas's theory of communicative action (Garnham, 1993; Bohman, 1997; Kögler, 1997; Taylor, 1999: 29–44; Vandenberghe, 1999; Poupeau, 2000: 69–87), to articulate a political philosophy of anticapitalism (Pinto, 1999: 88–104) and to argue against various prevailing liberalist doctrines (Eagleton and Bourdieu, 1992). What these share is an appeal to Bourdieu's academic authority. On his own terms this suggests that we should be mindful of the often unacknowledged rules of the game which underpin academia as much as any other field.[1] It also means that it is important to be clear about which Bourdieu forms the theoretical backbone of this book – without assuming that there is a uniquely authentic Bourdieu to discover – and that is what follows in this chapter. After setting out working definitions for some of the core concepts in Bourdieusian theory, we will locate Bourdieu in the context of a tradition in philosophy and political theory which aims to reconcile structuralism and phenomenology (e.g. Jung, 1988). This will then be developed into a consideration of how a field of cultural production is experienced by those immersed in it, and the extent to which this can be said to be politically implicated. And, since a discussion of Bourdieu's philosophical framework inevitably tends towards the abstract, I will end with a brief summation of what it means to build a research project around the concept of habitus.

The journalistic field

What does it mean to characterise journalism as a Bourdieusian field? First, it means that journalism at any given place and time is structured according to a praxeological system – that is, that it has an established logic of practice which precedes and exceeds (and indeed produces) both the subjects of the field (journalists) and its symbolic objects.[2] Second, this endogenous logic is sufficiently coherent and distinct for journalism to be labelled 'relatively autonomous'. This proposition is controversial given journalism's exposure to market forces, but there is a broad consensus (Deuze, 2005; Hanitzsch, 2007) that there is in the US, the UK and many other countries[3] a culture of journalism internally coherent enough to distinguish it from other forms of cultural production. It does not mean that journalism exists as a discrete, self-contained world.[4] Together, these two propositions underpin journalism's 'rules of the game': the locally universalised set of principles, internalised by field actors as the natural state of things, which establishes the dominant forms of capital in the field, the means by which individuals and groups vie for association with or embodiment of this capital and the status and power that come with it, down to the unspoken rules of interaction – self-presentation, addressing, soliciting, negotiating, socialising – in everyday situations.

Next, the field is relational. This means that one cannot look at either individuals or institutions in isolation. The conscious experience of the individual journalist is not self-contained but the product of that journalist's position in various hierarchies and other relationships, according to the proposition that journalists only exist insofar as they differ by age, gender, class, medium, affiliation, employment contract, education and so on.[5] Likewise, it is impossible to grasp the institutional character and power of, say, *The Times* by looking only at its management structures, budgets,[6] position within News International, principal advertisers and the like. A relational situating would include such factors as the relative weight given to its market share, influence over public policy, advertising and the combined cultural heft of its columnists. As a relational field of forces, journalism is marked by constant and permanent relations of inequality. Domination and dominatedness are a given; what changes over time are the individuals and institutions occupying positions of domination and, more slowly, the stakes of the game by which domination is achieved. The field of journalism itself consists of subfields (Tunstall, 1971) which 'compete' against each other for dominance over what constitutes authoritative journalism, but which may also have their own relatively autonomous logics of practice. Distinct modes of cultural production can co-exist peaceably enough, though we return below to the question of whether tabloids constitute their own relatively autonomous subfield or are instead engaged in a struggle for forms of symbolic capital universally relevant across journalism.

But our aim here is to tie down the specifics of fields and their symbolic economies and conditions of possibilities. In the execution of Bourdieusian case studies, to construct the generative principle which objectively grounds observed differences is ultimately a matter of explaining the structure of the distribution of the forms of power or the kinds of capital which are most effective in the social context in question at a particular point in time. These principles of 'vision and division' (Bourdieu, 2005: 36), which are equatable to social categories of perception, are manifest in all behaviour: Bourdieu notes that the differences in practices, in goods possessed and opinions expressed constitute a veritable language (Kögler, 1997: 145; Bourdieu, 1998a: 8). Bourdieu argues that differences associated with social positions – goods, practices, manners and so on – function in each society in the same way, that is, by the same processes, as differences which constitute symbolic systems. He thus uses the same terms to speak of social differentiation as one could apply to the set of phonemes of a language or the distinctive signs ('differential écarts') that constitute a mythical system (Bourdieu, 1998a: 9).[7] Bourdieu terms such differentiated constituents symbolic capital (Bourdieu, 1990a: 112–21; 1991b: 72–6; Beasley-Murray, 2000),[8] of which there are two subsets: cultural capital and social capital.

'Cultural capital' has been misappropriated and employed against its intended usage (Neveu, 2005), and this has doubtless contributed to the categorical misapprehension of Bourdieu in some quarters as being adjacent to Robert Putnam.[9] Cultural capital in the Bourdieusian sense is best understood as those advantages accrued through specialised knowledge or skills, and encompasses education, taste, frames of cultural reference and bearing (Bourdieu, 1990a:

124–5; 1993a: 270n.24; Robbins, 2005). Adjacent to it is the category of 'social capital', defined as relations and networks of influence amongst colleagues and acquaintances (Bourdieu, 1990a: 108–10; Anheier and Gerhards, 1995: 862).[10] Properly deployed, Bourdieu argues, these terms allow for the depiction of fields as systems of dominant and dominated positions in which each epistemic position, which is empirically realised in the form of a concrete institution, organisation, social group or individual, derives its distinctive properties from its internal relationship with all other positions. The Bourdieusian field may then be defined as a structured space of social positions in which the positions and their interrelations are determined by the distribution of different types of economic and symbolic capital.

Next, we need to identify the social agents active in the journalistic field. This incorporates not only journalists, but all those with a vested interest in influencing or benefiting from the shifting power relations in the field. Writing about the artistic field, Bourdieu posits that:

> the 'subject' of the production of the art-work – of its value but also of its meaning – is not the producer who creates the object in its materiality but rather the entire set of agents engaged in the field. Among these are the producers of the works classified as artistic (great or minor, famous or unknown), critics of all persuasions (who themselves are established within the field), collectors, middlemen, curators etc, in short, all those who have ties with art, who live for art and, to varying degrees, from it, and who confront each other in struggles where the imposition of not only a world view but also a vision of the artworld is at stake, and who through these struggles, participate in the production of the value of the artist and of art. (Bourdieu, 1993a: 261)

In journalism, such a group would comprise editors in their various guises, technical staff, advertisers, media buyers, politicians, regulators and other cultural producers (both individual and institutional) such as writers, academics and bloggers. As this book deals with a particular journalistic subfield, interviewees were drawn from politics, the military and academia as well as journalism. The Bourdieusian field is constructed such that agents or groups of agents are arranged in it according to their relative position in distributions based upon two fundamental principles of differentiation of capital: first, the volume of capital, and, second, the relative weight of the different kinds of capital (Bourdieu, 1998a: 6–7). For Bourdieu, for the purposes of studying late capitalist society, the most efficient categorisations to employ are economic and cultural capital.[11] More broadly, one may say that the space of social positions is recast into a

space of position-takings through the mediation of the space of dispositions, that is, through the principles of the habitus. As Bourdieu puts
it:

> the system of differential deviations which defines the different
> positions in the two major dimensions of social space corresponds to the
> system of differential deviations in agents' properties (or in the proper-
> ties of constructed classes of agents), i.e. in their practices and in the
> goods they possess. (Bourdieu, 1998a: 7)

If cultural capital is defined in strict terms according to prestige and
authority, journalism is located in a dominated position relative to,
say, academia or literature, which more effectively determine that
which is systematically recognised as culturally valuable. This is
Bourdieu's stated position on journalism, evident in his critique of the
blurring of the boundaries of philosophy and journalism in 'L'Emprise
du journalisme'. Once the position of the field to be analysed is established in relation to the metafield of power (Bourdieu, 1989: 263–71),
the next task is to uncover the objective structure of the relations
between positions occupied in the field by agents or the institutions
which are in competition with each other in the field. The internal
structure of the journalistic field, it is hypothesised, extends in one
dimension from a pole at which economic capital is relatively (and
apparently) unimportant and cultural or social capital is held to be
valuable, to another pole where the reverse is true.[12] It is problematic
at the outset to assign positions at these extremities labels such as
'analytical journalism', 'investigative reporter', 'quality newspapers',
'scandal-mongering' or 'gutter press'. Deciding who and what constitutes and legitimates, for example, 'quality journalism' is one of the
struggles of constitution and legitimation in the field of cultural
production: investigative journalism, quality papers and tabloids are
not trans-historical categories but sites of competition over specific
forms or combinations of capital. No objective position in the field is
essentially captured by such conceptual categorisations; rather, these
categorisations are used by individuals and organisations in an
attempt to inhabit those positions and to monopolise the symbolic
capital associated with them. Individuals and organisations do not
become identical to objective positions (though they may be perceived
to do so); instead they are disposed to adapt to the conditions or
demands of those positions. For Bourdieu, then, it makes little sense
to speak of a figure such as Rupert Murdoch as having a conscious
plan to dominate the media world, for what determines an individual's strategies are practical, em-bodied (i.e. not simply willed)

dispositions (Bourdieu, 1990b: 59–75). By virtue of his own particular habitus Murdoch is a practically engaged player in the media 'game' (Cook, 2000: 171); within this game position-takings are also always 'semi-conscious strategies in a game in which the conquest of cultural legitimacy and the concomitant power of symbolic violence is at stake' (Bourdieu, 1993a: 137).

It is important not to overstate the extent to which Bourdieu sees fields as neat and delineable objects of social scientific analysis. By characterising a field as relatively autonomous he is not suggesting it exists in a vacuum, but rather that in order to understand it we need to pay heed to its peculiar internal logics as well as its external relations in the broader field of power – what would typically be called macrostructural factors. All the same, several questions suggest themselves. At what point does a journalist become inculcated with the operating principles of the journalistic field? Is a more experienced journalist to be assumed to have assimilated and naturalised these principles more totally, to have taken on a journalistic disposition more wholly? From Bourdieu's writings on the academic world, the answer is unequivocally affirmative. There is for Bourdieu a collective habitus which unites all actors in a field. This is not to say that all journalists think the same, but instead that they share a common logic which generates all the various dispositions, professional ethics, political viewpoints and so on in a field.[13] Further, there must be a substantial amount held in common between the habitus which 'produced' the would-be journalists as they were socialised, in order for journalism or a particular speciality to be an option to them, for them to have considered it as a potential objective, and for them to have succeeded to some degree in that arena. Some basic, hypothetical generative logic is assumed as common to all journalists, though the influence of age, amount and range of journalistic experience, and exposure to other fields, are all to be taken into account. Bourdieu's emphasis on the temporal aspect of strategy extends from the microscopic level of individual instances of practice to the long-term acquisition of dispositions or 'personalities'; the latter is brought visibly to bear in works such as *Distinction* and *Homo Academicus*.[14]

As a social space, the journalistic field is the locus in which actors struggle for the transformation or preservation of the field in its current state (Bourdieu, 1993a: 82–3). The power at their disposal defines their relative position and, subsequently, the strategies available to them (Poupeau, 2000: 76–7). Overt competition between journalists is underpinned by competition which is not recognised as such, and this second-order competition is best thought of not as

between individuals or institutions but field positions and the configurations of symbolic capital – including dispositional – endemic to
them. Whether or not it is defensible to characterise all behaviour as
competition (Bourdieu, 1993a: 34; Berard, 1999: 145) remains an
open question, but we can say that practices such as self-identification
and interaction will be governed by the field's internal laws. The
assignation of meaning to cultural production – here, what counts as
valorised journalism and journalists – is also constituted relationally
according to the praxeological structuredness of the field as a whole.
The 'raw' information of the event – what happened, where and when
– is inseparable from its reception. What is to journalists the more
salient information is whether something is worth reporting, which
angle to focus on and what a report's perceived value is anticipated to
be. That is, what counts as news is a product of the interaction
between journalists and editors, rather than some universal or extra-
discursive criterion of newsworthiness. Further, these connections
between journalists, editors and other field actors remain hidden to
the readers of newspapers, if only because of the oft-cited maxim that
only journalists read all the papers. As Bourdieu observes: 'to know
what to say you have to know what everyone else has said' (Bourdieu,
1994c: 5). This is not to attribute to journalists a privileged status
through insight into a world about which the public is ignorant. In
fact, journalists tend to overstate the differences between newspapers
or television networks. More accurately, perhaps, the differences of
which they speak (who got the story first, who got the angle 'wrong',
who got the exclusive interview) are irrelevant to most news
consumers. The perceived best managers, editors and journalists,
Bourdieu argues, are those for whom all significant information is
obvious, he who is 'perfectly adapted to the objective exigencies of his
position' (Bourdieu, 1998b: 26; Dreyfus and Rabinow, 1993: 38). It is
this embodiable, highly adaptable code which dictates what is given
to constitute news, how it is reported and gathered, and whose
opinions are recognised as legitimate and authoritative.[15] There is no
law set in stone. Journalists are in a sense free to form whatever
opinion they will and to pursue any strategy conceivable. But each
knows, or instinctively anticipates, the judgement which practices will
receive, since judgement is foremost a recognition of the position from
which an opinion is expressed or a strategy enacted.

Bourdieu argues that, in the French context, the fundamental opposition which marks the print media field has not changed significantly
since the nineteenth century. This structure is based around the opposition between those papers which offer above all else news

(nouvelles), preferably sensational, and papers which give priority to thoroughness, analysis and commentary so as to emphasise their distinction to the former category 'by grandly affirming the values of objectivity' (Bourdieu, 1994c: 5). The social space in which the print journalistic field is located is thus a place of opposition between 'two logics and two principles of legitimation' (Bourdieu, 1998b: 70). These two principles are peer recognition, accorded to those who embody most completely the values or internal principles of the field, and recognition by the largest number, manifest in circulation figures and subsequent access to profitable markets such as advertising, book publishing, broadcasting and public speaking (Bourdieu, 1998b: 70; 1993a: 53–8). The first logic, determining what is regarded as professional honour, is manifest overtly as the journalistic code of conduct. It is also internalised as a sort of disposition by which an actor 'naturally' or 'instinctively' knows how to ascribe a value or particular angle to an event or article. The second is said to be expressed through a mindset which 'thinks', or more accurately, unconsciously anticipates, by way of categories such as 'it sells well', 'this will go down well with readers' and so on (Bourdieu, 1994c: 5). These examples are not journalists' reflective analyses of stories, but the 'natural' disposition of one who works at the commercial pole of journalism.

Bourdieu explains this opposition largely in terms of autonomy from one or other of the organising principles of a field (Bourdieu, 1994c: 4). Autonomy theoretically could denote independence from economic forces or from peer review. In Bourdieu's worldview, though, it is a thoroughly normative category indicating an actor's ability to act according to a noble esoteric principle in the face of market demands (Wacquant, 2000: 111). The autonomy of a newspaper will depend upon its market share and the concentration of its advertisers. An autonomous paper is by implication one which operates at the pole of restricted production, the position furthest removed from that at which economic capital is absolutely dominant.[16] The autonomy of an individual journalist is determined in the first instance by the extent to which press ownership is concentrated (with implications for job security), by the position the paper on which she works occupies in the larger space of newspapers (i.e. its relative position between the 'market' and 'intellectual' poles), and by the journalist's position within the news organisation – whether she is freelance or salaried, the level of the salary (resorting to producing 'potboilers' to supplement salary is cited as an example of loss of autonomy), her seniority and so on (Bourdieu, 1994c: 5). The type of articles produced will also influence the level of autonomy possible. Bourdieu notes that popularisers of science or economics are particularly dependent on other sources of authority. The scope for autonomy amongst war correspondents is considered in chapter 4.[17]

This opposition is, without doubt, overly simplistic. As a methodological tool it may help to conceive of the field in these terms, though it is easy to slip from this sort of conceptual model to a map of the existing journalistic field in which the tabloid with the largest circulation 'naturally' takes up residence at one extreme, the most 'weighty' broadsheet at the other. Certainly Bourdieu is guilty of this slippage in his limited analysis of the French media, and this may be explicable by his clear aversion to the sensationalising tendencies of all sectors of the press in France.[18] Actors within the field are predicted to betray a belief in the opposition inherent in the field to an extent that in fact exaggerates the actual opposition in the field's objective structures, since this is how their distinction is constituted. The interviews conducted for this book reveal a more complex picture. While distinctions are drawn, a lot of differentiation is made on the basis of the principles of distinction other than those conventionally attached to mass versus restricted circulation or sensationalising versus serious news. Within the field, the British tabloids are regarded not so much cynically as sensationalising and therefore worthless by 'rigorous' journalistic standards, but as sensationalising and as such subject to different criteria for judgement. Several elite journalists and editors of broadsheet newspapers betrayed a view in the interviews, whether consciously or implicitly, that tabloid journalism is a separate artform altogether and as such requires its own critical standards. Tabloid articles can be (and are) described as 'brilliant', 'wonderful', 'terrible' and so on, on the basis of wholly professional (i.e. not only commercial) values which are not accounted for in Bourdieu's analysis.

For Bourdieu, the continued existence of a coherent journalistic field depends on *illusio*, the collective sense amongst all actors that a game defined according to a universalised set of principles is worth playing. In theory this would be sustained by the quality press dismissing tabloids as cynical and mercenary, the tabloids delegitimising the quality press by branding them aloof and elitist. In practice neither pole matches the description of its ideal type. At the restricted end of the industry, that which is meant to guarantee quality – peer review – is at best inconsistent, with light formal regulation in countries such as the UK and few examples of transgressors of journalistic principles suffering long-term damage to their careers (Bourdieu, 1998b: 53). It would also be naive to suggest that popularity does not count amongst the quality press. At the other end, the propensity of tabloids to stage political campaigns demonstrates that the capital they seek to accrue is not only economic – though campaigning journalism does have its financial rewards. I would suggest that the polarity of the field is compromised, in the UK to a greater extent than the US, by the engagement by individuals and institutions from all sectors in competition over capital which is neither purely popular nor purely professional, but moral. That is, claiming a position defined according to principles of democratic probity on the one hand, or speaking for ordinary people on the other, may obviate both the requirement to cleave to professional codes of conduct, and the assumption that commercial success translates into negative cultural capital. Adding moral authority to the mix usefully complicates Bourdieu's neat delineation of the field. There are many moral positions which can be assumed, as well as amoral ones, and these muddy the distinction between prestige and profit. It is only by accepting the variegation of authority in today's journalism that we can understand both the broader contests that permeate the field and the proliferation and endurance of niche markets. The latter is simply a recognition of complexity in the news media and its audiences, while the former is potentially more significant. Along with occupation of positions of power in a field comes the possibility of cultural consecration: the ability not only to acquire symbolic capital but also to shape what is collectively recognised as such. Thus, the tabloid press can be seen to be not only forces of marketisation, but engaged in a strategy to remould the terms of cultural legitimacy according to principles of populism and anti-elitism.

How are fields lived? Bourdieu and phenomenology

If all of this appears more political economical than phenomenological, this is indicative of the mix of quantitative and qualitative approaches that Bourdieu deploys. Field maps based on exhaustive data collection have taken on a certain iconic status in the reception of books such as *Distinction* and *Homo Academicus*. They are useful insofar as they indicate centres of power in spaces of cultural production, the relational positions of institutions and subfields (such as genres of newspaper) and, perhaps most importantly, the dominant forms of capital by which distinctions between these are sustained. But they also tend to be descriptive rather than analytical, establishing what the status quo is without asking how it is constantly, temporally, renewed. This is the aim of focusing on how a field is inhabited on an everyday level – not so as to produce an authentic account of their experiences, but because it is at this level of practice that political reproduction is effected.

By focusing on the material determinants of social phenomena, and specifically on the political determination of subjectivity, Bourdieu can be classified as a neo-Marxist phenomenologist.[19] He is one of a long series of scholars in the history of ideas to attempt to synthesise phenomenology and structuralism, a tradition dating back to Hegel's delineation of the mediation of the material and ideal in *The Phenomenology of Spirit*.[20] One of the key tenets of this tradition is that the human subject never just is. Subjectivity emerges only through successive objectifications, especially through being an object for other subjects' consciousnesses across an array of material and social relations. Bourdieu's starting point is Marx's contention that Hegel ultimately fails to supersede idealism, and that later phenome-nologists, in particular Husserl,[21] fail to overcome the opposition between objectivism and subjectivism[22] because they misunderstand the role that intention plays in the experience of the lifeworld – the taken-for-granted stream of everyday routines, interactions and events that constitute individual and social experience. Bourdieu's claim is not that intention is irrelevant, simply that it cannot be under-stood in voluntarist terms, for it is in part determined by a material context which exceeds its symbolic apprehension.[23] In short, we do not fully understand the multivalent determination of our experience, since our facility to understand is itself materially determined in ways to which we usually do not have access. Bourdieu is convincing in arguing that historically phenomenology is mistaken in its view of society as an emergent product of 'decisions, actions and cognitions of conscious, alert individuals to whom the world is given as immedi-ately familiar and meaningful' (Throop and Murphy, 2002: 190), but his corrective to voluntarism leaves itself open to charges of hyper-politicisation – positing ever-greater and necessarily intangible determinations of consciousness at every turn. In fact, though, Bourdieu does not posit an all-pervasive and all-productive set of determining structures, but rather an ever-present regularity which can be traced back to historically and culturally specific generative conditions of possibility.

Is Bourdieu's critique based on a fair reading of Husserl? The central thrust of his argument is that Husserlian phenomenology cannot describe how lived experience is produced by a dialectic of internalisation of previously externalised structures, because its conception of 'genetic' explanation remains overly descriptive

(Throop and Murphy, 2002: 201). But this rests on the assumption that traditional phenomenology only seeks to understand the world as it appears to consciousness, as self-evident – an assumption tied to the assessment routinely made about Husserl (Ricoeur, 1967: 143–74; Bell, 1990: 230–2; Smith, 1995: 394–432; Smith, 2007: 402–24; cf. Thierry, 1995), that he is not a 'political' thinker. In fact Husserl's natural attitude – the naturalised set of implicit assumptions about ourselves, the world and the relation between the two (see especially Husserl, 1982: 184–92; 1970: 148–54; Luft, 1998) – is as immersed in power relations as Bourdieu's doxa,[24] and Husserl does aim to account for the forces which produce and sustain the lifeworld, rather than insisting that the means of describing experience (scientifically or otherwise) are as enclosed by the parameters of the lifeworld as the primary subjective experience of it (Husserl, 1970: 233).[25] Bourdieu's claim (consistent with the earlier work of Foucault and Butler) that the subject is always-already over-determined, and especially that that excess of determination is politically implicated, is a normative commitment (Ortner, 1996: 11; Bouveresse, 2004), not one that can be derived from scientific or phenomenological first principles. The main difference between the two is that Husserl treats the content of conscious experience as meaningful data in itself (Husserl, 1970: 115–16), while for Bourdieu its content is secondary to its function, namely the reproduction of power relations.

Throop and Murphy depict a substantial divergence between the two theorists, in that Bourdieu locates the internalisation of structure as itself determining of consciousness, while Husserl posits that internalisation can only proceed with pre-given structures of consciousness in place. This does not, however, amount to the postulation of a pure subject which does the internalising: while it may exceed internalisation, it is also changed by it. Instead of working from the assumption that Husserl is an idealist, Bourdieu a determinist, it is arguable that Husserlian genetic description avoids the subjectivist fallacy of positing pre-given consciousness (Husserl, 1970: 8), while space for agency in Bourdieu's habitus model is, if not explicitly detailed in his phenomenological work, is commensurate with it. And, further, it is arguable that establishing differences in approaches to qualifying and unpacking subjectivity is secondary to a greater priority in each body of work: making explicit the implications of objectivism both in interpreting lived experience and in social science generally.

In developing his philosophy of social science, Bourdieu also draws on the phenomenological principles of Alfred Schutz, in particular Schutz's ordering of knowledge distinguishing between common

sense and scientific thought (Schutz, 1972: 220–4).[26] Bourdieu
extends Schutz's proposition that second-order scientific thought is
properly located in the social world (Schutz, 1972: 241, 1973: 212),
by calling for a double epistemological break.[27] For both theorists a
'science of science' (Bourdieu, 2004) is possible, though Bourdieu
emphasises that this cannot proceed on the basis of the assumption
that the social scientific analysis of the pre-scientific is itself a science
(Throop and Murphy, 2002: 191). We saw earlier that Bourdieu's
generative or genetic structures produce the means of their own
apprehension, although the social scientist is able to break with that
determination to enable a properly objectified, if not objective,
analysis of those structures. While Bourdieu claims a degree of innovation in this regard, it is not the case that Schutz treats the
pre-scientific as a realm which can be coldly described by the scientist,
rather than as a realm which determines to an extent the terms of
reference of its observation and interpretation (Schutz, 1972: 220–4).
As for Husserl, Schutz does not place generative structural determination at the centre of analysis, but neither is the category of natural
knowledge characterised as undetermined (Schutz, 1972: 70–4). It is
rather a difference of emphasis, with Schutz seeking to compartmen-
talise different categories of social scientific data rather than rule one
category or another untainted, irrelevant or unknowable (Throop and
Murphy, 2002: 195).

But while Schutz by no means depicts the taken-for-granted as
unstructured or intrinsically meaningful (Schutz, 1972: 74), like
Husserl he does nonetheless prioritise its content. There is an imperative in *The Phenomenology of the Social World* that analysing the
interpretations that people make about their interactions with the
objective world is essential to understanding that relation between
subject and object (Schutz, 1972: 83–6). As becomes clear in
Bourdieu's often dismissive position on the reflections of social actors
– in no field so much as the journalistic – Bourdieu can be read as
claiming that all that matters is to demonstrate a fit between fundamentally arbitrary subject–object relations. Bourdieu's dismissal of
agent reflection is a recurring theme, but for present purposes the
more interesting contrast is between the objects of knowledge in
Bourdieusian and Schutzian theory. While for Schutz common sense
knowledge will often reveal something of the meaning of
subject–object relations, for Bourdieu this type of knowledge can only
be seen as particular instances of the possible. This distinction matters
because it means that for Schutz, the content of natural knowledge is
scientifically productive, whereas for Bourdieu it is something which

can only be rationalised after the fact. The import of this is that it demonstrates the heightened scepticism with which scientists should approach the basic units of data they encounter. But it also points to a more political implication: sense-data, common sense and everyday reflection are then not only not natural, but are structured in such a way as to reproduce hierarchies of power (Bourdieu, 1990a: 58–9). And the postulation of necessary politicality renders Bourdieu's specific criteria for politicality unclear: if coercive power is not only everywhere but productive of future configurations of power, then it is difficult to conceive of political agency, or indeed differentiation between levels of coercion. I would suggest that while Bourdieu's more rhetorical writings on journalism suggest the inevitability of endless layers of political domination behind the seemingly natural and conventionally received, the emphasis on finite reflexivity in *The Logic of Practice* and *Outline of a Theory of Practice* does open up the potential for a practical delimitation – in the neo-Marxist phenomenological sense described here rather than the mere bracketing-out of the intangible (Bourdieu, 1990a: 64–5) – of political analysis. Maintaining the possibility that, while common sense knowledge and first-order reflections are not pre-given they are not inevitably complicit in the reproduction of domination, means that a (contested) separation can be posited between the politically meaningful and meaningless. It means that some unreflective data can be taken on their own merits, some can be classified as without relevance and the remainder can be properly identified as structurally strategic: that is, contributing to or evidence of the reproduction of domination defined in particular terms. Establishing the possibility of effective political meaninglessness would thus allow the Bourdieusian model to be specific about what forms of domination are or should be central to it. For present purposes these may be summarised as hierarchisation and structures of distinction and exclusion, reproduced by the complicity of their victims through naturalisation and internalisation. Establishing these specifics then allows for a more specific statement of what would count as a political goal in Bourdieu's model: qualified autonomy from the dominant principle of differentiation which characterises a field and which is geared towards its endurance.

While Husserl and Schutz do allow for investigation into the material determinants of consciousness, it is only with the contributions of Merleau-Ponty and Goffman on the micro-determinations of the everyday experience of spatiality and temporality that phenomenology takes on an explicitly political hue. Specifically, the subject–object dualism is reworked so that instead of addressing itself

to interactions with the social world as such, or to the role of the
senses in constituting experience, the body as a mediating ground is
brought centre-stage (Schatzski, 2001: 8; Kelly, 2002). Instead of
being cast as a mechanistic matter of stimulus and response, rule
following and habit formation are recast in terms of corporeal
knowledge. Goffman in particular stresses the variety of ways in
which socioeconomic status and social signifiers (in Goffman's words,
'totalitarian institutions') are manifest in seemingly incidental body
movements in social interactions. Bourdieu adapts both Goffman's
concept of bodily performance and Merleau-Ponty's body hexis –
defined as 'the socially inculcated ways an individual moves, carries
and positions his or her body in the lived world' (Throop and Murphy,
2002: 188) – to develop a model of corporeal memory consisting in
structures which pass from practice to practice without the mediation
of consciousness, but which help to shape that consciousness (Streeck
and Jordan, 2009). As Merleau-Ponty writes:

> We said earlier that it is the body which understands in the acquisition
> of habit. This way of putting it will appear absurd, if understanding is
> subsuming a sense datum under an idea, and if the body is as an object.
> But the phenomenon of habit is just what prompts us to revise our
> notion of 'understand' and our notion of the body. To understand is to
> experience the harmony between what we aim at and what is given,
> between the intention and the performance – and the body is our
> anchorage in a world. (Merleau-Ponty, 1962: 167)

There are four points worth making here. First, to focus on the
corporeal is not to restrict phenomenology to an idiosyncratic analysis
of posture, movement and so on. In this model language too is
corporeal, such that what someone says is inseparable from the way
in which they say it, and the way they speak is the product of the
incorporation of social structures. Second, what Mauss called body
techniques[28] are collective rather than individual: the unremarkable
taken-for-grantedness of minutely structured and contextually
contingent practices is only sustainable insofar as everyone is 'in the
game'. Third, this approach offers an effective response to the claim
that Bourdieusian phenomenology simply seeks to locate over-
determination at ever-more microscopic loci. In Bourdieu's words, it

> has the virtue of recalling what is most particularly ignored or repressed,
> especially in universes in which people tend to think of themselves as
> free of conformisms and beliefs, namely the relation of often insur-
> mountable submission which binds all social agents, whether they like it
> or not, to the social world of which they are, for better or worse, the
> products. (Bourdieu, 2000: 173)

Finally, it allows us to talk about why people act the way they do, following customs and rituals but also acting strategically, in a way that is neither brutally deterministic nor idealistically voluntaristic. The body is not simply a conduit for structural reproduction, though nor is conscious intention the primary motivator of everyday actions (Anderson, 2004). The mediation of subject and object here is essentially a temporal one: the body is not a passive object on which structures are (in Foucault's term) inscribed, but nor is there an ideal subject which becomes progressively objectified. Structures are productive rather than constraining, and the subject emerges through (not in spite of) structured cultures of practice of socialisation. As Goffman puts it:

> To walk, to cross a road, to utter a complete sentence, to wear long pants, to tie one's shoes, to add a column of figures – all these routines that allow the individual unthinking, competent performance were attained through an acquisition process whose early stages were negotiated in cold sweat. (Goffman, 1972: 293)

Subjectivity may then be thought of as acquired corporeal memory, or what Bourdieu terms practical reason. The first part of this term is meant to encapsulate the hard-wiring of habitus, such that bodies function as 'depositories of deferred thoughts' or, paraphrasing Proust, 'arms and legs are full of numb imperatives' (Bourdieu, 1990a: 69). The second word does not indicate a rational, cognitive reasoning but instead that practices have reason, in J.S. Mill's ([1872] 1987) sense of the term. And this describes not only the structuredness and regularity of behaviour but how it is experienced as reasonable or appropriate. The experience of habitus is thus one of instinct, spontaneity and tacit understanding rather than belief, purpose or intention. Bourdieu and Merleau-Ponty in particular both emphasise the dynamism of habituation, arguing that even repetitive, unreflective applications of (generative) logic are never only reproductive: even if we cannot say that they carry a natural potential for reflexivity, they nonetheless enact the potential for their rearrangement (Marcoulatos, 2001: 7). [29] The principal point of divergence emerges in Merleau-Ponty's characterisation of the 'phenomenal body' as the arena in which 'significance and intentionality come to dwell' (Merleau-Ponty, 1962: 409). Habitus in this sense is more than the sum of a set of dispositions, rather something which itself comprises a living presence; this, in turn, is predicated on Merleau-Ponty's positing of an 'original' (Merleau-Ponty, 1962: 157; Husserl, 1982: xxii) intentionality. For Bourdieu, while embodied significance

(Marcoulatos, 2001) is pervasive in its domination of subjective experience of a field, it is nonetheless an effect of that field. This in itself does not demonstrate that Bourdieu is excessively objectivist. Rather, it points to Bourdieu's failure to construct the pre-reflexive on phenomenological grounds, opting instead to characterise the pre-reflexive normatively as a domain of political coercion.

It remains an open question across the phenomenological tradition whether subjectification is complicit in structural reproduction (Crossley, 1994). For a structuralist like the early Foucault (Flynn, 1985) there is a sense that subjectification exists primarily to reinforce power relations of which the individual is inevitably unaware: he coined the term *assujetissement* to make clear that subjectification entails subjection.[30] For Bourdieu too there is a kind of conservative inevitability in that being disposed to act in anticipation of the likely outcome of events over time makes more likely the occurrence of those events – in effect, all behaviour tends towards normalisation (cf. Gartman, 1991; Crossley, 2003; Fowler, 2003). Further, the phenomenological model developed in *The Logic of Practice* and *Outline of a Theory of Practice* makes clear that the symbolic content of those practices is of little import: practices simultaneously express the quasi-arbitrariness of cultural norms as well as their near-absolute pervasion of behaviour. The practices through which the concretisation of power relations is effected could conceivably be anything – from the discernment of what counts as good art or sound journalistic practice to cultural identity and one's sense of selfhood. It certainly makes sense to challenge the naturalised ascendancy of fine art or academia and the power that accrues to practitioners in these fields, and it is not unreasonable to question why cultural identity is an unremarkably significant facet of subjectivity in contemporary Western societies. But the same logic leads Bourdieu to characterise journalistic ethics and professional identities as primarily functional (the function being structural reproduction), even though he makes the case for defending the authoritative social scientific subject. We will see in chapter 5 that there are grounds for arguing with Bourdieu against Bourdieu (King, 2000) over the idea that moral codes have less to do with the practice of professional journalism than with hierarchical relations of power within journalism and the wider field of cultural production (Evans, 1999).

Does all this imply that individuals are genetically incapable of seeing the bigger picture, and that their conscious experience is a field effect which has reason but no more than any number of other possibilities? It is difficult to avoid the conclusion that subjectification is coerced, and that subjectifying practices are in Austin's terminology no more than the forced iteration of norms. Bourdieu (1990a: 69) writes that the reproduction of power is invested in the belief that is given by 'the collectively recognised capacity to act in various ways on deep-rooted linguistic and muscular patterns of behaviour, either by neutralising them or by reactivating them to function mimetically'. But while mimesis might be forced, it never results in seamless reproduction of power structures because, to make a technical point, these structures do not have a solid existence and only endure insofar as they are enacted in practice. Since interpellation is an active process with temporal and material conditionality, there are gaps between local iterations of collective templates of the practices which give rise to lived experience (McNay, 1999; Marcoulatos, 2001). This means that while the theory tends to treat as literal the universalised dominance of symbolic forms and cultures of practice, in reality the determination of consciousness is always partly haphazard. Becoming a subject may, then, be inextricably linked with structural reproduction – the two are mutually constitutive – but conscious experience is not a simple expression of structure, nor does it simply and neatly serve a structural function. Subjectification is political, then, but it is also many other things besides.

John Simpson as Martin Heidegger

This raises a difficult question about the status of the individual: how do we reconcile the fullness and seamlessness of individual experience with a phenomenology which characterises that experience as a reasonable but essentially interchangeable expression of a collective genetic template? It is easy to infer that Bourdieu is not interested in individuals, only in how collective practices of individuation form part of a broader interplay of forces, and indeed this book constructs such cultures of subjectifying practice in strategic terms. But that is not the same as writing off the individual. Bourdieu pays detailed attention to individual lives in works such as *The Weight of the World*. Determining structures may more or less complete the lived experience of a field, and there is certainly nothing special about specific individuals. But this is only to say that a sociologist analysing a field is unsurprised by the behaviour or insights of individuals – because they are always, technically, reasonable – not that they are not meaningful. Bourdieusian analysis does not suggest that figures of authority in journalism are accidental, or that there is no connection between their personal qualities or skills and their professional status. Rather, it emphasises that we should not see the rise of one elite actor or another as a unique event explicable on its own terms, nor believe that his rise was in some sense inevitable. We should instead, as with morality or authority generally, see John Simpson, for the sake of illustration, as a particular manifestation of a number of hypothetically conceivable emergences to prominence.

The parameters for explaining generational change or the rise to prominence of a new elite in a field of cultural production, avoiding both historical determinism and relativism, are set out in *The Political Ontology of Martin Heidegger* (Bourdieu, 1991c). Bourdieu argues that Heidegger's rise to a position of eminence in the philosophical field should not be interpreted as pre-ordained or predictable; nor, however, should it be regarded as *sui generis* or surprising. Instead, Heidegger's ascent should be interpreted as reasonable, explicable after the fact as a particular case of a wider field of possibility. This does not detach the author from his work, recasting it as the inevitable product of historical forces. But it does indicate that Heidegger's occupation of an elite position in the field is a particular observed instance of the generative structures of the field, which provide its conditions of possibility. Heidegger's authorial voice should thus be seen not as generic but as deriving from generic cultural (and political) origins, rather than as the embodiment of individual genius whose meaning is self-evident. Thus, while the precise content of Heideggerian philosophy cannot be derived from structural principles, it is reasonable to see it as an example of a set of practices endemic to the philosophical field and wider field of cultural production.[31] By this logic, what is predictable is that in each successive generation a relatively small number of individual producers will emerge who overthrow certain key sacred texts in the field, and in so doing lay claim not only to a position of authority but also, crucially, to the power to consecrate future dominant criteria of cultural value. In political terms what is most significant about this process of usurpation is that the taboos broken must be recognisably sanctified enough to indicate that a sea-change has taken place, but at base it will usually be a 'conservative revolution' which leaves in place more than it revolutionises: while the stakes of the game may change, the game itself will not be radically changed.[32] For Bourdieu, Heidegger's rise to prominence does not amount to a philosophical revolution, but the overthrow of specific philosophical tenets, necessary to effect a generational shift of authority, and masking the enduring supremacy of a particular reading of neo-Kantian philosophy (see also Rose, 1984).

If we transfer this logic to war reporting, then we might start by characterising John Simpson's rise to eminence in terms of the accrual of different types of symbolic capital, in particular cultural capital in the form of status and influence over (or valorisation by) peers, as well as the social capital of being a trusted 'star' reporter. Now, the phenomenological approach tells us that this ascent is not explicable by some essence of John Simpson-ness – but nor is it the case that John Simpson is reductively one of a set of interchangeable clones, and that if we did not have John Simpson we would have someone virtually indistinguishable assuming the same position in the field. Instead, John Simpson is very much an individual, but one whose individuation proceeded from a generative set of principles held in common by those collectively oriented by class habitus. 'Oriented to what?' remains unresolved: for Bourdieu immersion in a relatively autonomous professional field is sufficient to produce group habitus, but in this book no such hermeticality is assumed. The pool of possibles out of which Simpson emerged may not be as narrow as those working a threshold number of years as a journalist at the BBC, but it is unlikely to be as wide as society generally; the alternatives include immersion in the field of cultural production more broadly, or a specific demographic of socialisation and education. In any case, for our purposes Simpson's authority tells us less about him than it does about the conditions of possibility of the journalistic field. If our premise is that Simpson's seniority is reasonable (in whatever sense: it makes no difference conceptually whether authority consists in gravitas or *Heat* magazine visibility – the same logic could be applied to a Paris Hilton), then we can work backwards from his current position to the preconditions of that state of affairs.

First, an environment has to be in place in which the public admires or trusts war reporters embodying a specific set of qualities – there will be more on this in chapter 4, but the crux is that the perceived personal qualities of an authority figure are as significant as the successful execution of professional duties (see also Livingstone, 1998). Crudely put, John Simpson exists because there is a market for him. We could then feasibly ask what it says about contemporary British society that such symbolic capital as, say, gritty integrity is admired, and recognised in the form of an individual journalist rather than a media institution or a politician. Second, and more significantly in the Bourdieusian model, we should understand Simpson as a manifestation of the internal logic of the fields of war reporting journalism and cultural production. The starting assumption is that the valorisation of the specific configuration of symbolic capital that he appears to embody does not emerge simply out of the work in which he is engaged, and chapters 4 and 5 are devoted to delineating what these other symbolic economies might be. Third, Simpson's rise should be seen in strategic terms. This does not mean looking at how competitive journalists are – and they undoubtedly are – but thinking in terms of a group habitus (of which Simpson is one manifestation) oriented towards the pre-reflexive pursuit of power in the field at the expense of other groups – distinguished perhaps by generation, or perhaps by professional ideology (just-the-facts versus attached journalism, for example). Speculatively, Simpson's progression represents a group strategy which would preserve some existing forms of valorised capital – unflappability, for instance – while challenging others, perhaps including deference and stiffness. This in turn points us towards broader conditions of possibility, potentially including a cultural shift in how authority is perceived, from institutional to individual and from expert to authentic, themes to which we will return.

Habitus in theory and practice

The political phenomenology of journalism thus aims to unpack the determinants and implications of those practices which underpin the correspondent's experience of the lifeworld of journalism as pre-given. For instance, while it is experienced as pre-given that the journalistic field is made up of individuals and institutions, the phenomenological approach attempts to disaggregate how individuation proceeds (and also how institutions come to exist and be recognised as such, though that is not our concern here). We have seen here that this means investigating habitus: the collective logics which structure practices at the pre-conscious level, practices which are not owned by individuals but which are experienced as such, through the embodiment of historical contingencies, as personal character, professional identity and gut instinct (Schultz, 2007).

Habitus is characterised both as a product of history and, since it produces individual and collective practice, history itself.[33] It is instituted through a system of dispositions, themselves a past which survives in the present and 'tends to perpetuate itself into the future by making itself present in practices structured according to its principles' (Bourdieu, 1977: 82). The system of dispositions may thus be said to act as an internal, 'natural law' which relays the continuous exercise of the laws, again conceived in the Millian sense, which comprise the regularities of external objective structures. As such, any form of objectivism which identifies these regularities manifest in observed behaviour, without reconstructing the external structures which perpetuate themselves by transmitting their regularities into local laws, is essentially missing the point. Events are not caused by agents, nor, contrary to some readings of Bourdieu (Harland, 1991; Pellerin and Stearns, 2001), may they be structurally inferred from the networks of differentiated positions of power which form the focus of Bourdieusian field analysis.[34] Instead, events (including speech acts in interviews) are the product of the synchronic combination of dispositions and situations which are themselves never entirely independent.[35] Habitus, as it is rendered methodologically, is the logic by which structured, structuring dispositions and situations interact and produce social effects.[36] And insofar as this is a practical logic, it makes sense for Bourdieu to use the same language to speak of the logic of practice in the philosophical-theoretical sense as he uses to speak of its methodological sense, that is, the principles of production of fields and strategies within fields in a given social context. The sociological construction of habitus is thus the reconstruction of the logic which governs the dialectical relationship between objective structures and the cognitive motivating structures they produce and which tend to reproduce them. And it is precisely in this mutual constitutivity of habitus and field that Bourdieu locates politics: that is, the structured, structuring differential relations of power which are prior to and exceed our pre-reflexive experience of the world – and ourselves. In Bourdieu's words it is:

> between the feel for the game and the game itself, that the stakes of the game are generated and ends are constituted which are not posited as such, objective potentialities which, although they do not exist outside that relationship, impose themselves, within it, with absolute necessity and self-evidence. The game presents itself to someone caught up in it, absorbed in it, as a transcendent universe, imposing its own ends and norms unconditionally. (Bourdieu, 2000: 151)

Individuation is both collective and relational: the template upon which selfhood is apprehended as given is shared amongst actors in any field with a base level of internal coherence, and that selfhood is ultimately constituted in the hardwired sense, again collectively held, of how one differs from others. A corollary is that valorisations of others are similarly relational, based on common principles of differentiation, and made as much according to ineffable categories perceived as personal authenticity as the successful execution of professional practices judged against explicit standards. This is what allows the analysis presented in this book to move from positionings of self and other in the interviews to the construction of a symbolic economy of war reporting – that is, a locally universalised set of principles of differentiation which are decontested through collective internalisation and routinisation and misrecognised as natural and more or less neutral rather than the stakes of a 'game'. Evidence of collective practices of individuation and (mis-)recognition is to be found in the fact that the way someone talks is experienced as unremarkable, even if it is similar to others, and that one's tastes in culture and leisure 'just are', though they are distributed according to relational structures in which the occupation of a position of authority (or lack of it) is similarly felicitous.

Such an analysis will inevitably talk about journalistic dispositions, but this is not to suggest that all journalists act, talk or dress alike. First, to say that dispositional practices – those signifying selfhood to self or other – are collective simply indicates that they are not 'owned' by discrete individuals. They are practised, but variably across different spaces in the field, and with consequences which are often unpredictable. If there are specific dominant dispositions which are collectively (mis)recognised as being associated with a specific form of authority, this is not because there are ideal types which individual professionals either innately or progressively come to resemble, but because their collective embodiment and recognition are strategies associated with the accumulation of symbolic capital.[37] Dispositions are never a perfect fit with some pre-existing individual's essence, but through the nonconscious mastery of specific practices – practices performing authenticity, especially – they may come to be seen as such (Alexander, 2004). If we call this misrecognition, it does not mean that journalists fail to recognise each others' 'true selves', since such a concept has no meaning here outside the purely functional. Misrecognition, too, is a structured practice which consists in the collective failure to recognise the historical and political dimensions of disposition. Bourdieu writes in *Outline of a Theory of Practice* that while habitus is marked by double historicity it is experienced as atemporal (Bourdieu, 1977: 82). The upshot is that while journalists may be fiercely competitive, they are never fully cognisant of the collectively internalised 'rules' by which the accumulation of symbolic capital and the occupation of positions of power in the field actually proceed.

For journalism, the upshot is that both professional practice and practices of subjectivity are not what they appear, that there is a kind of systemic obscuration of their political function. It means that professional values such as ethics, as well as professional identity and phenomena like talent, need to be analysed in strategic terms, by asking who stands to benefit either from their recognition in discrete situations or their ongoing dominance as symbolic forms in the field. This is by no means nihilistic or conspiratorial. Ethics, professionalism, a nose for news – all of these things are important and remain theoretically defensible as categories, but the specific forms they take are only particular instances of the possible and should therefore be challenged. The seemingly unremarkable dominance of particular symbolic forms in journalism is not a natural development unimplicated in structural reproduction, and if an individual is an expert in her enactment it is not because it comes naturally to her, but rather because individual variation on the collective journalistic habitus is, at a given time and place, ideally oriented towards the journalistic field's power structures. There is no presumption of cynicism or calculation; orientation concerns structured anticipation and memory which operate at the level of the corporeal, underpinning but not necessarily present to a consciousness which unproblematically perceives their professional environment in terms of flair, principle and common sense.

The political import of this is that the internal hierarchies of the journalistic field and its external barriers should not be thought of as static monoliths. Instead, they are reproduced in quotidian contexts through the instinctive, ordinary practices of individuals immersed in a symbolic economy whose demands and incentives are hypothesised to go largely unacknowledged.[38] But it is worth stressing that there is nothing intrinsically wrong with hierarchies or boundaries as such. While recent theories of networked communications collaborative media production promote horizontal rather than vertical relations between media professionals and publics (Delli Carpini and Williams, 2001; Bentivegna, 2002; Platon and Deuze, 2003; Gillmor, 2004; Lievrouw and Livingstone, 2006; Pickard, 2008; Fenton, 2010), a quality like experience is irreducible to simply more complete indoctrination in a field's arbitrary codes and offers one possible means of bestowing authority in a world in which the division of labour between management, editorial and journalistic positions remains inevitable – and defensible. Similarly, there is no reason to presume that war reporting would benefit from being opened up to all comers. While this may be seen as democratising, it relies on an epistemological claim that is at least questionable – namely that maximising the number of accounts of an event is the best way to capture its truth (see Allan, 2006). We return in chapter 7 to the implications of media organisations using local-foreign correspondents, effectively employing media producers who are not immersed in the Western journalistic field. For present purposes it bears underlining Bourdieu's argument that in fields of cultural production there is a need for a pole of restricted production which is protected from the exigencies of mass production, for the simple reason that there are certain cultural products which can only be produced in isolation from principles of popularity or marketability. In journalism, investigative and war reporting are two such subfields which can only subsist in a climate of relative rarefaction. Autonomy of a subfield for Bourdieu typically means that its internal logics are shielded from external forces, but there is a difference between exposure to critical contestation and exposure to market forces. The aim here is not to undermine the relative autonomy of war reporting, but rather to disrupt that which is experienced by its inhabitants as unremarkable but is in fact associated with power and status. The exposure of otherwise unacknowledged competition is not to suggest that competition is a bad thing: access to sources and timeliness depend on a degree of competitiveness. But it is worth knowing if unacknowledged distinction making is associated with economies of influence and status, and if there is a strategic interest in the collective normalisation of symbolic forms, whether they be the more acknowledged values of professionalism or subtler things such as mode of expression and professional instinct.

In particular, this book is interested in the possibility that the meaning that journalism and journalists come to assume has less to do with the content of the news produced and more to do with the way that journalists position themselves in relation to their work and to peers. This positioning is experienced by and large simply as what feels individually appropriate, but Bourdieusian phenomenology directs us to the collectively internalised structures that underpin this sense of felicity[39] – what makes it possible for practices of valorisation, subjectification and so on to just happen. It means looking at the naturalised orientation that war reporters have to the world around them and asking how such an orientation comes to be experienced as a natural fit, at least by some. This in turn leads to the more specifically political question of authorisation, with the expectation that those who are authorised to speak as and for war reporters are those for whom it is naturally appropriate to do so. The task at hand is to unpack the collective logics of practice which allow for appropriateness to be recognised as given. Of course, such logics do not only structure instinctive apprehension in war reporting or journalism more broadly, but also in other fields of cultural production including academic research. This raises a raft of methodological questions, both at the level of the philosophy of social science and in terms of logistics, to which we now turn.

Notes

1 Bourdieu's call to dissect the symbolic economy that characterises the academic field stems from his antipathy towards what he regarded as an overly theoretical focus in French academia: 'the philosophical babble found in academic institutions'. Bourdieu (1987: 13), quoted in Lane (2000: 11). See also Chomsky et al. (1979); Wilcken (1995: 48–9).
2 The upshot of this is that the logic of the journalistic field produces the categories and value systems of news, not the other way around.
3 For example, India (Ståhlberg, 2006); Brazil (Herscovitz, 2004; de Albuquerque, 2005); the Arab world (Pintak and Ginges, 2009).
4 While it has been argued (Bourdieu, 1994c) that the pack mentality means that journalists rely too heavily on peers for information, and that internet research and other deskbound work practices are undermining journalism done 'on the beat' (Davies, 2008), journalists nonetheless interact with non-field members on a routine basis.
5 Bourdieu writes that 'to exist is to differ' (Bourdieu, 1993a: 170), a statement of relationalism which marks a clear adjacency to the double meaning of Derrida's 'différance' (Derrida, 1991: 59–79): that is, to exist is both to differ and to defer.
6 This is not to underestimate the impact of differential economic resources on reporting. As the editor of a US quality newspaper (Interviewee 6) put it: 'You're competing with the wires though, it's, I mean, they've just got so many resources, so many people on the ground and everything, they get their news out quick, you know, real quick. But they're huge organisations, you know, they can afford to spend a lot of money on putting people out there. It's a different way of operating.'
7 Mannheim also sought to formulate a conception of the symbolic which was nonreductionistic but correlated to social structures, though he eventually reverted to the philosophy of consciousness as his conceptual framework (Kögler, 1997: 147).
8 Bohman (1997: 175–6) contends that Bourdieu's definition of symbolic capital (and symbolic violence) is so broad as to render it unworkable, implying that Bourdieu, like Foucault, merely implies symbolic coercion at every conceivable locus without offering an explanation for its generation. See also Dreyfus and Rabinow (1993: 42). In this book I argue that it is the normative loading of the priority of determination, rather than the symbolic forms of capital, which manifests the ubiquity of coercive power in Bourdieusian theory.
9 On the misapprehension of Bourdieusian concepts, see Neveu (2005); Bourdieu (1992); Lizardo (2004); Shusterman (1999). In the United

States in particular, Bourdieu's model is often applied selectively. Weininger and Lareau (2003), for example, explicitly reject 'abstract debates about reproduction theory' in applying Bourdieu to the American educational context.

10 Putnam (2000: 3–12) traces the history of the term back to 1916, and posits that it has been defined in at least six significantly different ways since. For a critical survey of different models of social capital, see Swain (2003) and Johnston and Percy-Smith (2003). Social capital is in general of only secondary significance in Bourdieu's work, though it is a principal focus in, for example, his discussion of structures of socialist societies.

11 Anheier and Gerhards (1995), however, argue that Bourdieu assumes a correlation between distribution of economic and cultural capital.

12 This will usually correspond to a continuum between high circulation and 'high quality' (Anheier and Gerhards, 1995).

13 As Goffman puts it: 'In analysing the self, then, we are drawn from its possessor, from the person who will profit or lose most by it, for he and his body merely provide the peg on which something of collaborative manufacture will be hung for a time' (Goffman, [1959] 1971: 245).

14 Vandenberghe (1999: 54) further develops the use of 'personal biographical trajectories' in post-structuralist methodology.

15 Legitimacy is inextricably connected to symbolic violence: 'An institution, action or usage which is dominant, but not recognised as such, that is to say, which is tacitly accepted, is legitimate' (Bourdieu, 1980, cited in Moi, 1991: 270).

16 Or 'the field of large scale production' (Bourdieu, 1993a: 125–31).

17 The rise of digital media has also necessarily reshaped the relative positions (and thus possible position-takings) of the journalistic field, both as a professional social space and a site of cultural production (Davis, 2005; Klinenberg, 2005). We return to this issue in chapter 7.

18 Bourdieu attacked *L'Indépendant* in scathing terms on several occasions for its publication of scare-mongering articles.

19 'The knowledge we shall call *phenomenological* ... sets out to make explicit the truth of primary experience of the social world, i.e. all that is inscribed in the relationship of familiarity with the familiar environment, the unquestioning apprehension of the social world which, by definition, does not reflect on itself and excludes the question of the conditions of its own possibility' (Bourdieu, 1977: 3). Bourdieu counterposes this with objectivist knowledge, referring to the material conditions of possibility of phenomenological knowledge, which is identified by Tilley (1990: 65–6) as demonstrably neo-Marxist.

20 See especially 'Independence and dependence of self consciousness: Lordship and bondage' (Hegel, [1807] 1977: 111–18).

21 Bourdieu concludes that Husserl is unable to escape transcendental idealism, or 'disembodied solipsism' (Lizardo, 2004: 379).

22 'One has to construct a materialist theory which (in accordance with the wish that Marx expressed in the *Theses on Feuerbach*) is capable of taking

back from idealism the "active side" of practical knowledge that the materialist tradition has abandoned to it' (Bourdieu, 2000: 136).

23 'Social relations cannot be reduced to relationships between subjectivities driven by intentions or "motivations", because they are established between social conditions and positions and therefore have more reality than the subjects whom they link' (Bourdieu et al., 1991: 18).

24 Bourdieu defines doxa as the beliefs of an individual, as 'a quasi-perfect correspondence between the objective order and the subjective principles of organisation [with which] the natural and social world appears as self evident' (Bourdieu, 1977: 156).

25 Likewise, if Bourdieu criticises Sartre for not recognising the durable dispositions of habitus which constrain subjectivity (Bourdieu, 1990a: 42), he does so only by reading a volitional intention into Sartrean subjectivity which is at best contestable (Fox, 2003: 47–53).

26 For a personal reflection on how Bourdieu first read phenomenological philosophy, see especially 'Fieldwork in philosophy' in Bourdieu (1990b).

27 The double epistemological break means that Bourdieu categorises three orders of experience constructs, augmenting the traditional division of cognition into directly experienced reality and knowledge about social reality.

28 Mauss (1979: 101) also sets out the conceptual structure of habitus thus: 'Please note that I use the Latin word – it should be understood in France as *habitus*. The word translates infinitely better than "habitude" (habit or custom), the "exis", the "acquired ability" and "faculty" of Aristotle (who was a psychologist). It does not designate those metaphysical *habitudes*, that mysterious "memory", the subject of volumes or short and famous theses. The "habits" do not vary just with individuals and their imitations; they vary between societies, educations, proprieties and fashions, prestiges. In them we should see the techniques and work of collective and individual practical reason rather than, in the ordinary way, merely the soul and its repetitive faculties.'

29 Butler's (1997) theory of performativity develops the notion of subjectless performance to theorise the possibility of insight into subjectification. McNay (2000: 38–9) argues that linking the anticipatory dimension to Husserl's concept of protension establishes an 'active and creative relation ... between the subject and the world', concluding that 'the uncertainties and anticipatory elements immanent in the way in which these potentialities are lived renders this an active, interpretative process rather than a merely receptive one'. Adkins (2003) locates reflexivity in the lack of fit between the female habitus and the public sphere. See also Sweetman (2003).

30 Bourdieu (1990b: 4–5) distances himself from 'faddish' structuralism, which he suggests could be explained generationally, by the need of Foucault, Althusser and others to overthrow the dominance of existentialism.

31 On this point Bourdieu is clearly adjacent to Winch (1990: 92), who notes

that 'the rule here does not specify any determinate outcome to the situation, though it does limit the range of possible alternatives'.

32 This is similar to Foucault's qualification of the transgression of limits as not inherently transformative. In the words of Simons (1995: 69), 'Transgression does not overcome limits ... but shows that what we are, our being, depends on the existence of limits.'

33 Bourdieu introduces the concept as follows: 'The structures constitutive of a particular type of environment (e.g. the material conditions of existence characteristic of a class condition) produce habitus, systems of durable, transposable dispositions, structured structures predisposed to function as structuring structures, that is, as principles of the generation and structuring of practices and representations which can be objectively "regulated" and "regular" without in any way being the product of obedience to rules, objectively adapted to their goals without presupposing a conscious aiming at ends or an express mastery of the operations necessary to attain them and, being all this, collectively orchestrated without being the product of the orchestrating action of a conductor' (Bourdieu, 1977: 72). See also Bourdieu (1990a: 54).

34 This study thus does not seek to infer practice from observed structure, nor to prove the existence of structures from observed practice, but to examine *how* practices in the field of war correspondence are structured, and with what structuring effects. In *Distinction*, Bourdieu (1984: 107) argues against 'linear' inference from cause to observed phenomena, and for the establishment of 'networks' of possibility.

35 'If agents are possessed by their habitus more than they possess it, this is because it acts within them as the organising principle of their actions, and because this modus operandi informing all thought and action (including thought of action), reveals itself only in the *opus operatum*' (Bourdieu, 1977: 18). See also Bourdieu (2000: 146–50).

36 Observed practices, Bourdieu writes, can only be explained by 'relating the objective structure defining the social conditions of the production of the habitus which engendered them to the conditions in which the habitus is operating, that is, to the conjuncture which, short of a radical transformation, represents a particular state of this structure. In practice, it is the habitus, history turned into nature, i.e. denied as such, which accomplishes practically the relating of these two systems of relations, in and through the production of practice' (Bourdieu, 1977: 78).

37 Bourdieu (1984: 12–13) explains that beyond seeking the 'phenomenal relation between this or that dependent variable' and some independent variable, the methodological aim is analytically to construct the dispositions which are the structured embodiment of strategies which are themselves effects of the prevailing symbolic economy. These dispositions are, like symbolic economies, always implicit, but in Bourdieu's words they are 'despite everything, recorded in analysis'.

38 Bourdieu (1977: 160) thus makes the distinction between the social recognition of the orthodox and the *doxic*, that is, that which is simply given.

39 In a critique of Austin, Bourdieu (1990a: 32) contends that 'ignorance of the conditions of production and circulation of commentary allows and encourages people to search solely in the discourse in question for the "conditions of felicity" which, though theoretically and practically inseparable from the institutional conditions of the functioning of the discourse, have been assigned to the domain of external linguistics'.

3

Methodological issues

I would like to show that with the same instruments, one can analyse phenomena as different as exchanges of honour in a precapitalist society or ... foundations such as the Ford Foundation, exchanges between generations within a family, transactions in markets of cultural or religious goods, and so forth. (Bourdieu, 1998a: 92–3)

Introduction

It is clear by now that Bourdieu's framework goes well beyond simply measuring different types of symbolic and economic capital extant in a given professional or cultural context. Field analysis has sometimes been interpreted as something akin to political economy (Martin and Szelenyi, [1987] 2000), but this is misleading for two reasons. First, while the more economistic readings of Bourdieu (e.g. Guillory, 2000: 29) may capture what he terms the structuredness of a field, they tend to fail to grasp the structuring aspect of a field – that is, the ongoing, temporal production and reproduction of relational structures through practice. Second, such an approach misses the lived aspect of fields – not in the sense of lacking a narrative account of what it feels like to inhabit a social space, but in terms of what shapes the conscious experience, largely as given, of being active in a field of power relations. We have seen that Bourdieu uses the transposable, durable dispositions of habitus to explain how the active, mutual constitution of structure and practice is embedded in everyday life, and it is the relation between habitus and field that any Bourdieusian analysis must target. This is by no means a simple task. This chapter sets out the parameters of Bourdieusian social scientific methodology, the problems it throws up as well as a methodical working-through of the discourse analysis constructed to address these aims and constraints, which forms the analytical core of this research.

Thinking about professional practice in the field of cultural production

Bourdieu invokes Gaston Bachelard to locate the generative function of habitus in professional practice. He calls for the reconstruction of what Bachelard termed the 'everyday' or unreflective philosophy of the scientist, that which is implicit and usually unconscious in spontaneous scientific practice (Vandenberghe, 1999: 37; Robbins, 2000: xviii). Pivotally, Bachelard held that this practical logic of the working scientist naturally transcends the philosophical oppositions of idealist rationalism and empiricist realism: unconcerned with the abstract causes and consequences of their actions, scientists 'spontaneously and eclectically' combine the creative, constructing imagination of idealism and the rationalising experience of empiricism (Vandenberghe, 1999: 37). Bachelard observed that the category of 'fact gatherer', which applies equally to scientists, historians and journalists, is meaningless in isolation. Scientists invariably construct abstract models of noumenal structures which necessitate the phenomena they observe, and they formulate experiments which technically realise the phenomena that the theory had hypothetically posed as a possible effect of those noumenal structures. While Bourdieu takes the step, characteristic of neo-Marxist phenomenology, of problematising as political and then attempting to overcome the division between idealism and empiricism, he does so in a way that defines Bourdieusianism as separate from the post-structuralism of, say, Lyotard, Derrida or Deleuze, insofar as Bourdieu posits symbolic systems which are misrecognised and disconnected from objective structures, though nonetheless not arbitrary or entirely self-contained.[1] These symbolic systems are the context in which professional practice emerges as meaningful and applies to the professional practice of the social scientist as well as the behaviour of any social group whose function is to gather, legitimate, produce and disseminate information: that is, the field of cultural production, which incorporates the journalistic field.

When analysing a locus of knowledge production such as social science or journalism, the reconstruction of the process, rooted in practice, by which internalised dispositions generate knowledge, knowability and legitimacy can be summed up by Bourdieu's overarching methodological mantra: an examination of the conditions of possibility of the knowledge in question. Bourdieu stresses that this is not a subjectivist approach but an exploration of the limits of objective exploration, or more specifically an analysis of the mode of production of the practical mastery (Bourdieu, 1977: 79–89; 1993a:

95) which creates the possibility both of objectively intelligible practice and of the lived experience (Bourdieu terms it 'objectively enchanted experience') of that practice (Bourdieu, 1984: 472). This clearly owes much to Marx, in particular the Marx of the *Theses on Feuerbach* (Bourdieu, 1984: 467; 1990b: 3), though Bourdieu is careful to emphasise the temporal discontinuities of practice and the impossibility of inferring behaviour from structure or vice versa. But it is also distinct from a hermeneutic approach which seeks only to give voice to journalists (see for instance, Faris, 2010). Bourdieusian philosophy of social science, then, aims to describe what makes possible the lived experience of journalism as a pre-reflexive, seamless lifeworld, by focusing on the symbolic worlds in which individuals as embodied dispositions interact and enact, in a temporally discontinuous though structurally enduring manner, relations of power.

Bourdieu's particular model has its roots in the Durkheimian principle of nonconsciousness, which posits that the social must be explained not by the conceptions of its participants, but by the structural causes which elude awareness but which necessitate the phenomena observed by the social scientist. In Bourdieu's words, 'It is the structure of relations which constitute the space of the field, which commands the form which the visible relations of interaction and the content itself which agents have of it take on' (cited in Vandenberghe, 1999: 42). To be sure, if this line of thinking is followed through the implications for sociological methodology are significant. It is accepted, after Durkheim, that social facts can only be explained by conscious facts, and these conscious facts must be systematically constructed against common sense and objectified into a system of relations in such a way that the objective structural relations between the phenomenal elements necessitate and explain the behaviour of the elements of the constructed relation between the elements (Kauppi, 1996: 46). This programme is at the heart of Bourdieusian methodology, and any case study carried out along Bourdieusian principles must be designed within these parameters. The reconstruction of facts 'against common sense' is not intended to produce objectivity, but rather a description of a relation between social fact and its perception. As a corollary, the reconstruction of the scientific fact against the spontaneous perceptions of the 'real object' is inseparable from its systematic construction as a theoretical object.[2]

The motivation behind exploding the ontological division between the theoretical and the social, by casting both as material and constituted in practice, is clear enough: Bourdieu intends to escape a philosophy of consciousness which adheres to what he regards as an indefensible idealised (meaning non-materially mediated) concept of theoretical abstraction, with an eye to rejecting 'the alternative between an internal interpretation and an external explanation' (cited in Vandenberghe, 1999: 51).[3] Thus, while it is true that the concept of the field demonstrates the influence of Saussurean relationalism on Bourdieu's work, the practical grounding of both habitus and field means that Bourdieu cannot be simply labelled a relationalist (Schinkel and Tacq, 2004). In fact, the Bourdieusian programme is better characterised as an attempt to establish a middle ground between relationalism and rationalism (Vandenberghe, 1999). Bourdieu suggests that the opposition between formalist analysis, with its immanent interpretation of meaning, and reductionist analysis, with its external reading that directly relates meaning to social forms, can be overcome by demonstrating that the external influences and constraints of a theory or analysis are always mediated by the structure of the particular field which intervenes between the social positions of the producer of social theory and the postures in which they are expressed and whose principle lies in the structure of the field of relative positions. As a result, the 'immanent' approach of, say, anthropology or semiotics, as well as the argued reductionism of Lévi-Strauss (Bourdieu, 1990a: 95), can both be avoided by training an analytical eye upon the field (academia, art, science, journalism and so on) in which that knowledge is produced.

In practice, the social scientist constructs a field which takes the form of a model of the range of social relations among the observed phenomenal relations; in effect, some relational superstructure is described, and particular observed social forms may then be seen as realisations of the same symbolic function. The goal of Bourdieusian methodology is to identify the generative relations, patterns, tendencies and so on that could create a finite range of actual outcomes – one example of which is the observed set of social facts. Bourdieu surmises:

> The science of practice has to construct the principle which makes it possible to account for all the cases observed, and only those, without forgetting that this construction, and the generative operation of which it is the basis, are only the theoretical equivalent of the practical scheme which enables every correctly trained agent to produce all the practices and judgements of honour called for by the challenges of existence. (Bourdieu, 1977: 11)

Once the limiting, defining characteristics are established – incorporating *illusio*,[4] professional interests, struggle for monopoly of authority, circulation of capital, class differentiation, strategies of conservation and subversion – this model can be transposed to other fields of practice so as to offer functional and structural comparisons. Methodologically, this means that the codification and formalisation of the generative and unifying principles of a system of relations in the theoretical model allow for the meaningful comparison of the field of the analytic object and the academic field. This comparison of fields is held by Bourdieu to be crucial insofar as contrasting the application of generative formula can demonstrate to what extent structural 'invariance' can produce empirical variation. The result is that the analyst is less likely to reduce all analysis to a one-field perspective – though it is accepted that Bourdieu is criticised for overstating the closedness of professional fields in his own work.

Bourdieu's interpretation of relationalism and rationalism is not without its critics. Vandenberghe, for one, argues that Bourdieu finds himself trapped in the same predicament as Mannheim had foreseen in *Ideology and Utopia* (Mannheim, [1936] 1998: 74–7). Whereas Weber, rather than systematically relating social agents to each other, instead developed an ideal type of each of them that sought to define the characteristic of the actors themselves, both Mannheim and Bourdieu reject this 'substantialist' mindset and focus instead on the social determination of ideas. However, while Mannheim maintains that all knowledge is socially and historically determined, it was never his contention that all knowledge is reducible to the social circumstances of its production.[5] Mannheim fails to articulate a methodology which could properly explain the social genesis of ideas without finding recourse to reductionism; Vandenberghe argues that no solution has yet been found. The most widely voiced criticism (Martin and Szelenyi, [1987] 2000: 282; Kingston, 2001: 88–99) is that Bourdieu precludes a more nuanced, metaphysically relational or hermeneutic stance by reducing all behaviour to the pursuit, conscious or otherwise, of capital (Evans, 1999; Swingewood, 1999: 69). It is true that Bourdieu focuses for the most part on symbolic (or economic) struggle (Bourdieu, 1993a: 79–82), and specifically on competition for the means of determination of legitimacy and hierarchy. However, we have also seen that Bourdieu does not focus on systemic flows of capital to the exclusion of how such ubiquitous determinants of behaviour are lived (cf. Bohman, 1997). Bourdieusian generative structuralism concerns itself with every level of the operation of power – in particular with the corporeal and linguistic aspects of the individuation and internalisation of power relations. The methodology of field analysis is intended to provide access to the social conditions of possibility of agency, individuation and cultural meaning.[6] The analysis of the production of symbolic capital and its circulation through power structures is itself a constructed logic which may be pulled apart self-reflexively: it may (and, for Bourdieu, should) itself become an object of analysis. Capital, however, is not the ultimate end of Bourdieusian methodology.[7] Instead, the economy of symbolic capital and its institution in relational fields are conceived as means of redressing the reductionism attributed to Marxist analysis (Bourdieu, 1990b: 48–50), the limits of Saussurean relationalism (Bourdieu, 1977: 23–5), the philosophy of consciousness implied in Durkheim (Bourdieu, 1990a: 44) and the voluntarism of Weber (Bourdieu, 1990b: 49) – all of which are necessary in order to articulate explanations of authority and professional values as social, material, practical phenomena (Schatzski, 2001: 8). This is not to suggest that Bourdieu is uniquely successful in overcoming the limitations of previous social theory, and the analysis offered here is mindful of the allegations of determinism, elitism and culturalism in its execution and conclusions.

Constructing the interviewee

For now, we need to find a methodological resolution to a theoretical issue raised in chapter 2: how to conceive of and work with individuals and the words they use. The key issue here is the extent to which interviewees are capable of genuine insight into their own worlds, or whether their reflections are inevitably over-determined by the field they inhabit, and likely unwittingly complicit in the reproduction of coercive power relations (McNay, 1999: 100; cf. Sweetman, 2003). It was noted in more general terms in the previous chapter that in response to invocations of unconscious assent to domination and systematic misrecognition of symbolic economies, we can always point out that journalists (and other cultural producers) are only too aware of the constraints under which they work, of the dominance of market forces and of the hollowness of the pursuit for symbols of professional success which are held by agents to be valueless as anything other than career markers. Bourdieu's rejoinder, often implicit, is that while reflection does occur it cannot be properly critical, which is to say revealing to the level that the sociological analysis can be (Hamel, 1998: 9). The whole system of relations is predicated on the necessity of quasi-arbitrariness and structured, structuring domination remaining unknown and unknowable. Reflection may produce a degree of self-awareness, though it is always possible that the form the reflecting process takes will usually mask and reinforce deeper, pre-reflective structures by causing other fundamental questions not to be asked and by establishing contingencies as absolutes.[8] This contention has sparked a range of attacks on Bourdieu's theoretical recourse to insidious power relationships and unidentifiable microstructures. Garnham suggests that what Bourdieu seeks to account for through generative structures could in fact be explained by the fact that people are, at base, risk averse – and for sound, rational, historically supported reasons (Garnham, 1993: 183; Sparrow, 1999). However, Bourdieu's point is not merely to respond to consciously, inexpertly arrived-at revelations by invoking ever-deeper, increasingly unknowable structures. Bourdieu's intention is rather to demonstrate that the process of reflection, whatever the subjective experience may be, has a practical function (Bourdieu, 1990b: 52–3), and that it will tend always towards instituting a certain set of relations of meanings attributed to words, as much as of groups of actors, more firmly at the practical, unthinking level. For instance, the bulk of journalists are keenly aware of the economic constraints on their professional practice, from salary levels and job security to problems surrounding concentration of ownership, advertisers and so on; four interviewees made a point (without prompting) of emphasising that journalism is first and foremost an industry. But what is masked in the journalistic discourse is the symbolic capital which attaches to a detachment from either power or financial gain, manifest as a form of underdog status. That is, actors in the journalistic field (and other fields of cultural production) have an interest in being dismissive or ambivalent about wealth;[9] and decisively, the misrecognition of this economy is reinforced by actors' own insight into the iniquities of the field. This does not render those subjective observations wrong. Subjective insight does, however, serve a practical purpose which it itself cannot reveal.

None of this is to say that the political sociologist knows the journalist's mind better than she knows herself (Hamel, 1998: 9).[10] Instead, it means that even (or especially) in instances of 'nocturnal' philosophising – that is, overt reflection on one's professional identity (see Vandenberghe, 1999) – there may be nonconscious practices structured according to the demands of the field and with political effects in it. Matheson (2003) thus notes that it is precisely when journalists reflect on their profession that they – not cynically, but discursively – close down significant points of contestation and thus reproduce and rationalise field structures which are neither natural nor naturally defensible. Perhaps the clearest examples of this are

where specific discussions naturalise and legitimise broader commitments. For example, a discussion about particular ethical dilemmas or
priorities in war reporting precludes a debate over whether war correspondence is, can or should be an ethical pursuit. Likewise, by
discussing how best to guarantee objectivity or accuracy (Bowman,
2006), correspondents are embedding an epistemology of journalism
which is specifically instrumentalist, as though it is indeed possible –
and naturally culturally valuable – to 'collect facts' and describe the
world. I am not suggesting that journalists should not strive to be
objective: rather, the point is that embedding the notion that journalism is a natural repository for objectivity has broader political effects
in terms of the symbolic capital it wields both in the field of cultural
production and with relation to the public it serves (see Schudson and
Anderson, 2009). Similarly, if a journalist consciously reflects upon
what constitutes authority or professionalism in the field, the putative
effect is the reproduction of the idea that journalism is essentially
compatible with authority and professionalism more broadly – when
journalists are routinely polled as being less trustworthy than lawyers
or politicians (Committee on Standards in Public Life, 2008), and
where the status of journalism as a profession has been hotly
contested for well over a century (Deuze, 2005). To put it in phenomenological terms, there are aspects of the practice of reflection which
are structured according to the pre-existing power relations of the
journalistic field and which have structuring effects in that field,
without themselves emerging to consciousness. Significantly,
however, two respondents clearly pinpointed the 'game' of journalistic dispositions and their disconnection from the skills needed to do
journalism well:

> Now everyone thinks the way you present things is you know with a
> furrowed brow and an earnest manner. (Interviewee 5, male, 58, non-
> BBC broadcast war correspondent, British)

> these guys who come back from Afghanistan with their scarves around
> their necks, a little bit of dust on their shoulders... (Interviewee 14,
> male, late 50s, US correspondent of quality UK newspaper, British)

This may be regarded as a second-order strategy aimed at enacting a
higher-level authority than that available to 'ordinary' journalists
whose conscious experience is totally immersed in that lifeworld, but
that it may serve this function does not stop it being a substantive
insight into the workings of the journalistic field. We return to this
issue in subsequent chapters.

Authority, appropriateness and felicity

While care was taken to catalogue respondents' views on issues such
as military media management, overt currencies of authority and
changes in the field of war reporting, these were not the principal
target of this research, which instead takes its cue from Bourdieu's
maxim that the content of someone's speech is less significant than
what it has to say about their authority to speak. Bourdieu rejected the
tendency of structuralist linguists such as Saussure and Austin to
separate 'internal' and 'external' linguistics, which effectively amounts
to treating language as an autonomous object that can be studied
discretely (Bourdieu, 1991b: 107–16), insisting that language cannot
be conceived in isolation from its social uses. Against Habermas'
theory of communicative action[11] (and also Giddens' (1976; 1979)
structuration theory), people do not use language instrumentally to
get what they want; instead, the language we use represents where we
already are. As Bourdieu puts it, the power of words is the delegated
power of the speaker, while the way an individual speaks is the
guarantee of delegation which is vested in her (Bourdieu, 1991b:
107). It is this which marks the methodology of this book as political:
if what someone says is less important than their authority to say it,
then the question of access to the legitimate instruments of authority
in a given context is paramount. Access is not conferred on the basis
of the content of an individual's cultural production, but their appropriateness – the naturalised, unremarkable fact of their speaking
authoritatively. And this appropriateness is not something innate to
the speaker, but the product of the mastery of a distinct, and usually
misrecognised, set of practices. The upshot is that, after Goffman, we
need to unpack the collective skilled performances which underlie
authenticity. In terms of individuals this means identifying the ritualised practices underpinning that which is perceived as character
(i.e. practices of subjectification); and in wider terms it means identifying what Bourdieu terms the conditions of felicity – that is, what
makes it possible for certain actions and statements to 'just happen'.

So how do we measure appropriateness? The question is an
important one, since one's own sense of appropriateness and recognising it in others is pre-reflexive: the whole point is that it is
naturalised and thus does not need to be – indeed, it will be seen
sometimes cannot be – explained explicitly. The risk is that such an
approach will take a lack of explicit evidence in their words as
evidence of deeper forces at work, forces posited by the theory. There
are three necessary responses to this risk. First, the aim is not to get

inside the head of the war reporter. The aim is to identify collective practices of recognition and subjectification and their political effects; these certainly shape how the lifeworld of the journalist is experienced, but it does not amount to capturing the individual's psyche. Second, there is no assumption of some meta-structure of power underlying and determining all observed behaviour. The methodology used here owes much to the linguistic tradition of discourse processing (Beaugrande, 1996). This contends that we do not carry around complete linguistic structures with us and apply them from context to context; instead, we are 'primed' or predisposed to enact structured discourses more or less spontaneously. For Bourdieu it is the structuring of that spontaneity – how it is that anticipation feels instinctive but is both regularised and has regularising effects – that is critical. But that structure only persists so long as it is enacted in practice, so that while its enactment may become ritualised, it is not monolithic (Couldry, 2003b). I noted in chapter 2 that Bourdieu tends towards conservatism in his conception of historical change, but from his ethnographic work on the structuring of anticipation it is clear that structural reproduction constituted temporally is not linear and often leads to unexpected consequences (see also Butler, 1997: 151–6). The objects of analysis here are collective orientations towards specific practices of recognition and subjectification that are particular (out of many possible) expressions of a broad set of 'genetic' preconditions, not the linear determination of some 'deep' power structure.

Third, since power relations in the journalistic or any other field are not static backdrops but contingent upon repeated, structured enactment, there is likely to be evidence in the form of cultures of practice. If legitimacy is something conferred pre-reflexively, then it is not because this is a default condition of the field but because there are ongoing, active practices which make legitimacy pre-reflective. And this raises the possibility of constructing sociological meaning out of the structures of 'ordinary' language.[12] If appropriateness is experienced as natural, it is not because it is natural but because it is, repeatedly, naturalised; and what may be felt as a pre-given and continuous sense of self depends on the structured repetition of acts of selfhood. Sometimes the evidence for such practices is overt. Phrases such as 'He just has a feel for journalism' were widespread in the data, with both 'just' and 'feel' actively fencing legitimacy off from explicit delineation, simultaneously positioning an individual journalist as authoritative and marking the practice of recognition of authority as intuitive – as well as establishing the 'natural' appropriateness of the speaker to perform such recognition. In other cases the evidence is a kind of absence, in the form of sentences abandoned incomplete because of the ineffability or overwhelming obviousness of authority or its absence. This again is an active decontestation of what constitutes authority, as something which just is, which in spite of (or because of) the speaker's inability to express the conferral of legitimacy verbally nonetheless enacts his appropriateness to confer it.

More frequently, however, the decontestation of authority and appropriateness is effected not through direct ascriptions of such but specific styles of speech used when talking about external subjects and objects. Most often this is an aspect of journalistic work or other actors engaged in the field of conflict but, as Bourdieu demonstrates forcefully in *Distinction*, positionings and their decontestation can be achieved through a broad array of social signifiers that will also include taste, leisure pursuits and so on. This, again, does not suggest the instrumental use of language to appropriate authority,[13] but rather a shared culture of practice which actors in the field become more or less naturally oriented to enacting, un- or pre-reflexively, and recognising in the behaviour of others. For example, we will see in subsequent chapters that there is a collective culture of practice in which reporters respond to restrictions on mobility by way of pooling with ironic detachment and wry humour, rather than, say, outrage or a pious defence of journalistic autonomy. Thus, what could otherwise be seen as a dismissal or downplaying of the issue can instead be constructed as an active positioning. That this response is unremarkably appropriate across the interviews demonstrates a shared set of practices of self-positioning experienced as unreflective: it's 'just' a matter of being 'realistic'. The result is a common set of practices of subjectification or disposition – including traits such as world-weariness, misanthropy and ambivalence – which in part encode legitimacy in a way that necessarily, and strategically, evades description. By looking at common reactions to or ways of speaking about certain objects as specific cultures out of a range of possible cultures, it is possible to identify their decontesting effects and how appropriateness – that which is experienced as unproblematic, pre-given legitimacy – is constituted.

Coding the interview data

Focusing on shared sets of practices is one way of avoiding overloading every statement made by an interviewee as indicative of authority in a way that decontests what authority is and how it is recognised.

Even then, it is clear that there are some speech styles which are consistent across the sample but which do not say anything in particular about the fields of journalism or conflict. Where, then, to draw the line? When a respondent meanders off topic to ask me if I had seen the football match last night, is this to be read as a positioning of self within a complex symbolic economy according to interests – especially considering that legitimacy and authenticity among journalists appear to be tied to anti-elitist, demotic cultural capital? How different would the interview had been if I had arrived late? The Bourdieusian approach would hold that the particular speech acts emerging in a particular interview are expressions of the logic of the fields involved (journalism, academia etc.), without being inferable from the generative structures of those fields. Thus, while there is a (one-to-many) link between the underlying logic of the lifeworld of the journalist and the things he says, what does emerge cannot be predicted, nor can we work back from speech acts to build a definitive account of the field's generative structures.[14] What we can produce is an account of the symbolic economies extant in a field: namely valorised forms of symbolic capital and the (usually misrecognised) practices which must be mastered in order to appropriate this capital – and this is what follows in the next chapter. But it is not pedantic to stress that not all statements contribute to such an account. Bourdieu's genetic, microscopic conception of power is significantly insightful in uncovering the operation of coercive power relations in the seemingly quotidian and mundane. But the assumption of political pervasiveness must be seen as a normative commitment, and the social scientist is justified when objectifying interview data to distinguish the politically significant and insignificant.

Similarly, computational coding of interview text allows for the application of more or less infinite layers of codes, but it should not be assumed that the process will lead to some idealised point of satur-ation at which the true meaning of the text is grasped. In fact the main advantage of computational coding, bearing in mind that it remains a primarily organisational process underpinning qualitative analysis rather than doing the analysing, is flexibility. Codes and branches of codes could be easily moved around the overall tree, cutting where necessary for clarity, allowing for the development of a framework that is simultaneously systematic and intuitive to use. The first set of codes catalogued information about the speaker: their name (subsequently redacted), demographic details, current position and employment history, used in the analysis to answer broad questions about whether there are any cultures of practice among the interviewees which are structured by gender, generation, nationality, medium or market position. Next, text was coded for referent: what the speaker was speaking about, which ranged from other actors in the fields of journalism and war to statements about themselves and more abstract objects such as timeliness and danger. The aim here was to see if the correspondents tended to talk about certain objects in certain ways, which may be interpreted as a self-positioning in relation to that object. We will see in the next chapter, for instance, that speech style tended towards understatement when talking about elite power or high-risk situations, and that this can be interpreted as the enactment of an ambivalent attitude which marks an alternate (and unacknowledged) means of making distinctions against other actors (part of a wider alternate symbolic economy) as opposed to journalistic practice as such.

Next were codings of quality ascribed to an object, an expansive category of 47 often overlapping terms ranging from 'trustworthy' and 'courageous' to 'control freak' and 'risk averse', as well as more simple assessments of positive and negative attributes. These were grouped where possible into binary pairs, since to make a distinction against another's gullibility, for instance, is to signify one's own relative integrity. This was one category where, once all interviews had been coded, they were coded again for specific absences of ascriptions of qualities either where other speakers had made such ascriptions, or simply where they might reasonably be expected. Using the previous example to illustrate the point, the lack of any ascription of danger to a conflict situation described by others as perilous could be read in three ways. First, it could be that the danger of a war zone is simply presumed, too obvious to bear explication (see below). Second, we could take at face value the correspondent's fearlessness, shaped as it is by personal experience and professionalism. Third, the lack of a specific ascription can be read not as a simple absence but an alternate signification which is meaningful in the context of an economy in which unostentatious bravery is a valorised form of symbolic capital. This interpretation is consistent with explicit valorisations made in the interviews, in which integrity is associated more with 'grit' and 'just getting the job done' than overt heroics.

A similar line of reasoning applied to codings for speech style. While there was extensive evidence of what appeared to be genuine outrage, usually at the behaviour of other journalists, of particular interest were speech styles which actively decontest that which is being expressed: namely understatement and offhandedness. For instance when a respondent describes as part of her professional history 'doing a little bit on the fall of communism', she establishes not only the fact of this experience but the utter unremarkability that she would have done so, and thus her natural appropriateness as a journalistic authority. Humour played an important role in the discourse analysis, apparently having the functions of defusing more contentious statements and, more significantly, establishing an irreverence associated with anti-establishment authority. Irony, too, seemed to serve the purpose of establishing an ambivalent relation to an object, though it proved difficult to code – it is often open to interpretation whether a speaker is being ironic. None of this is to suggest that there is a singular journalistic voice, whether through journalists internalising a professional discourse or consciously mimicking perceived ideal types – indeed on the limited evidence available it appears that an idiosyncratic manner is linked to the specifically individualistic authority which dominates the field. Further, it is impossible from the interviews to discern the extent to which the interview context itself structures speech style. But there is clear evidence of similarities in the way that journalists enact principles of differentiation through the way they speak, which can defensibly be analysed in strategic terms in the sense developed in chapter 2 – that is, as the result of a naturalised orientation towards practices structured according to anticipation of likely outcomes in a field whose stakes are internalised as normal.

To these broad codes were added a series of more technical codes drawn largely from the discourse analysis model developed by Norman Fairclough (1995; 2003).[15] 'Experiential' codes included classification schemes (professional, moral etc.) and resignification of contestable terms, such as using 'code of conduct' to mean a mutual understanding between journalists rather than a technocratic or legalistic list of rules. 'Relational' codes were ultimately subsumed under style, and included euphemism, formality and informality: there were instances where an interviewee's speech style became more formal when talking about a sensitive topic or one about which they were defensive, and there was limited evidence of shifts towards looser language apparently aimed at establishing rapport with the interviewer. This is in line with a recurring theme of this book: that the mastery of practices enacting (i.e. being recognised as) informality or felicity is central to the performance and perception of authenticity (Ytreberg, 2002). Authenticity in turn is pivotal in the presentation of self in everyday life, and in the journalistic field in particular – both in the need for journalists to establish a sense of complicity or immediacy with their audiences, and in the context of a broader cultural shift away from institutional authority. Metaphors were widely used and proved significant in the analysis: using the metaphor of tourism, for instance, was a common way of establishing not only opposition to the pooling system, but a knowing, realistic opposition associated with naturalised authority. Grammatical codes paid particular attention to active/passive voice and overt/latent agency. Consider the contrast between the following statements by a war reporter and US government press officer, respectively:

> So the Americans were firing on them [Iraqi troops] from over there, behind the hill. (Interviewee 5)

> There was an instance where the coverage of the killed and wounded coming back from a friendly fire incident was not allowed and facilitated. (Interviewee 7, female, late 40s, US State Department press official, American)

While the obscured agency of the second quotation appears to indicate a reluctance to be frank about restrictions placed on the media, it can also reasonably be assumed to reflect (rather than provide evidence of) the institutionalised discourse of government media management. Likewise, while the first statement appears to be a fairly straightforward description of events on the ground, it must also be thought of as situated within the context of the journalistic field, in which it will be seen in the next chapter that a plain-speaking demeanour is a valorised, anti-establishment commodity. What Fairclough terms 'relational grammar' codes included authoritative modality, expressive statements (might, should etc.), statement grammar (imperatives, rhetorical questions etc.) and, significantly, inclusions and exclusions. This last subcategory catalogued the use of words such as we/they and us/them to track a speaker's distance or proximity to other actors; it will be seen in the next chapter, for instance, that newspaper war reporters frequently presented themselves as part of a group of elite actors alongside senior military personnel, in shared opposition to junior 'grunts' in the military and the lower echelons of the news media – usually meaning commercial television.

Let us consider two extracts to illustrate the coding and inference processes:

> You know, some of 'em are more used to human interest stories and that shit, you know, 'cause that's what they're used to, it's all nice stuff about Private Johnny and his kids back home in Nebraska. (Interviewee 10, male 28, war correspondent, US weekly news magazine, American)

This was coded first for the speaker's biographical details, in this case a younger (28-year-old) male American war reporter for a weekly US news magazine. The respondent's relative lack of experience (he had recently returned from Afghanistan, his 'first war', as he put it) is predicted by the theoretical model to play a part in a generational struggle within war reporting,[16] and it will be seen in the following chapter that there is sufficient evidence to bear this out. The divides between print journalists and the target of his ire here – television journalists – is evident, as is the connected opposition between hard news and human interest journalism, but these are clearly distinctions made at a very conscious level rather than in the unremarkable, pre-reflexive experience of the field. The phrase 'It's all nice stuff' was coded for dismissiveness: more than simple criticism, the style of this put-down is infantalising, casting its object as unserious and over-indulged. The implication is that war reporting should be the opposite of 'nice', a clear theme across the interviews which validates Matheson's (2003) claim that war reporters share an epistemological relation to the world which sees the process of fact-gathering as fundamentally onerous. Likewise, the mocking use of Nebraska to evoke parochialism suggests an opposite valorised form of symbolic capital – worldliness – whose naturalised centrality to the discourse of journalistic professionalism was evident in many interviews, but in particular amongst American interviewees. The reference to Private Johnny is an interesting one, suggesting practices of distinction made not only against positions in the journalistic field but the military field as well. There are also more generic forms of decontestation in this passage: the demarcation of 'them' as opposed to us serves the dual purpose of setting out a relational position according to principle, and characterising the speaker's opposites as an undifferentiated mass. The implication, and very much one that is implied rather than consciously argued, is that valorised authority amongst war reporters tends to be highly individualised – which points to a broader cultural shift that is a key theme of this book.

> They pointed their guns at us and shouted, 'Who are you? You don't have credentials.' And we were like, 'This is Pristina, we don't need credentials.' But it was all quite fun though. (Interviewee 13, male, late 30s, war correspondent, UK broadsheet, British)

This passage is quite different, in that rather than overtly expressing an opinion it forms part of a narrative about a past event, inevitably invoking assumptions and terms of reference as it develops in a way that appears significantly more likely to be instinctive rather than consciously thought through. A pattern emerged amongst war reporters, particularly male, with little bias in age or nationality, whereby speakers distanced themselves from the substance of their work by expressing an offhand, light-hearted or ambivalent response to a situation of real danger or involving powerful individuals. Here, the speaker, a late thirtysomething British reporter for a UK broadsheet, defuses what is clearly a tense situation first with a line 'And we were, like, "This is Pristina, we don't need credentials"' that was delivered with a defiance that sounded more than anything like a teenager dismissing a meddling parent,[17] and then with a sardonic meta-statement about it being 'fun'. Without doubting the speaker's sincerity there is the possibility that this, if mirrored in other interviews, indicates a culture of practice of positioning by establishing the speaker as a natural comfort with his professional world, expressed through an amused detachment in relation to his work. Importantly, and in contrast to reflexive statements about colleagues performing gravel-voiced stereotypes, there appears to be no premeditiation in such statements, suggesting that this may indicate the pre-reflexive enactment of strategies oriented to an economy of authority – we return to this issue in the next chapter.

To return to a point made earlier, references to symbolic economies should not conjure up mathematical models for inferring valorised forms of capital and the ways they are appropriated and made use of (Jones and Collins, 2006; Richardson, 2008). The aim of the discourse analysis is instead, first, to identify patterns in linguistic practice – if it is common to talk about an object in a certain way, for example – and, second, to attempt to establish what contingencies are decontested by their observed normalisation. To illustrate the point, one interesting finding was that the use of expletives was widely restricted to denunciations of peers rather than to accounts of dangerous or dramatic situations. This pattern seems to reflect that journalistic integrity in this context is connected both to irreverence in negotiating the professional environment (also observed in relation to more formal or restrictive contexts such as dealings with politicians and diplomats) and to an untheatrical attitude to the work of war reporting. It is worth emphasising that this is not a neat conclusion drawn from linear inferencing, and in this case the US news weekly correspondent provides a vivid counter-example. The significance of this example is that for a number of those interviewed, who are assumed by their common immersion in the field to share a group habitus, having an undramatic relation to one's work and a prickly relation to others are experienced as a natural fit, something which feels appropriate but would not (or could not) be consciously articulated. More broadly, this methodological approach aims to identify what is pre-reflexively recognised as obviously legitimate or illegitimate; and in Foucualdian terms, it aims to develop an account of what is speakable and unspeakable in the discourse of war reporting.

The political dimension of this is twofold. First, such a natural attitude will come more easily to some than others. Second, naturalisation decontests not only modes of expression but the collective recognition of professional norms and cultural values. Sometimes the unthinking shorthand used to recount a professional experience is just that: shorthand, a necessary component of all communication. But where there are collective, instinctive ways of expressing or responding to categories such as authority and authenticity, we can validly characterise these not as things which just are, but as practices which have to be mastered, practices which are simultaneously strategic and uncalculated. There is a wider school of thought (Andrejevic, 2008; Dent, 2008; van Dijk, 2009) that uses Foucauldian theory to investigate how journalism, and specifically news values, contributes to social reproduction by normalising the way we talk about certain things. Here, the focus is less on news values than a naturalised epistemological relation to the world (Höijer, 2008) and specifically how it structures relations between journalists and between journalism and adjacent fields. But this is not simply an intellectual exercise in identifying a new, arcane realm of determinism: it goes beyond news values to examine the contingently stabilised practices and principles which underpin, though usually unacknowledged, debates over values and ethics. Consider access to sources as an example. Debates over access in war reporting tend to focus on how it should be facilitated and when it can defensibly be restricted. But common to these divergent views is the centrality of witnessing, in particular first-person witnessing, to journalistic practice. This is not to undermine the importance of witnessing in war reporting, but it is worth pointing out that it is tied to a specific epistemology in which communicative authenticity is key – and authenticity is not a universal property but a collectively recognised symbolic form. If we can identify the cultures of practice which enable the enactment and recognition of authenticity, then it becomes possible critically to question broader commonplaces, such as the conflation of individualised authenticity and journalistic authority, which could after all take other forms. None of this is to suggest that authenticity is a bad thing – simply that it is situated in a relational field of forces in whose defence or overthrow different groups have a stake. Having established how we might move from observed patterns of behaviour to embedded schemes of recognition to naturalised norms in the field of war reporting and beyond, we can now turn to the main findings of this study.

Notes

1 Bourdieu (2004: 2, 91) consistently distanced his model from postmodernist history and sociology and the technique of deconstruction, labelling it 'relativist' and 'narcissistic'. On Bourdieu's opposition to Derrida and Lyotard, see also Lacey (1998: 174n).

2 Cassirer's influence is evident here. Cassirer developed the concept of 'lawful series of progressions' to describe the coherent network that scientific concepts inhabit. His form of neo-Kantian transcendental logic posits that the object is not presupposed by logic, but generated by it. See Bourdieu (1990b: 40); Vandenberghe, 1999: 33n.3; Bourdieu (2000: 175). Bourdieu published Cassirer's work in a collection he edited in the 1970s.

3 Kögler (1997) notes that it was Mannheim's inability to escape the philosophy of consciousness that led him to conceive of symbolic forms as pre-determined categorical apparatuses, or 'conceptual institutions'.

4 'Taking part in the *illusio* ... means taking seriously stakes which, arising from the logic of the game itself, establish its "seriousness", even if they escape or appear "disinterested" or "gratuitous" to those who are sometimes called "lay people" or those who are engaged in other fields' (Bourdieu, 2000: 11). See also Bourdieu (2005: 37).

5 Mannheim maintained that the proper object of sociology is pretheoretical cultural life, and to this end constructed a phenomenology of cultural meaning-constitution by which he claimed to be able to reach a level of interpretative and symbolic assumptions which may not be consciously intended by the subject (Kögler, 1997: 144–6).

6 This is also termed the 'space of possibles' of agency (Bourdieu, 1993a: 64).

7 Some critics, including Bohman (1997), have argued that it is Bourdieu's overpoliticisation of capital which is at the root of the determinism of his approach. In this book I take the view that capital is used by Bourdieu primarily as a methodological device to measure the enactment and embodiment of power relations in field contexts, and as such it is the structural determination of practice whose political teleology is suspect.

8 Hamel (1998: 10) notes that Bourdieu's position in this regard is adjacent to that of Giddens, who argues that 'any social agent has a high degree of knowledge which he invokes in the production and reproduction of daily social practices, but the greater part of this knowledge is practical rather than theoretical'.

9 This can be interpreted as a strategic positioning in relation to an

objective reality: the lack of wealth in the journalistic field. According to a National Union of Journalists Report (Slattery, 2004), nearly half of all UK journalists earn less than the national average wage of £26,151; almost three-quarters of journalists earn less than the UK average wage of a professional worker of £35,766; 80 per cent of journalists would be unable to obtain a mortgage to buy the average house in the UK.

10 Against this, Bohman (1997: 177) argues: '[r]eflexivity is not primarily an effect of theory, as Bourdieu often argues, but a component of the public, practical reason of agents who interpret and reinterpret their practices with others.'

11 Bourdieu (2000: 66) argues that Habermas simultaneously reduces and depoliticises social relations in his theory of communicative action.

12 'Ordinary language passes unnoticed, because it is so ordinary, but it carries in its vocabulary and syntax a petrified philosophy of the social, always ready to spring out of the common words, or complex expressions made up of common words, that the sociologist inevitably uses' (Bourdieu et al., 1991: 21).

13 Derek Robbins (2000: 297) explains this well: 'Every speech act and, more generally, every action is a conjecture, an encounter between independent causal series. On the one hand there are the socially constructed dispositions of the linguistic habitus which imply a certain propensity to speak and to say legitimate things (the expressive interest) and a certain capacity to speak, which involves both the linguistic capacity to generate an infinite number of grammatically correct discourses, and the social capacity to use this competence adequately in a determinate situation. On the other hand, there are the structures of the linguistic market which impose themselves as a system of specific sanctions and censorships.'

14 This is consistent with Derrida's (1991) claim that the unpredictability of language and its inevitable failure to describe what it intends to, means that observed utterances cannot be read as simple expressions of discourse.

15 See also van Dijk (1998); Wodak (2001); Hammersley (2002). This form of discourse analysis is distinct from critical discourse analysis (CDA), which seeks to effect social change through its practice. See, for instance, Hammersley (1997); Carvalho (2008); Scheuer (2003).

16 One editor (Interviewee 6) explained that generation becomes more significant the longer a war goes on: 'Well there was this situation in Vietnam where the longer the war went on the younger the journalists became, you know because young journalists are cheaper.'

17 This metaphor recurs in chapter 7, to demonstrate an interviewee's wish to keep his editor at arm's length.

4

Practical mastery of authority, authenticity and disposition

As the preceding chapters have made clear, the purpose of this book is not to tell the personal stories of individual war reporters, but to describe the structured, structuring logics which determine how the field of war reporting is experienced. In fact the two are related, since individuation, along with professional identities and values, is among the common matrices by which individuals make sense of their professional lives. However, the political phenomenological focus on generative logics necessitates a distinctive way of engaging with field actors, with three factors worth foregrounding. First, the symbolic meaning attached to a journalistic subject or object – an individual's status or the value of a piece of journalism – is produced not individually but collectively by everyone with a stake in what is valorised in the journalistic field. To understand journalism we need to take into account the interest that external as well as internal actors have in changes and continuities in how the symbolic world and relations of power in journalism are structured: editors, proprietors. For this study, interviews were carried out with 14 actors with an active interest in the field of war correspondence in the period 1990–2004. Eight of the interviewees were war correspondents, of whom 5 were journalists active in the British media, 3 in the American media; 5 worked in print media, 3 in broadcast journalism. There were 6 male and 2 female correspondents, and ages ranged from 28 to late 60s. In addition, interviews were conducted with two newspaper editors (one of whom had been a war correspondent previously), a US government official, a think tank president and a (retired) US Army general, who at the time of the interview also advised a think tank.

Second, since the journalistic field is conceived as a differential space, particular attention was paid to self-positionings and distinctions made between different objects, subjects and symbolic values. The positions identified in the interviews are in fact moving points in time and space, and individuals are repositories of internalised structures or matrices of practice, inscribed with a socially specific past and orienting themselves towards their possible futures (Bourdieu, 1996: 258; see also Ekelund, 2000; Power, 2004; Philo, 2007). I thus began by asking interviewees for their professional histories: their reasons for entering the journalistic field, how they came to specialise in war correspondence (and equivalent questions for those working in governmental and military positions), which newspapers or broadcast corporations they had worked for (and in which capacity). This did not lead to the construction of an overall personal trajectory for each respondent, but the interviews did track in particular whether moves in respondents' careers were horizontal or vertical – whether, for instance, a reporter moved from one paper to another of similar symbolic status, working in a position of similar esteem or influence, or instead moved from a desk job to working in the field, or from writing copy to editing or writing comment pieces. An interviewee's accumulation of cultural and social capital derives not only from professional seniority, but also in how professional success has translated into connections and achievements outside the subfield of war correspondence. Participants were thus asked, usually indirectly in response to an aside, about their activities in other media and their liaisons with academic and political institutions.

Third, it has been established that phenomenology seeks to construct methodologically the taken-for-granted symbolic world individuals inhabit, and political phenomenology seeks to document those mechanisms, experienced as given, that naturalise and reproduce hierarchies of domination and dominatedness. This means identifying through the interviews which symbolic forms are instinctively valorised and who is pre-reflexively authorised to consecrate symbolic forms as meaningful. Any interview inevitably captures only a fragment of the naturalised distinctions that individuals instinctively make, and overly directive questioning runs the risk of over-determining the responses given. Bearing this in mind, the interviews were only semi-structured, with interviewees allowed to meander from the core questions at will.[1] This allowed for unforced descriptions of whatever came to an interviewee's mind, with an abundance of more or less spontaneous evocations of principles of differentiation which did not have to be articulated or explained because they were seemingly experienced as entirely ordinary. While this kind of interview is not unstructured or more authentic than a formal question-and-response style, it does produce solid evidence of the collectively internalised and normalised principles of differentiation which shape individuals' experience of their lifeworld as given. Reflexive, in vivo distinctions between valued and unvalued symbolic forms in journalism took three broad forms: those differentiating between journalistic practices, those identifying personal qualities needed to be a good war reporter, and distinctions about personal character which are not obviously connected to the demands of war reporting. We will discover here that in fact for all of these categories it is the case that there is no natural connection between the job itself and the valorised forms routinely associated with doing it well, and that there are alternate, misrecognised, symbolic economies which determine the structures of the latter.

Pronouncements about news values largely confirmed the values commonly identified in the literature (see for instance Deuze, 2005: 446–7): objectivity, autonomy, public service, neutrality, protection of sources, timeliness and impact. However, reflexive valuations of other journalists did not usually proceed on the basis of these values: it was rare for respondents to explain another's worth (or lack thereof) as a journalist in terms of their timeliness or respect for source anonymity. Instead, reporters were judged on their perceived professional authority, which was predominantly associated with a number of character traits which suited or ill-suited their working in journalism – they were either naturals or completely lacking the qualities needed ever to become a good journalist. Specifically, authority largely took the form of integrity, conceived in terms of being quietly, unproblematically principled, and can be broken down into several categories. First, while autonomy was listed above as a criterion for establishing the value of a journalistic output, it also applies to the type of journalist someone is. Most obviously this means independence from undue influence from censors, military media managers and political representatives, though it was more frequently evoked in relation to independence (or lack of it) from non-elite military personnel and other journalists. The latter is an unequivocal and effective means of establishing a speaker's distinction against the vast majority of peers, who are described as an undifferentiated mass using terms like 'sheep' and 'herded', or simply 'everybody else' – in each case, recognition of their authority as sentient professionals is withheld. The inability to keep a professional distance from the military on which they were reporting, and indeed their barely disguised glee to gain proximity, was a common focus of criticism of pooled journalists:

> Bottom line was that a lot of the press you know thought this was wonderful, because they were given backpacks and they were you know

given chocolate chip trousers and jackets and all the fucking paraphernalia of military status ... a lot of journalists love it, they love it, they get sucked in by the military, which is of course the idea. (Interviewee 5)

I think he was tricked into becoming too close to the armed forces. (Interviewee 4, female, 38, BBC/ABC broadcast journalist and producer, Australian)

In the first quote, the word 'wonderful' was emphasised with a derisiveness that bordered on campness, not merely stating disapproval but doing so in a way that implies a natural personal disinclination to be easily impressed. 'Love it' likewise suggests that these journalists' delight is immature and irrational while 'which is of course the idea', rhetorically emphasised by its position at the end of an utterance, neatly demonstrates the speaker's ability to see through military media management strategies and remain level-headedly, calmly autonomous. It will be seen below that this sort of distinction making, setting oneself apart from the pack, is underpinned by structured significations of personality, and is consistent with the distinctly individualised form that authority has traditionally taken in war reporting. The word 'tricked' in the second quote signals a similar consecration of independence of mind, as well as an established trope amongst war reporters that there is a game (the precise nature of which varies from conflict to conflict) played by military and media personnel in which each tries to outwit and second-guess the other. While it is not our intention to downplay the dangers inherent in conflict situations, interviewees evidently did do so, performing a distancing of their professional selves from the visceral nature of their work, and an emphasis on the criterion of guile – often described in a way that almost suggests cheekiness – over formal objectivity or bravery.

A second key principle of differentiation was selflessness, set in opposition to egoism. This was most commonly invoked in criticisms of journalists being more interested in their profile rather than 'the story':

I have seen times when there's just a certain mentality in a war correspondent which is after self-glory, and cameramen as well. I mean, to really stand out from the crowd, you have to do the crazy thing. Like what's-his-name, the Telegraph guy who walked into the Falklands ... (Interviewee 8, female, 40s, non-BBC broadcast journalist, American)

'Self-glory' is otherwise expressed in descriptions of reporters as 'self-obsessed', 'narcissistic' and 'pompous'. It will be seen below that, at least amongst that culture of war reporting that sees its role as prioritising facts over moralising, authority is in part contingent on a self-effacing disposition, which is to say the embodiment of practices which are recognised or misrecognised as constituting self-efface-ment. This is an instance of what I referred to earlier as the 'interest in disinterest' (Bourdieu, 1993a: 154) – an apparent disavowal of status or riches which may be strategically oriented towards achieving exactly that (see below). Selflessness is also sometimes used to mitigate another quality, such as adventurousness, which elsewhere would be expected to be valued. In the following, Interviewee 4 recounts the story of a colleague ignoring travel restrictions in East Timor:

> And they were ambushed. And they shot the driver, and he [the journalist] managed to jump into the bushes, and fortunately he had a mobile phone he was able to phone the soldiers who then risked their lives coming to find him. I remember we were about to do a live interview with him, we had the camera there and this woman comes up and she's just tears streaming and she's screaming and she just comes up and starts hitting him around the face and it's the driver's wife. Now up until that point he has been talking quite happily, you know the brave journalist, how I got the story, and he seemed a little bit shocked after the interview but he got through it fine, did a live interview for the ABC, but I found it quite shocking, because his stupidity had meant this person's life. I don't like that and I've met other war correspondents who are more interested in telling you what they've done than the actual situation or what the local people are doing or suffering. (Interviewee 4)

This is an illustration of the point that the struggle between groups characterised by distinct class habitus is never only about accumulat-ing dominant symbolic capital but also pursuing the power to determine what that dominant form is. The last quote can thus be seen both as an expression of genuinely felt outrage and a delegit-imising practice. The interviewee's opinion that audacity and relishing danger amount not to courageousness but recklessness may be experi-enced as authentic while still being, in phenomenological terms, a structured strategic practice determined by a sub-culture of practice the individuated members of which have an interest in overthrowing the dominant culture, itself characterised by determinate, naturalised norms and practices. While it is impossible to extrapolate from a rela-tively small sample, it is interesting that this oppositional opinion is expressed in a distinctly measured tone, evidence perhaps of the maxim that the content of what is said cannot be decoupled from the manner in and position from which it is said.

More ineffably, integrity is also instantiated in the quality of substance, an extension of the traditional distinction between hard and soft news to personal character. Substance is used to encapsulate a variety of aspects of a journalist's authority that would otherwise be difficult to define, such as worldliness and gravitas or their opposites:

> that's not a press issue, that's not the kind of thing that I think about, it's analysis, it's soundbites on television. What's my concern is, what news editors' concerns are, reporters' concerns are, news reporting, access to news, not whether someone calls this a quagmire on the editorial page. That is true, that is carried in newspapers and in all 24 hour cable channels, that is not news, that is thumb sucking. (Interviewee 3, male, 50s, US think tank president, American)

Here, comment and analysis are that to which real, substantial journalism is diametrically opposed. Even though the newspapers being discussed are the *New York Times* and *Washington Post*, uncontroversially categorisable as elite media institutions with high amounts of consecrated cultural capital, the same type of infantalisation is deployed to make clear that the speaker does not recognise these journalists as authoritative. As with the critique of egoism above, this should be regarded both as a genuinely felt opinion and a collective strategy, of which he and his practices are an individual manifestation, to accumulate and determine valorised forms of symbolic capital in the field. The following comment by Interviewee 10 shows how substance and insubstantiality are often expressed through strikingly literal metaphors:

> But TV, fucking fluff monkeys. On TV all they want to do is put on familiar faces, instead of good journos. It's all about face time to them, so they put these fucking fluff monkeys out there. See with TV the standards are lower, and that's producers too, not just the journos. There's not as many of 'em, and they don't know anything. It's like you'll get a guy and it's like the most exciting thing he'd ever done was the floods in Chicago or something. (Interviewee 10)

The pervasiveness of nodes of grit and dirt, opposed to air and 'fluff', is an important component of the symbolic world of the journalist which is simultaneously experienced as pre-given and is contingent on specific cultural and political conditions. This is a world in which facts have to be captured or liberated – and we could add in which a willingness to get one's hands dirty goes hand in hand with an unshowy, ruggedly individual correspondent disposition.

Economies of esotericisation and ambivalence

We saw in chapter 2 that this disposition or any others are not owned by individuals: they are a template of dispositional practices which precede individual journalists and in fact are central to their becoming conscious professional subjects. Dispositions are generative templates rather than identities or ideal types, and their enactment is heterogeneous – both because of natural variance within the parameters of the journalistic field and because they overlap and potentially pull in different directions from other determining forces. The specific practices underpinning dispositions are discussed below, but first we need to ask how it comes to pass that an individual's enactment of structured, structuring practices is recognised by others (and self) as personal character trait. There are two symbolic economies which underpin this transaction, economies which are presumed to proceed below the consciousness of the professional in normal circumstances.

The first of these is an economy of esotericisation. In accordance with the sociology of professions (Johnson, 1972), it was found that ascriptions of journalistic success were expressed in terms which defied questioning or disaggregation. Authority figures were said to have a 'feel' for journalism, a verbal invocation of the Bourdieusian habitus naturally aligned to the contingencies of the game in which it finds itself.

> He's just a better journalist; he always had a feel [gestures] for the job which Fialka doesn't ... it was like he had a sense for these things. (Interviewee 1, male, 65, retired army general, American)

> they get a really good sense of what a reporter is. (Interviewee 2, male, late 50s, UK broadsheet columnist and former war reporter, British)

> He did his job very well, really good at just like sniffing a thread, you know getting a hint of something, some movement or something and ... uncovering what's going on there, really quite insightful. (Interviewee 9, male, 50s, public radio broadcaster/editor, American)

In these brief examples are an array of indicators of esotericisation, including 'just' and 'feel' in the first and 'sense' and the emphasis on 'is' in the second. Beyond explicit invocations of the 'feel', there were many instances where participants literally shut down the possibility of contestation by trailing off in mid sentence. The apparent suggestion in these cases is that a journalist's authority, where present, is self-evident – literally too obvious to be able to explain. The inability to articulate this verbally comes with the implication that one just knows: it cannot be described let alone explained or deconstructed, and if you have to ask you'll certainly never understand. For several participants these utterances were accompanied by gesticulations (seemingly) indicating frustration at attempting to give form to the self-evident.

While there are clear pathways by which an individual can acquire the requisite skills to practise journalism, there is no obvious route by which an inexperienced journalist or outsider can acquire the talent – often referred to as a 'nose' or an 'eye' for news – to become a 'good' journalist, more precisely to accumulate the symbolic capital needed to be widely recognised as authoritative in journalism. The implication is that good journalists are good journalists from the start – before entering the field – or have some natural instinct by which their progress towards the top of the professional media hierarchy is more or less predestined. In Weberian fashion, actors occupying specific objective positions in the field of journalism – or, before embarking on a career, positions in the hierarchical social, cultural and educational spaces endemic to the society in which an individual grows up – with which at a given place and time particular configurations of symbolic capital are associated, over time come to embody those position-takings and capitals through the collective misrecognition of immersed actors of contingent symbolic forms as natural. What is demonstrably a socio-historical specificity assumes the deontological status of a mystic good, all the more valuable for being unattainable by those who do not already possess it.

The political effects of misrecognition are clear. First, by esotericising the constituent parts of journalistic skill, contestation of what it means to be a good journalist is effectively precluded. Second, through recognition by other actors of natural repositories of authority, field actors are able to extend their dominance over determination of the principles of legitimising good journalism. The reproductive aspect of legitimising power through esotericisation is readily describable: those regarded as natural personifications of journalistic values regularly gain employment as commentators, columnists, analysts, editors and consultants,[2] positions in which ruling on journalistic and broader cultural legitimacy and merit is a basic part of the job. Since senior journalists routinely come to have influence not only within journalism but in politics and over the public, and since gaining such authority is not so much an individual achievement as a set of collective strategic practices, then esotericisation can be seen as a deep-rooted strategy by which journalism competes with other subfields of the wider field of cultural production, specifically enshrining journalism's unique authority to rule on what counts as public knowledge:

> I don't mean an egotistical, egomaniacal role, I mean our very basic role, which is our basic mandate, of going in and bringing information back to people wherever they might be. (Interviewee 8)

> You gotta open people's minds to the world out there, you know? (Interviewee 9)

There is a contrast here between a principled, even pious statement about the role that journalism serves in contemporary society, which makes use of a word usually associated with political legitimacy ('mandate'), and a more rough-and-ready perspective that sees journalists as having a basic duty of care to clueless audiences who do not understand how things really are. It will be seen in chapter 5 that these are associated with two forms of authority in war reporting which have traditionally competed for dominance.

The second systematically misrecognised symbolic economy evident among the war reporters interviewed, which is to say a coherent system of positioning, appearing and contesting, was one of ambivalence towards power and danger. While there was scattered evidence of disavowing economic gain as a goal, with a few instances of colleagues deemed to have 'sold out',[3] there was a far more systematic ambivalence towards power of the type wielded by the military and political professionals with whom they interact, and a routine playing down of the risks and drama of the work of war reporting.

> journalists who have been wounded or killed or otherwise prevented from doing their job. (Interviewee 8)

> you could get shot at and strafed if you played your cards right. (Interviewee 5)

> Drew would be great if you want to talk to the bang bang guys. (Interviewee 10)

> I'd done a little bit on the fall of communism .... (Interviewee 8)

It is difficult to draw definitive conclusions, and advisable in any case to remember that the determination of speech style in the context of a field is always to a degree unpredictable. However, in the interviews it was clearly evident that an interviewee's tone was likely to be more offhand, irreverent, often playful and frequently modest when either directly describing, or evoking as context for specific referents, situations involving significant risk, personal achievement and powerful figures.[4] These modes of playing down symbolic capital which have high value outside the journalistic field can be explained in two ways. First, at the level of the field of cultural production, the fact of dealing with extraordinary situations on an everyday basis, and embodying these practices in a way that appears quite normal, allow the symbolic form of individual as recognisable war reporter to be concretised. Broad recognition of this specific authoritative status is contingent upon established cultural identities of war reporter in a given context, and thus is more correctly described as the misrecognition of professional identity. This misrecognition is a practical act which consists in the iteration and reiteration of the possession of something which cannot be possessed, with the ultimate end of naturalised embodiment of a property which, in absolute terms, is unembodiable. However, because recognition of authority in those best oriented towards practising professional dispositions occurs pre-reflexively and universally across a finite cultural space, the power (in the form of status and influence) it accords a field actor is very real. The transformation of war reporting's object from one of obvious drama to one of ordinary reportorial material thus involves the esotericisation of journalistic professional practice and, by extension, the mystification of the journalistic subject.[5] Coming to inhabit the field position of 'war correspondent' entails a transformation inconceivable to other cultural producers, the public and arguably other journalists, which means that the finite conditions of possibility of the symbolic forms that individual reporter-subjects and the genre of war reporting assume are effectively obscured.

It is worth taking seriously the argument that all interactions – not just communicative ones but practices of recognition and authorisation – are at base interactions between fields (see for instance Bourdieu, 2005). But chapter 2 established that while Bourdieu often appears to dismiss the individual as a valid locus of meaning, individuals do matter insofar as there are locally stabilised individuations. That is, while the primary focus of political phenomenology is the generative structures that make individuation possible, and while there are no discrete, essential individuals in this philosophy, the actions of individuated field subjects are important because their actions have real effects. This leads us to the internal logic of the subfield of war reporting and how it structures competition between journalists (and groups of journalists) and shapes the discipline's internal hierarchies. In this vein, it is valid to hypothesise that as war correspondents share a journalistic object – conflict – then they will find recourse to other means of enacting distinctions. Specifically,

competition will proceed over the ground of objectification rather
than object – how the 'stuff' of journalism emerges to the subject's
consciousness, with a posited second-order competition over domination of the principles of legitimisation of objectification determining
the terms of first-order strategic practice. This does not mean that
journalists do not compete at that explicit, first-order level: they
undoubtedly do compete over access, timeliness and quality:

> I want to be the best, I want to get the best copy, I want to be foreign
> correspondent of the year, this is my chance. (Interviewee 8)

It has also been seen above that reporters also compete by making
implicit self-positionings through criticism of others, often expressed
in terms of individual exceptionalism – where 'everybody' else thinks
differently. And while journalists' style of speech is in part the expression of field positions through habitualised dispositions, there was
also extensive evidence of intentional use of common rhetorical
devices traditionally conceived, such as irony, humour and metaphor.
The metaphor of hunting was often used to describe the relationship
between war correspondents as military officers; another common
example was tourism:

> They were like, 'We'll tell you if anything's going on, if you're especially
> nice to us we'll give you a trip so you can see something or other'.
> (Interviewee 2)

> The authorities have organised an excursion to cover the protests.
> (Interviewee 6, male, 50s, senior US broadsheet editor, American)

Both of these also deploy a sardonic kind of humour to make their
point, which positions the speaker authoritatively in relation to the
object of lack of access without becoming moralising or shrill about
press restrictions, practices which it appears are judged as naive.
Another example of humour not only confirms that embedding journalists is increasingly standard procedure, but that reporters have
become just another piece of kit to manage:

> It'd be like, You got your gun? Check. Your gas mask? Check. Your
> reporters? (Interviewee 5)

The extent to which these rhetorical strategies are consciously
enacted is open to question – it will be seen in the following section
that these too may be interpreted as instincts produced through the
internalisation of field structures, and it bears emphasising that, at
least in post-Husserlian phenomenology, intention is regarded as a
determination rather than an origin of practice.

Another common form of conscious competition was identification with positions of authority in journalism, politics and especially the military. In one respect this took the form of an understanding of a military characterised, like journalism, in esoteric terms. Mutual mystification is sometimes used to criticise military personnel:

> they don't know how journalism works, they don't understand how we do our job. (Interviewee 6)

This was a standard response to situations in which war reporters' presence was resented by military actors: in place of a direct confrontation of principles of differentiation between dominant and dominated subfields in the field of war, journalistic values are bracketed off as esoteric – a strategy which depends on a relatively stable professional discourse in which journalists reinforce the idea of their exceptionalism. Alternatively, interviewees claimed unique insight into the military, an understanding of the inner workings of a world which to the public and most journalists remains unknowable:[6]

> You gotta understand that the military is a machine. Once you get to know how it works it all makes sense, it's got its own sort of logic. (Interviewee 10)

> Which is not to say they were all bad but ... as a system they were ... as a machine it was always working against the journalists getting their stories in. (Interviewee 6)

As an act of distinction, this self-authorisation has the secondary effect of reinforcing an effectively naturalised but not absolutely given idea of what journalism is about: getting access to and understanding a mystified other, and translating this alien world into terms that non-journalists can understand – a norm which helps to concretise journalism's public status as gatekeeper of public knowledge, in principle at least.

More commonly, however, interviewees personally identified with elite individuals in the military, a move which can be characterised as using these authority figures as symbolic capital to enact their own authority – not through specific journalistic practices but (supposedly) mutually recognised personal qualities.[7] Such identifications serve the function of positioning the speaker in opposition to both other war correspondents (in the case of print journalists this usually means television journalists, while for the television journalist interviewed the distinction was made against competing US television networks) and to more junior military personnel – PR officials and the 'grunts' (using the army term for ordinary soldiers forms part of the

strategy of identification). Another striking pattern of relational positioning is the alliance of independent war reporters, opposed to
embedded or pooled journalists, with special or elite forces, opposed
to regular military personnel portrayed as more institutionalised and
highly regulated:[8]

> They're [US special forces] like, 'We're professionals, you're profession-
> als', there's that understanding and they're happy to just you know leave
> you to it. (Interviewee 2)

> and they're [US special forces] like, hey he's known, he's a cool guy.
> Once they know who you are, once they know you're cool they like
> completely trust you .... (Interviewee 10)

> and there were American special forces and Brit special forces, and they
> said if you got this far, fine, you know, don't get killed, and it worked
> okay. (Interviewee 5)

This can be seen as both oriented towards establishing the authority
of the journalist and concretising the centrality of autonomy – specifically conceived in terms of mobility – to that authority. The disavowal
of drama noted above is also present in these identifications, opposed
to actors in the journalistic, military and political fields who are
judged to be histrionic, bureaucratic, rule-bound or self-interested.
Further, beyond the explicit authorisations by military figures in the
quotes above, several interviewees engaged in practices of identification that indicated a personal as well as professional kinship, going so
far as to express sympathy with senior military personnel who have to
deal with 'clueless' journalists:[9]

> A lot of journalists are just really stupid. Especially these guys at the
> BBC, they think they're God's gift to journalism, and they piss him
> [military commander] off and they piss me off too. (Interviewee 2)

> I do sympathise to some extent because the pillock factor rises amongst
> journalists, and I mean I say that as a 58–year-old who's been doing it
> for a long time, but I don't think I was as much of a pillock as the ones
> I see now. I think it might be quite a pain being a PR man, even if you're
> the greatest PR man, subtle, gentle and understanding, probably even-
> tually the journalistic pillocks piss you off so much that you become
> unreasonable .... (Interviewee 5)

Misrecognised economies of subjectification

While linguistic practices such as irony, humour and metaphor are
available to actors in most contexts, codings for speech style point to
other practices with particular currency in war reporting and perhaps

journalism more broadly. For instance, cynicism appears to play a role in establishing individuals as naturally, unproblematically authoritative, distancing themselves from negative capital or obstacles to positively valued symbolic forms but in a way that is knowing and worldly:

> Oh yeah. There was a clever and unfortunately successful press policy. If you look at their press conferences, they stuffed them with people, right, a: they trusted, and b: didn't know a thing, got it? They didn't have to worry about getting misquoted or challenged 'cause they had reporters in there who didn't know a thing, and they were basically doing the work for them and were, well you know, they were a bit in awe of Powell and of Schwartzkopf to be frank. And then they had people who they knew would write what they wanted them to ... I mean write stuff that they weren't told to write but that they knew whatever they wrote would be OK, it wouldn't rock the boat so to speak. (Interviewee 6)

> You know the press spokesman actually said 'you better watch what you say', and you know then he showed how much he meant that by erasing that from the official transcript of the press conference. (Interviewee 9)

The form and function of cynicism in the interviews were not unambiguous, but it does appear to underpin the symbolic economy of ambivalence by positioning the speaker in opposition to the naive and romantic, not through argument but instinctive, implicit self-presentation. Other practices serve the same purpose, most noticeably irreverence, offhandedness and a knowing or reflexive form of humorous offensiveness. While it is clear from the interviews that war reporters (and others) use ironic distancing to position themselves in relation to their work, what the political phenomenological approach uniquely allows for is an excavation of the interests – not conscious, but strategic nonetheless – individuals have in embodying the valorised symbolic forms of ambivalence. Further, it pushes the social scientist to unpack the specific practices on which that embodiment is predicated. Cynicism, irreverence, offhandedness and faux-offensiveness thus represent effective practices whose mastery consecrates the field actor as authentically ambivalent towards the objects of the trade, and thereby as speaking from a field position associated with a specific authority: one which is individualised and anti-institutional. Authenticity depends on the internalisation of cynicism, irreverence and so on as an anticipatory structure: it must be experienced as second nature if it is reliably to signify that an individual possesses it. In theory, at least, it cannot be wielded disingenuously, though the ambiguous status of reflexivity in the interviews questions this premise: in short, it is indiscernible whether those peers mimicking war correspondent stereotypes are doing so cynically or if they experience such practices as authentic practices of self.

None of this is to suggest that all war reporters are cynical or irreverent, or that even if they are not they will learn to be so in a way that will seem increasingly natural as they make their way through their careers. Nor does it mean that mastery entails a seamless embodiment of pre-determined practices: embodiment, while constrained by the generative structures of the field, is always to a degree haphazard and unstable. However, these practices do appear to be associated in the field with an unpretentious, anti-elitist and realistic kind of authority – one which is obviously apparent rather than needing explication. Now, the crux is that these practices are not only relevant to the doing of journalistic work; they are also subjectifying practices. The upshot is that their misrecognition as markers of distinction is a (mis)recognition of disposition: extending the argument that journalistic skill is perceived as innate character, we can now isolate the practices on which that instinctive but determined recognition of character is conditional. We have seen that dispositions are not the same as Weberian ideal types, in the sense of monolithic symbolic configurations which individuals come to assume. Rather, they are habitus: structured, structuring schemes of anticipation which exceed the individual and which are experienced by the individuated subject as a pre-given orientation to the world. Among those alternately individuated by this group habitus, subjects may be perceived as natural embodiments of one or other of the dominant forms of symbolic subject in the field, which is to say that they appear as unproblematic manifestations of personalised authority, consciousnesses that are unstructured and simply a happy fit with the demands of the field.

These dispositional characteristics can be grouped into three rough categories, again without overstating the homogeneity of their members or suggesting that group habitus are static and immune to contestation. First, there is a misanthropic aspect, perceived not as a way of doing journalism but in personal terms, as one who 'does not play well with others'. This is based on the naturalised performance of cynical linguistic practices, not only towards journalistic objects but to social situations and, perhaps, family life (see chapter 5).[10] It is marked in particular by an apparently congenital inability to be impressed by consecrated symbolic forms, whether they be individual authorities or cultural objects: a peer's interest in fashion, for example, is written off by one respondent as vanity, which operates as negative capital according to the endogenous logic of the journalistic field. This disposition is consistent with the broader dominant principle that war reporter authority in particular is individualised, in line with the historical romanticisation of the war correspondent (Pedelty, 1995; McLaughlin, 2002; Knightley, 2003; Tumber and Webster, 2006). It is a disposition enacted through subjectifying practices as much as professional codes, with a personal distaste for social niceties, readiness to criticise and irreverent sense of humour indicating the speaker's occupation of a rarefied field position whose symbolic capital consists in the perceivedly professional qualities of directness, impartiality, autonomy and a lack of interest in playing the game in which colleagues and others are engaged.

A second and related dispositional characteristic, or structured set of subjectifying practices, might be labelled 'underdog' or 'terrier'. Here, the authority unreflexively accorded by other individuations of class habitus consists in symbolic capital which can be described as secondary journalistic characteristics: not just doing the job well, but being personally tenacious, adaptable, ingenious, tireless and on the side of 'ordinary' people.[11] There is a corresponding interest in disinterest here too, taking the form of being unfazed by elite or institutional power, which again suggests an individualised authoritativeness but one more grounded in locally valorised anti-elitism or anti-institutionalism. While there is no suggestion that this group of reporters has a generic mode of speaking, there appear to be some common practices whose mastery underpins the recognition of the requisite personal qualities: in particular, self-effacement in the sense of playing down personal achievements, relishing chaos, expressing pleasure at being engaged in a 'battle' (either of attrition or cat and mouse) requiring guile and cunning, demotic popular references and gallows humour. None of these guarantees authorisation, but their unremarkable presence does contribute to the recognition that a journalist is in his element – a recognition which, I have argued, is not a deontological feature of the journalistic field but a contingent culture of practice.

The third dispositional characteristic, journalist as moral authority, is in contrast to the others and is marked by a distinct lack of ambivalence in the journalist's personal ambitions and his relation to objects of power and danger. Morality and moral authority are tackled in detail in the next chapter, but the symbolic capital associated with positions of moral authority are readily describable: they remain personal qualities, but ones which are aligned with the overt moral principles of journalism: a commitment to justice, a deep-seated belief in holding power to account and humaneness. Since authorisation is often explicit here it might be thought that there is less contingency on unspoken attributes, but the data, albeit tentatively, suggest that here too there are cultures of practice which ground moral authority as something given: expressions of personal outrage, latent rather than overt agency in speech act architecture, little humour, little irony or vituperation, and a heightened tendency to speak on behalf of the journalistic community or western nations. Codings for the word 'I' showed up an interesting distinction: it was used comparatively rarely when describing a sequence of events, and more often when giving second-order reflections on the moral implications of such. By contrast, speakers identified as closer approximations of the first two dispositions threaded themselves more thoroughly into event narratives, while judgements were more likely to be made on the basis of what is 'obviously' right or wrong, rather than what they as individuals think. It is arguable that speaking on behalf of others represents a more collective notion of authority in this third type of position, but it is equally plausible that the speaker is claiming unique delegation to do so.

Gender

The number of women working in war reporting has increased significantly over the last 20 years (Chambers et al., 2004: 196–215; Tumber, 2006: 444), and in the interviews there were no explicit suggestions that women should not work as war correspondents (cf. de Bruin, 2000). However, there were sharp distinctions between descriptions by male correspondents about male and female colleagues; further, the three female correspondents interviewed all saw the field as heavily, and problematically, gendered. There are some principles of personal valorisation which were applied uniformly – intelligence, substance, autonomy and the ability to communicate and sustain productive relations with contacts were used regardless of gender. However, two descriptors were only used about male correspondents. In terms of valorisation, only males were described as having a natural talent or feel for war correspondence. With regard to derision, it is interesting that alcoholism emerges as a key form of negative symbolic capital (five respondents mentioned it in this sense) and that it was only applied to male correspondents. Alcoholism in the interview data is conceived quite specifically in distinction against 'good' or functional drinkers, rather than against abstinence. There were no forms of positive symbolic capital used exclusively to describe female correspondents, but two negative forms were readily apparent. The first is physical attractiveness:

> There's another one, really ugly girl, working in New York, really thin face with sort of lank hair, and she was in Africa before. And she became a moral authority. (Interviewee 5)

The second is sexually inappropriate behaviour. One war correspondent, for instance, expressed a negative opinion about the professional ability of a prominent female colleague and, when asked the reasons for his judgement, recounted a situation in which she had gained access to senior military sources by gambling with them and 'dancing around in her knickers' (Interviewee 14). A female reporter used the same example to illustrate the gendered structural bias of the field:

> It is really quite hard, I think it's quite hard for women. I mean [name removed] is a good example of someone who had a good relationship, but it's not really relevant but you get a lot of gossip about [name removed], you know [name removed] hangs around with her underwear on with the army officers that kind of thing, which makes it really hard for women ... I think you're battling against two quite chauvinistic cultures, both army and the press corps. (Interviewee 4)

There is an interesting parallel to this last example, insofar as it can be reconstructed strategically as resentment of intimacy with sources or figures of authority. Two of the female correspondents believed that the men were *too* likely to become close to powerful sources, that they were unable to retain a professional distance when embedded with military personnel. This was ascribed to their being overly impressed by traditionally masculine manifestations of power: fire-power, machinery or the adventurousness of special operations:

> Anyway he was covering Kosovo and I think he was a journalist who had been tricked into becoming too close to the armed forces, and I think it happens a lot with especially male journalists, who like to see themselves as one of the boys. (Interviewee 4)

Ultimately, however, there was no evidence that there is a single masculine or ungendered disposition to which any actor in the field would come increasingly to embody in professional practice.[12] What we can say is that of the multitude of differential field positions which characterise war reporting, some are associated with symbolic capital which is either recognised by field actors or has been interpreted by scholars as gendered in other fields (Krais, 1993; Reay, 2005), and particular individuals may inhabit such positions (or be seen to do so) under certain temporally specific and unstable conditions. There is no sign of systematic decontestation of gendered symbolic forms in war reporting.

The particularly individualised form of authority that characterises war reporting means that correspondents have a stake in resisting the conventional, institutional game in which they perceive others as being invested. In short, the lack of interest is itself interested; refusing to play the game is part of another game with its own distinct but generally unacknowledged rules. None of this is intended to suggest conspiracy, nor the tendency in some readings of Bourdieu and Foucault always to posit deeper, undetectable power determinations at every turn. But it is plausible that war reporting is sustained by illusio: the collective, and collectively forgotten, sense that makes immersing oneself in a field inherently, instinctively meaningful. It is also significant that the criteria by which symbolic forms are valorised as symbolic capital in this field – in more practical terms, the criteria by which authority is recognised in a very normal, pre-given fashion – do not emerge simply out of the demands of the job. This necessitates neither the willed performance of cultural ideals nor the non-conscious, enforced enactment of subjectivity which characterises Judith Butler's performativity model. But it does mean that authority is tied to dispositions as orientations to the world, dispositions which are not coterminous with discrete individuals and which are revealed in a range of non-specifically professional practices. And in turn, identifying these practices may tell us something significant about norms of authority in the broader field of cultural production – specifically as individualised, anti-institutional and anti-elitist. Next, let us turn to some more specific themes revealed by the discourse analysis: the roles played by morality and moral authority.

Notes

1 The decision to conduct semi-structured interviews is based on the methodology used by Bourdieu in *La Misère du monde*, published in English as *The Weight of the World* (1999). See also Mayer (1995). Bourdieu calls sociological interviews 'provoked' and 'accompanied': 'provoked', because they take place when requested by the sociologist in order to pursue the object of his or her study; 'accompanied', in that the interviewer both observes and participates in objectifying participant responses, as well as engaging in self-analysis (Hamel, 1998: 8). McRobbie (2002) criticises the methodology of *La Misère du monde* on the grounds that it ignores recent debates over methodology in the field of cultural studies.

2 Marchetti (2005: 193) notes that while professional success initially depends on specialisation, successful journalists eventually become generalists.

3 This may also apply in the military field; the retired army general interviewed suggested that some colleagues were resentful of his media profile.

4 It was noted in chapter 3 that, conversely, vituperative language was largely absent from such descriptions, reserved instead for denigrations of colleagues and other actors.

5 Bourdieu (1998a: 99–101) has also called this transformation 'symbolic alchemy', likening the 'magical power' of symbolic capital to Weberian 'charisma' and Durkheimian 'mana'.

6 Several interviewees talked about the media and the military as different 'worlds'. In the US context, one ascribed the gulf between the two to the end of the draft.

7 For a dissection of such distinctions and identifications, and their implications for the relative autonomy of the field of war reporting, see Markham (2007: 178–89).

8 The close relationships between senior military and media personnel were confirmed by the retired US army general: 'See in Bosnia the journalists had been there longer than the military, a lot longer. I mean Amanpour had been there three years, she was there, also Kirk Short, you know who died in Sierra Leone, real tragedy that, they'd been in Bosnia for a long time. And we used them. I remember when I first got there I met them, we went to a bar and looked at maps and they basically explained to me what was going on, I asked Christiane a lot of questions 'cause well I really wasn't well informed about the situation on the ground … she explained who was who and what was what, really helped me find my feet as it were. I trusted them, you know' (Interviewee 1).

9 The same retired general (Interviewee 1) said of unprepared reporters: 'When they arrived it'd be like "have you got a gas mask?" Right then .. and you know some of them were like, we'd ask them "have you got a tent?" and a torch, and you know they'd just arrived and this is two days before the offensive.'

10 On the gendered dimension of 'emotional capital', see Reay (2005).

11 Marchetti (2005: 67) identifies resourcefulness, rapidity, brashness, the ability to get there first and independence vis-à-vis sources as the most valuable journalistic assets.

12 It has been argued, however, that journalistic values are strongly determined according to masculinist norms. De Bruin (2000: 232) writes: 'But is it that journalism "accords" with masculine values or is it perhaps that its values have been constructed to fit masculine values? Traditionally developed by male decision makers, who used to monopolise decision making positions, certain styles and values will have become accepted as professional standards, at the same time will have become part of the organisation's house-style – "that's how-we-do-it-here."'

5

Journalistic ethics and moral authority: being right, knowing better

As a sociologist, I know that morality only works if it is supported by structures and a mechanism that give people an interest in morality. (Bourdieu, 1998b: 56)

Is it futile to discuss journalistic ethics? Relativism versus strategism

Previous chapters have set out the case for interpreting journalistic principles primarily as strategic. While this could reasonably be understood to indicate that the particular content of journalistic ethics is inconsequential, in the following it will be seen that debating ethics remains viable despite their broader role as symbolic capital in the journalistic field. In theoretical terms the basis for this assertion is that the lifeworld which professional journalists inhabit is not a self-contained, discrete phenomenal realm (Reckwitz, 2002). It is similarly not a direct expression of the material differential space in which journalism subsists. The journalistic field as experienced by its agents is completed by the symbolic world of the journalistic game, such that there is not, as Adorno had it (see Hull, 1997), a material remainder which generates the possibility of access to a 'deeper' reality. But this is not the same as saying that the symbolic form of the journalistic field is wholly arbitrary or unrelated to its political and economic context (Smith, 1988; Fiske, 1992b; Wilcken, 1995; McGuigan, 1996). Instead, the journalistic world is characterisable as a particular case of the possible: it is a reasonable expression of the generative structures of the field, but its particular emergence from those structures could not have been predicted. Likewise, journalistic ethics should be seen neither as natural responses to the objective reality of journalistic practice, nor as arbitrary clusters of symbolic forms whose particular shape is inconsequential next to the strategic role that journalistic ethics play. They are reasonable manifestations of the conditions of possibility from which they emerged, but should be seen as only one of a set of possible manifestations. This effectively means that journalistic ethics make sense in retrospect, but their observed practical universalisation (Laclau, 2000) in specific contexts should not be misinterpreted as absolute. There is a one-to-many correspondence between the generative structures of the journalistic field and its observed manifestations, and it is on this basis that comparison of such manifestations is valid. Conceiving of journalistic ethics in these terms is thus not nihilistic but unsettling, suggesting that we should reject seeing contemporary codes of practice as the inevitable product of incremental refinement and instead asking, given a common generative origin, how different things could be.

This theoretical grounding of the viability of contesting ethics then leads us to the question of how such discussions should proceed. Journalists debating ethics among themselves is perhaps the obvious starting point, though the relative autonomy of the journalistic field which is essential to fostering uniquely journalistic cultural production also limits the reflexivity of field actors. This is best encapsulated by the maxim that fields produce the means of their own apprehension: that is, the conceptual apparatus with which agents make sense of their context is itself a determination of the field. As such, the way that journalists reflect upon ethics, however frankly, will necessarily misrecognise the radical contingency of ethics as such. This is consistent with Matheson's (2003) observation that journalistic discussions of ethics tend to be conservative insofar as they implicitly reinforce more than they submit to scrutiny, and it is also in line with Pöttker's (2004) contention that ethical debates tend towards dogmatism because they remain blind to the existence, and possible normative merit, of an 'outside' of ethics. It is further consistent with those theories of professionalism in which professional identities and discourses are reproduced by mutual performance and projection as such by individuals (Carpentier, 2005; Frith and Meech, 2007; Schultz, 2007). According to this position there is no solidity of identity or discourse beyond the structured practices enacting them. But while this suggests fluidity or transience, the durable logic of such practices means they do have a localised stability. The upshot is a pragmatic one: even if journalistic ethics have no stable ontological basis, they matter because they have effects in the world we experience as given. This chapter aims to unpack how ethics and morality come to have practical durability and what it tells us about authority in war reporting and the field of cultural production generally.

Dispositional ethics

Does it matter if journalists perceive authority and value in cultural production according to explicit or unacknowledged criteria? It does, in short, because these misrecognised symbolic economies reproduce both the gatekeeping mechanisms by which entry into the journalistic trade is strictly controlled (Shoemaker et al., 2009) and the internal hierarchies of the field. The conceivability of going into journalism and assuming a privileged position within it depends upon the extent to which one's habitus is already aligned to the unspoken rules of the game – and this appears to be related to socioeconomic (McNair, 1998; Marchetti, 2005), educational (Sutton Trust, 2006) and ethnic status. Part of this alignment relates to how naturally specific ethical commitments 'fit' with one's disposition as it is lived in our everyday experience. Let us consider some examples to explore what this means in practice.

While it cannot be assumed that any journalistic ethics are universal, the literature confirms several which are systematically recognised across geographical, cultural and historical contexts. These include a commitment to objectivity, respect for privacy, protection of sources, and autonomy from undue political, economic or other external influence (Hafez, 2002; Deuze, 2005; Himelboim and Limor, 2008). This is not to suggest that journalistic ethics are homogeneous the world over: these are common categories at present, but each may take different forms and priorities over other categories (Wasserman and Rao, 2008). Further, there are other ethical questions over which there is less universalisation, both internationally and between different journalistic genres – the use of subterfuge in the public interest, for example.[1] But let us consider the practical implications of some of the core journalistic ethics, beginning with objectivity. A more or less universal principle in the abstract (Boyd-Barrett, 2004), in practice it breaks down to a commitment to accuracy, neutrality or balance (or a combination of these), weighed against a sense of news values which vary according to context – impact, novelty, public service and so on (Bowman, 2006; Thomson et al., 2008). In any case, however, the principle of objectivity also enacts a hierarchy of truth which the journalist is given to be uniquely authorised to discern. While we may fairly play down the effect this has in terms of the journalist's status in society more broadly, within the field taking up the position of truth-speaker is not reducible to the fact of writing accurately but instead consists in a recognition by peers and audience of truthfulness. This in turn is dependent upon collective normative commitment to speaking truth to power, which is recognised dispositionally as not just getting things right, but being right. And this status, described in the previous chapter as a kind of 'terrier' outlook, is by no means pre-given but instead enacted through a practical mastery of a set of linguistic (and potentially corporeal, though the evidence here was inconclusive) signifiers of symbolic value – which come more easily to some than others. Consider the following statements:

> You'll be reliant on briefings and on a few happily released pictures to keep the television people cheerful. (Interviewee 14)

> Those guys [the UN] used to water things down a lot. We'd like make bets over how watered down things were, the reports of bombs dropped by Nato. (Interviewee 13)

While such comments are necessarily equivocal, the coding categories applied here and elsewhere suggest a commitment to objectivity which is worn lightly, an uncomplicated sense of right and wrong, and an understated and knowing reaction to obstacles to objectivity.

Next, autonomy from undue external influence. While autonomy is unproblematically regarded as a *sine qua non* of ethical practice (McLaughlin, 2002; Tumber, 2004), its recognition both within the journalistic field and the broader field of cultural production (Bourdieu, 1993a: 115) appears in the data to be tied to a disposition of rugged individualism enacted not only through explicit acts of resistance but more broadly being the sort of person who is not impressionable or conformist and in many cases who actively enjoys disobeying authority. This is a generative template for subjectifying practices which accommodates a substantial degree of heterogeneity, rather than an internalised instruction manual for how to act in order to be perceived as a natural journalist. But there is localised stability in how such practices are collectively recognised, and the theory predicts that their performance will come more naturally to those entering the field already closely aligned to its structures. As with objectivity, there is a pervading sense of autonomy being worn lightly, as an instinct which is in an individual's nature, though it will be seen in chapter 7 that alternative strategies may come into play when autonomy is compromised in the field. Third, consider protection of sources. This is widely agreed to be essential to the ethical 'doing' of journalism, though there is considerable disagreement around the 'of' and 'from' of protection. Whichever permutation it takes, it bears emphasising how this institutes the source as an elevated, almost mystic source of truth (Deuze, 2005; cf. Liebes and Kampf, 2004) and the journalist as uniquely (though naturally) capable of simultaneously safeguarding this epistemological origin and acting as its conduit and translator into the language of public knowledge. Around this ethic in particular in the interviews, any qualification is regarded as taboo, effectively closing down any questioning of journalistic authority.

Morality: getting it right versus being right

To journalists immersed in their field, its objective relations of domination and dominatedness are obscured in the lifeworld which underpins their conscious experience of being in the field. This experience is, in Hardt's words, 'superficial, positive and full' (1993: xii) and is characterised by a quasi-arbitrary set of rules, stakes, strategies and cultures of practice which are misrecognised as the natural state of things. We have seen that the journalistic habitus is experienced as instinct or spontaneity insofar as it operates in unfamiliar situations as much as the routine or banal, but in fact it is very much a product – and productive – of history. The journalistic 'game' is not a monolithic or oppressive institution but a relational space with numerous sites of relative power and its absence. And importantly, here are multiple forms of recognised symbolic capital both within the subfield of war reporting and the field of journalism more generally: journalists are not all competing for the same field positions via the same symbolic configurations attached to them.[2] There are distinct types of authority with which one might come to be identified – popular, highbrow, public-spirited and so on – and these can and do co-exist. However, if the symbolic economy in which these particular forms of authority are currency amounts to a self-contained professional world – that is, one which is relatively autonomous and internally coherent – then the import for ethics in war reporting is significant. In each, what is ethical is conflated, because of the dispositional nature of recognition, with morality, embodied according to a symbolic economy that is simultaneously misunderstood and potentially profitable. This is the essence of the quotation at the beginning of this chapter: a quality such as morality should not be seen as a natural attribute of journalism, but rather as a dominant criterion by which individuals and groups vie for status and influence – morality is always a claim to authority. The upshot is that any discussion of journalistic ethics reduces to the strategic effects of individuals and institutions enacting certain ethics, and the implications of particular ethics achieving effective universality as the dominant principles of differentiation in the journalistic field.

This undoubtedly attracts allegations of nihilism in Bourdieu's work (e.g. Evans, 1999), and as such it is worth taking seriously the inference that not only ethics but the moral principles they supposedly protect are themselves primarily strategic. The question of morality leads us back to the recurring theme of esotericisation, in that instead of codes of conduct, interviewees invoke principles which are simultaneously ineffable and hardwired in those who understand. The phenomenological approach questions not only the basis of individuals' association with morality but the very idea that journalism naturally has a moral aspect, even if it often fails to live up to expectations. My intention here is not to assess whether journalism as a profession is moral, immoral or amoral, but rather what forms morality takes and what are its strategic functions. As with ethics, let us consider some examples.

Forms and functions of moral authority in war reporting

The distinction between institutional and individual authority discussed in the previous chapter has an inexact counterpart here: the divide between journalism valorised for its factual authority and that valorised for its moral authority. Recent research suggests that moral authority is increasingly valuable as symbolic capital recognised by peers and audiences alike, from compelling explorations of the implications of an increasingly moralising tabloid media in the UK (Conboy, 2006, 2007; Tulloch, 2007; cf. Örnebring and Jönsson, 2004), to research which associates moral authority with particular political and geographical contexts (Herscovitz, 2004; cf. Anderson, 2007; Ståhlberg, 2006; Tsfati et al., 2006). In reality, both just-the-facts or *pur et dur* reporting and morally motivated or 'attached' journalism (Bell, 1995, 1997; Champagne, 2005a: 52; Seib, 2002: 39–66) have always existed. And while one could ostensibly point to times when one or other mode of judging 'good' journalism has dominated, I would suggest that to describe the journalistic field as being structured primarily according to this dichotomy itself leads to a reductive and exclusionary view of news making. Rather, we need to look at how moral authority is constituted, recognised, rationalised and embodied in war correspondence; and, if there were an expanded public or professional market for morality in the news media, what the preconditions for this increase might be. In the first instance, this means establishing the relational structure of the economy of moral authority: namely its poles, and the types and amounts of symbolic capital which operate as the dominant differential criteria for these poles and the economy as a whole. This is relevant for two reasons. First, it allows us to sketch the misrecognised strategic matrices which underpin both the nonconscious enactment of field norms and conscious reflection (see also Tumber, 2006) and how they structure internal competition, professional motivation, professional identity and journalistic instinct within the field of war reporting. Second, it underpins an investigation of the possible broader cultural determinants and implications of journalistic moral authority. That is, since journalism is only partly autonomous, it is characterised by both internal and external principles of differentiation, and it will be seen here that morality plays a distinct part in each.

In one sense it is problematic to separate moral and other criteria for ascribing value to journalistic production, because morality's 'other' – defined by respondents as a combination of neutrality, disinterestedness, accuracy, facticity and balance – can itself be characterised as a moral claim. But insofar as we are concerned with the systematic (mis)recognition of symbolic capital it will suffice to begin by defining journalism's moral aspects as those identified by respondents in talking about how journalism should contribute to the social or public good, however defined, or how journalists should behave towards those with whom they interact in their work. The most commonly evoked moral principles in the interviews were selflessness, giving voice, bearing witness, public service and holding power to account. Let us look at each in turn.

First, selflessness[3] consists in a moral prioritisation of others' interests over one's own. This downplaying of self has the effect of decontesting an individual's position in the journalistic field: it is an ethos of not self-aggrandising and just 'getting on with the job' which positions a journalist as a reliable professional. But beyond operating as a potentially pre-reflexive individual strategy, this also has a broader field effect. The interviews and any glance at war reporters' memoirs demonstrate that ego is a given in war reporting, but the prevalence of selflessness as a valued norm establishes that there is a limit to ego, beyond which decency and camaraderie come into play. This is a collective disavowal of competition, contributing to the collective misrecognition of the field as, at base, a collective enterprise: it may be every man for himself in the pursuit of a story, but in peril reporters will look out for one anothers' interests. This has two consequences: first, it romanticises the journalistic profession as a kind of tribe, suggesting a common ethos and cohesive professional culture which is at best questionable. Second, it legitimises cynicism as a default orientation to the world by implying that it is qualified by a basic sense of humanity, in the process masking its potential value as symbolic capital.

Next, giving voice to and respecting sources combine an ethos of representing the under-represented (there were several explicit references to this ethos) with an enactment of the journalist's powers of authorial consecration, potentially alongside the ability to determine mediated identities of victimhood. There is immediately a problem with 'giving' voice, as it suggests that subjects have to be authorised to speak, and the journalist's act of authorising another is first and foremost self-authorisation. The represented 'other' is at best a by-product of journalistic authority claims and, at worst, a constrained, disciplined subject produced by the eliciting of expression, itself a form of coercion by the instituionalised will-to-truth that some argue journalism represents (Dent, 2008; Markham, 2010). Even if this strongly Foucauldian reading is set aside, there remains a case for interpreting giving voice as a form of de-authorisation, effectively amounting to nothing more than confirmation of the dominatedness of the journalistic object. If recognition is largely pre-reflexive, then voice can only reveal its position, dominated or otherwise, and not through its content influence how it is heard. We return to this point in relation to audiences in the following chapter.

> But you do have some responsibilities, you do have to think a little bit about what you're doing, both to the people you're in contact with and the impact it will have on their lives. (Interviewee 4)

Third, bearing witness (see Seib, 2002; Tumber, 2006) carries with it a signification of personal ability to deal with the horrors of conflict and deprivation which others by implication would find intolerable, and can thus also be seen as strategic positioning or distinction. This usually takes the form of a systematic downplaying of ostensibly traumatic situations, using understatement ('untidy' to describe a scene of carnage, 'hairy' to describe a life-threatening situation, etc.) and metaphor. As with giving voice, bearing witness also carries the possibility that it rationalises suffering by processing it according to journalistic principles which are also economic and industrial. It might be said that the competitive economy underpinning war reporting is masked by a collective emphasis on authenticity encapsulated in the prioritisation of eye witnessing, an authenticity predicated on a problematic conception of immediacy. We return to this point in the context of new technologies in chapter 7.

Fourth, keeping the public informed or serving the public is a clear positioning of self as authority figure:

I'd say papers do a better job of finding ... ways to satisfy the commitment to the readers, you know compared to the military satisfying their
need to report on how things were going. (Interviewee 6)

You know the anecdote, the episode when the friendly fire evacuees
were being evacuated, that was sort of the first real test of whether there
would be access and they shut the reporters and photographers down
immediately. They apologised later, which was nice [laughs] but you
know, they apologised later. And any time this could happen in the
future, you know, the press will scream, but no one else will.
(Interviewee 6)

As well as being disposed towards reinforcing the gatekeeper role for
journalists, such a normative commitment may also be seen as a
strategy to enshrine journalism as a dominant epistemological orientation to the world (Glasser, 1996; Höijer, 2008), specifically one
which is rationalising and instrumentalist. Journalism by this view
has the effect of imposing categories, criteria and value judgements
where there is no ontological imperative for order to exist. Following
this line of reason, scholars are divided as to whether the motivation
for such a strategy is psychological – our basic need for structure – or
political, in the sense of discursive reproduction (Johnson-Cartee,
2005; Dent, 2008). Either way, it suggests that the journalistic
influence on what counts as public knowledge, and how journalists
conceive of 'the public', should not be underestimated.

   Fifth, holding power to account likewise has a flipside to its moral
claim: the enactment of competence and positioning of self as capable
of taking on elite power, while remaining very much on the side of
ordinary members of the public. Yet this anti-establishment authority
glosses over the conflicted, arguably complicit relationship that journalism has with the elite institutions of society. And it is only viable as
an authoritative form in the context of a broader anti-elite or anti-
establishment cultural moment, in which the rules for enacting and
recognising it have been internalised and normalised by cultural
producers and consumers alike.

   For each of these, it bears repeating the argument that whatever the
particular moral claims made, their performance or discussion
contributes to the decontestation of the idea that journalism is a
naturally viable repository for morality – whether or not it lives up to
this responsibility in practice – and this has broader strategic implications regarding journalism's position in the field of cultural
production.

Disavowing morality as a moral claim

In the interviews, however, most respondents (especially male, under 40 or over 55) in fact played down the moral dimension of their work, were actively dismissive of others seen as overly moralising and declined to discuss any specific moral issues, such as the dilemma of representing distant suffering, in detail. Thus, the empirical data would appear to contradict Bourdieu's claim about journalists being 'full of moralising' in their 'theoretical' reflections on the nature of their work. This can be explained in two ways. First, for some correspondents the disavowal of morality represented a projection of authenticity – which is interpreted here not as a natural quality but as a field-constituted configuration of symbolic capital enacted by an individual and recognised by peers or public:

> I mean, war is the best spectator sport in the world. It's fun, I love it, it's just such a rush … it's kind of like watching sport, but much more intense. So I kind of tend to say if people ask me why I'm a war correspondent, it's like, well if I didn't I'd have to have a fucking job. I mean, this isn't work, it's fun. I'm getting paid to do all this stuff which is totally amazing and I love it, we all do. (Interviewee 10)

While not widespread amongst interviewees, two younger war correspondents engaged in this type of practice, and the underlying, nonconscious strategy generating its possibility appears to be one of disarming self-effacement. This can be seen as strategic insofar as it establishes the actor as unencumbered by norms traditionally publicly attached to the profession, and thus interested only in the ethically procedural, technical or morally 'neutral', practical aspects of good war reporting – access, exclusivity, timeliness and so on. This orientation is only viable alongside the perceived possibility that journalism can be practised in a moral vacuum.

Second, and more commonly, interviewees disavowed morality by depicting it in others as hypocrisy or self-indulgence. For example:

> He became like that [a moral authority]. He was going and pontificating on things. I mean I don't mean to backbite, I've got nothing personal against him, I don't know him, in fact I avoid him, I avoid people like that. As soon as I see them I avoid them, because they are busy getting things wrong, and they're busy pissing me off if I'm standing anywhere nearby. You know [name removed] did this whole unctuous thing about staying in Sarajevo, how it was his duty and he felt that he owed it to the people of Bosnia, I heard him going on about this on the radio, he was really just turning himself into some great moral arbiter. And the fact is, he's got a broken marriage at home, and he was shagging the

most sexy Sarajevo interpreter you've ever seen in your life – what's the point of going home? He was having a good time. I don't say that because I disapprove of that, but don't turn into moral arbiter and say that you've, it's because you want to see the story through and all that, just say nothing. (Interviewee 5)

The charge of hypocrisy usually relies upon a contradiction between public avowals of morality and private immorality. There is not space here to unpack the contingency of such claims – namely that the criteria for each category are not the same (see also Runciman, 2008) – but it is interesting that in the interviews, it was the public moralising rather than the personal behaviour which was criticised. The implication is that all journalists (or simply all people) are personally immoral at least some of the time, and this can be interpreted as a signification of realism or pragmatism, which appears systematically throughout in the data as a marker of embodied authority. Attributions of worthiness are expressed with particular distaste:

I hate worthy. People who take themselves seriously. Last night – fuck. Did you see *Newsnight* last night? It was Jackie Rowland's thing at the trial, and it's the front page of the *Guardian*'s magazine. That's what I hate. She came out and she said 'Oh I felt great, I was on a roll,' and I thought 'You stupid cow, you stupid, stupid woman.' You know whatever you think of Milosevic, I mean he's killed a fair few people but actually, what he was doing made some sense, because we've now got a Kosovo which instead of being a drugs corridor, is now a drugs plateau, and that's what he was aiming at. So okay he's a pretty bad guy but how dare Jacky Rowland go in there and grandstand? We shouldn't be doing that. (Interviewee 5)

The implication is that 'naturally' talented journalists do not have to engage in such 'indulgent' debates about morality and ethics. Several respondents, when talking about moral issues (or moralising journalists), stated as entirely obvious the idea that the media industry, as well as political and military institutions active in conflict situations, are fundamentally corrupt, and that all actors' motivations are self-interested. While such observations may be accurate, their prevalence in the field can also be constituted as performing a function, that is, signifying the embodiment of cynicism or world-weariness, themselves recognised as indicators of authority. This was expressed by three respondents as the ability to see through the 'bullshit' of the game in which journalists, politicians and military personnel are collectively engaged. However, the above discussion suggests we should construct this enactment of disinterested insight not as dismantling or seeing through strategising in journalistic practice, but (also) as enacting alternative strategies itself.

The common theme in disavowals of morality is that acting 'properly' in a field is simply a matter of common sense or professionalism. That is, one should be suspicious of those espousing 'woolly' moral principles because the journalistic instinct is given more or less naturally to incorporate a sense of right and wrong in any given professional context. Here, the disavowal of morality can thus be seen as a moral claim itself: the obscured strategy is to establish an actor as unremarkably, uncomplicatedly morally oriented. As described above, it means being the right sort of person rather than doing the right thing by, say, following ethical codes of conduct. This constitution of a journalist as the natural, common sense embodiment of moral authority should be seen as the result of a context-specific, structurally contingent process of symbolic projection and reception.

What's wrong with moral authority as a culture of strategic practice?

The observed pragmatisation of morality – the idea that it should be a matter of common sense, not pontification – is parallel to but distinct from the 'secularisation' and 'rationalisation' accounts of morality developed by Weber and Foucault respectively, in which ethics are institutionally bureaucratised. It is also a finding one would expect of a Bourdieusian analysis: structured, structuring anti-moralising valorisations are cultures of practice largely internal to the professional field (i.e. by and about peers), and the Bourdieusian model lends itself to explaining economies of practice in terms of endogenous field logics. What, then, explains the durability of explicitly moral journalistic authority? The first option is that as a subfield of war reporting it does not pose a threat to other modes of journalistic practice, and is thus left to its own devices by the majority who oppose overt moralising. The second, and I would argue more likely given the weakness of journalistic autonomy in relation to external economic forces, is that moral authority can only endure as a dominant principle of differentiation if there is a market for it. I return in this chapter's conclusion to the question of why this should be the case, but first it is important to flesh out what the institutionalisation of a differentiating principle based on popular mandate means for journalism.

If moral authority were to be conferred by the public, rather than by peers, it would have the potential to short-circuit endogenous principles for ascribing cultural value (iniquitous as these are), substituting principles of popularity (Bourdieu, 1994c; Champagne, 2005a: 58). However, while the internal mechanisms of a field are invariably skewed towards the reproduction of hierarchy, it is only with the preservation of a pole of restricted production – that is, a position in the journalistic field where access is limited to those deemed deserving of such a position-taking by their peers – that 'quality' cultural production is possible. This does not equate to the fencing off or depoliticisation of what constitutes 'quality' war reporting, but rather suggests that while the contestation of this category should be encouraged (and indeed institutionalised), the tenability of the category of endogenously determined cultural value should be accepted on normative grounds. To be sure, this Bourdieusian argument applies more to the 'purer' cultural subfields of art and literature (Grenfell and Hardy, 2003), and it is readily demonstrable that journalism is already more susceptible to market pressures. But it is also valid to argue that the mediated negotiation of public issues and conflicts in terms other than the consumerist or populist is only possible if the internal logic of peer-determined value endures.

In our present context, the upshot is that while it is important to uncover the misrecognised economies underpinning authority in war reporting, it is nonetheless cogent to defend those forms of journalism created and consecrated by a self-selecting clique against that consecrated to the values associated with unrestricted, or popular, consecration. Thus, authority which is conferred on reporters by the public – the star correspondent who appears to speak directly to the public rather than on behalf of an establishment institution – can be seen as a dilution of journalistic values intrinsic to the field, as much as those values are unjust and unnatural. The impact of public consecration is mirrored in the political field in Patrick Champagne's (1994, 2005b) position on opinion polling. What is problematic is not that consecration is based on public popularity per se, but that what is essentially an economic principle of valorisation is misrecognised as democratic legitimacy (Chouliaraki, 2000; cf. Fiske, 1992a). It is this misrepresentation of a cultural phenomenon as political which leads to the rationalisation of mass-conferred symbolic capital as the dominant principle of vision and division of journalistic value, with two implications. First, it means that which is ascribed value according to market principles is authorised as a moral good, insofar as it points to a democratic legitimacy opposed to the implied corruption of establishment institutions. Second, it means that journalists best oriented towards projecting popularly perceived journalistic value are regarded as democratically legitimated public figures and natural embodiments of morality, while the relation between the star war reporter and his audience is misrecognised as immediate and unconflicted (Livingstone, 1998)[4] – again in comparison to the mistrusted mediating institutions of state.

This does not necessitate that the public recognition of a journalist as a dependable ethical practitioner is inevitably misplaced, or that journalists are necessarily (and perhaps unconsciously) disingenuous when they appear to be acting morally. Rather, the point here is to emphasise that invoking or enacting a moral code should be seen as (also) strategic, performing a function beyond its overt motivation. It is not intended to indicate that any principle established and conferred by popularity is inherently misplaced, though there is the possibility that it may be complicit in an obscured structural repro-duction. This possibility amounts to a reasonable justification for analysing the unrecognised political implications of moral authority conferred by public sanction: that is, without positing that cultural forms produced according to market criteria are necessarily sinister, it is worth decoupling market and democratic principles of differentia-tion and establishing, if there is a market for moral authority in the media, what conditions of possibility underpin its operation.

Why is war reporting morally implicated?

How is it that the production and consumption of war reporting have a moral dimension? We have seen that even when disavowing moral-isation, war reporters see themselves and others in moral terms. Further, as part of the habitualised process of decoding news consumers are oriented towards recognising or according moral value to information as they process it. While this may seem an obvious aspect of consuming news, the phenomenological approach followed here emphasises the importance of understanding how such a practice has become naturalised and unremarkable. We turn to audiences of conflict reporting in the next chapter; first, however, let us assess the status of morality in war journalism by considering five possible responses to this question.

For the majority of scholars the moral dimension of war reporting is a given. The question of how we should react to human suffering is inextricable from moral considerations (Moeller, 2004), and the fact that war involves political as well as military decisions about who it is acceptable to kill and to ask to risk their lives means that there is an obligation to disseminate the reality of conflict in the name of demo-cratic oversight. Morality in this way of looking at war reporting is related both to compassion towards casualties and the bereaved, and to democracy itself: journalism's traditional role as fourth estate is a moral imperative rather than a procedural check and balance. Much research on war reporting (Young and Jesser, 1997; McLaughlin, 2002; Brown, 2003; Tumber and Palmer, 2004; Fahmy and Johnson, 2005; Brandenburg, 2007) thus discusses issues such as censorship, restrictions on access and mobility and military PR not just in terms of how they hinder journalists trying to go about their work, but the injustices that these entail, preventing reporters performing an essential democratic function. This emphasis on the political importance of war reporting and the personal sacrifices it involves leads to a further focus on the risks war reporters face (Feinstein, 2003; Boyd-Barrett, 2004; Tumber and Palmer, 2004; Tumber, 2006; Tumber and Webster, 2006; Lisosky and Henrichsen, 2009; Murrell, 2010). While this book takes a more strategic approach to the way that reporters talk about danger, and while the cultural icon of the war correspondent has sometimes been romanticised (McLaughlin, 2002; Evans, 2003), it bears emphasising that casualty rates amongst journalists at war have risen to unprecedented levels over the past decade (International Federation of Journalists, 2009), and that respect for war reporters within journalism remains high:

> There's certainly been some excellent reporting, some really good stories, and you know they're not all Dan Rather, they don't operate with TV networks and with ah large support systems, most of them are individuals who are extremely vulnerable, who have no protection, who have no support networks, who are loaded down with batteries and generators, and loaded down with cash in a very dangerous situation in which they're sort of virtually walking ATM machines, they're you know vulnerable to robbery, extortion or worse, so the reporters have gone in there on their own in a total no man's land, and I think we're all in their debt for their excellent, excellent reporting very different from any other situation we've had. (Interviewee 6)

Second, if external critics can routinely deride journalists for moral turpitude, they can only do so if they see the trade, in the same way that journalists have been argued to do here, as naturally having a moral dimension. I would argue that this is only plausible if the media themselves are seen as naturally morally implicated (see, for instance, Chouliaraki, 2008). There is certainly strong support for this view. Silverstone (2007), for example, argues that insofar as the media are in the business of mediating relationships between global citizens, their very essence is irredeemably moralised – and Western media in particular fall short on moral criteria by failing to sustain an effective distance or framing of the global other (see also Seib, 2002). This

position effectively, and usefully, establishes media morality as deontological (which is not to say unproblematic), and as such provides a
stable basis for critiquing the media on moral grounds and allowing
for guidelines for media production and representation which, if not
universal, are broadly applicable and relatively uncontroversial. While
this entails a strong refutation of moral relativism, it goes further: the
suggestion is that since representation of humanity is inevitably
morally implicated, then the argument that the ethics of representation can ever be a purely technical, disinterested matter does not
stand. The strength of Silverstone's argument is that it allows us,
without resorting to dogmatism, to see the moral commitments and
implications of all media practice and reflections upon the journalistic trade, including those which on the face of it disclaim any moral
interest. In this chapter I have suggested that morality should not be
conceived in deontological terms, but there is nonetheless much
common ground – not least Silverstone's contention that since the
media determine the dominant modes of orientation between publics
(a view similar to that of Michael Ignatieff: see Plaisance, 2002), then
journalism needs protection from the vicissitudes of market logics.

Third, and at the other end of the spectrum, morality could in the
same vein as giving voice above be read as a regulatory regime,
systematically legitimising and delegitimising cultural forms and
social groups, and disciplining the individual by inciting internal
discourses of morality through media coverage of anything from
conflict to celebrity. This possibility has been much discussed
elsewhere; Dent (2008; see also Andrejevic, 2008), for instance,
writes in Foucauldian terms about discipline being effected by journalists acting as the public's 'confessor', eliciting, externalising,
categorising and discursively processing the internal monologues of
its members. We return to this question in the next chapter. A fourth
possibility, and one that is more journalistically focused, is that
morality serves a primarily narrative function: that is, journalists are
better able to construct an article and consumers more easily digest
news when it is framed according to well-established moral (among
other) norms. This would be in line with research by Conboy (2006;
2007) which concludes that effective (especially tabloid) journalism
relies upon a sense of intimacy between journalist and consumer,
and that this relationship is predicated upon the deployment of
cultural references and a common worldview. A shared sense of
morality, or an authorial voice which is readily dependable, could
also feasibly serve to support the constitution of journalist–audience
intimacy, and it will be seen in the next chapter that morality in the

form of unsentimental, common sense decency has particular currency in some cultures of media consumption. There is clearly a market for morally attached war reporting, even if on the basis of the interviews discussed here it is a minority interest both amongst correspondents and their audiences. If war reporting as an area of cultural production is romanticised, it bears emphasising that the basis of this is not unrealistic – there is no reason to assume it is nothing other than a genuine respect for the perilous work that war reporters do. But in specifically moral terms, it appears that for the majority of field members and news consumers alike, authority consists in an individualised, unfussy form of morality that does not need to wear its heart on its sleeve. It is precisely this downplayed sense of right and wrong – characterised as something obvious and practical rather than sentimental – which enables the recognition of a reporter's moral instincts. These instincts, according to the phenomenological approach, are not his: they are collective practices increasingly recognised as innate character, such that it is not about sizing up individual decisions he has taken but simply knowing that he is the sort of person who knows what is appropriate in a conflict environment. This certainly doesn't imply that there is a collective recognition that war reporters are morally pure – indeed, from the profile of many star reporters there is a clear attraction towards the roguish and raffish – but the discussion above suggests that this comes with a caveat. It appears that acting inappropriately in certain contexts is itself appropriate according to the internal logic of the field of war reporting, establishing a renegade quality associated with ruggedly individual authority, but there is also an unspoken line beyond which a basic decency is pre-reflexively attributed. With the odd exception, encapsulated by the 'Anyone here been raped and speak English?' (Behr, 1992) folk legends of the genre, that audiences perceive morality-as-common-decency in war reporters is entirely warranted. But we can take a step back and ask why this type of morality dominates rather than others, and what are the constituent elements and broader cultural preconditions of its collective recognition? This is not the same thing as saying that morality in war reporting is somehow inauthentic: rather, its authenticity is not something which just is, but a set of practices acknowledged as such. To be sure, for Bourdieu that unthinking acknowledgement amounts to misrecognition based on the perception of a form of symbolic capital rather than an objective value, but as the symbolic *is* our experience of the world then the values that dominate the symbolic economies we inhabit still matter. That is, we can point to

the contingency of specific forms of symbolic capital without anni-
hilating the case for moral standards.

The fifth alternative is that regardless of what reporters think of the
moral aspect of their work, there is a broader interest, amongst
reporters and audiences generally, in perceiving morality in the field.
If we start from the position, by no means unproblematic, that our
orientation to the world naturally has a moral component, then it may
be that the perception of specific forms of morality in the news media
reflects a broader shift in what that orientation articulates with. The
combination of a sense of morality which is neither bureaucratic nor
histrionic, as well as the continued prevalence of star reporters,
suggests that the object of articulation is the perceived authentic individual. By this view, morality is a resource that we use to position
ourselves in relation to the world around us, and the trend is towards
using persons rather than institutions as relational markers. The
problem, at least for the phenomenologist, is that what is being recognised (as moral, amoral, decent, irreverent etc.) is definitively not a
person, at least not in the essentialist sense, but a collective set of
dispositional practices whose enactment forms the basis of interactions between journalists and between journalism and the rest of
society – interactions in which much is at stake in terms of status and
power.

Misrecognition is a given. The point here is not to realign journalistic principles according to a purer relation to the world, but rather to
explore the symbolic world of war reporting and journalism more
widely – how it is instinctively experienced by its members and how
it is regarded by its publics, and why. Individualised authority might
suggest that audiences' orientation to the field is a more emotional
one, based on a perception of personal admiration, identification or,
for that matter, revulsion. This would certainly fit MacIntyre's
argument (1981; see also Wessler and Schultz, 2007) that the decline
of institutions such as organised religion and the family has coincided
with increasing emotivism in public life. Using media as an emotional
resource is a well-established phenomenon, explained variably as
substituting pararelations for intimate relationships in the face of
anomie and atomisation, as a way of making sense of our selves, as a
status claim or as entertainment. But while all of these are plausible,
it is necessary to take into account the compelling correctives put
forward by Boltanski, Moeller and, more recently, Chouliaraki. While
these are of course significantly distinct contributions to the literature,
they share a common thread: that we cannot assume the emotionality
of audiences' experiences of war reporting and that visceral responses

to war reporting are increasingly absent from practices of news consumption.

Leaving aside the status of the distant others represented in war reporting, I have suggested here that morality plays a dual function. First, its disavowal operates as a field strategy, leading not to the negation of morality in war reporting but its more lightly worn and hence more plausible embodiment. Second, it does moral work for society at large by presenting a reference point for self-positioning, while itself positioning the war correspondent in a privileged position. In this regard I would argue that eliciting emotional responses is not a *sine qua non* of being recognised as authoritative by either peers or audience. If Chouliaraki is right in describing audience responses to representations of distant suffering as increasingly unemotional and reflexive, it might be assumed that this would lessen the gap between news consumers and producers, where part of the latter's mystification consists in unflappability in the face of mortal danger. But such a shift in viewing behaviour simultaneously opens the door to another possibility: complicity. Complicity is a long-established strategy deployed in particular by mid market and tabloid newspapers in the UK and elsewhere, using informal language and exclusive cultural references to foster a bond between a paper and its readers. It seems likely that a shared sense of ambivalence about violence and suffering will produce similar intimacies, leaving the war reporter no less authoritative. But instead of authority consisting in superhuman bravery and compassion, here, though these qualities remain valued, they are in the context of a culture of ambivalence worn in a more human way: being perceived to be pragmatic, unsentimental but decent.[5] In short, if war reporting as an emotional call-and-response is losing ground to a shared understanding of the complexities of conflict and uncertainty about how we should respond, then there is greater scope for authority taking the symbolic form of (performative) authenticity.

But there remains an important difference between the recognition of authority by peers and the wider public. The public status of the war correspondent does not depend on perceived piety, and a degree of ambivalence is unproblematically presumed, but recognition of integrity or decency is a necessary requirement of authority. I would argue that this is explained by audiences' immersion in a game of their own, to which we turn in the next chapter. Belief in a base level of goodness is part of their own illusio: whatever cynicism people might harbour about journalism, this belief sustains the sense that the game is worth playing, which in turn is necessary if war reporting is to do the moral work they rely on it to do. But amongst the war reporters interviewed, four implied that any claims even to integrity or decency were suspect. It is not that these respondents undermined the importance of their own profession, rather that its importance – for them, its principle of consecration – is distanced from questions of right and wrong. The sense was that morality was something strictly for others; if one knew of the side of war reporting that the public generally does not see – the compromises, futility, degradation and corruption – then one would instinctively recognise the naivety of talking about right and wrong; instead, it is a matter of professionalism.

There is in effect, then, a kind of meta-game at work here, in which a war reporter is instinctively oriented towards being publicly recognised as essentially good, which is not the same as well behaved, and within the field as knowing this to be a ruse. The trope that the public have no idea what really goes on in war was a common one, and fairly straightforwardly positions war reporting as a rarefied field of unique knowledge, or symbolic capital.

> Unfortunately the public don't know, I mean they thought *Bonanza* was live, so there is a sort of duty to try to get it right. (Interviewee 5)

In some cases public ignorance was defended as necessary, though this can still be regarded as strategic in that it places the speaker as able to process appalling horrors in a way that most cannot. In one case (Interviewee 2) it went further, effectively infantilising the audience by claiming that the bowdlerised conflict reporting that Western audiences see allows them to 'feel better about themselves'. In any case, this double strategy is difficult to negotiate, requiring as it does a level of hypocrisy while, as noted earlier, nearly all interviewees were quick to spot hypocrisy in others, interpreted as a sign of inauthenticity. But in the case of the reporter who explicitly presented himself as a moral authority while having a supposedly compromised private life, the criticism directed at him is not that he is a hypocrite – it is that he is the wrong kind of hypocrite, specifically one who preached to colleagues as well as the public. The dispositional best fit is that which knows in its bones that hypocrisy is inevitable, to the point of being ironic or playful about it or else simply implying its obviousness. This is the journalist for whom the dual consciousness fits seamlessly and appears as character, instantly recognisable as naturally, authentically authoritative (including by myself at several stages on the analysis). Again, this does not rule out good war reporting or war reporters,[6] and I suggested earlier that Bourdieu overstates the malevolence of this dual consciousness in journalists. If there is a game it is one common to many professions in which what is said publicly is at odds with what we tell each other, and in which to see this not as wrong but as absurd or simply the way things are is an effective means of performing experience and insight.

Notes

1 Henningham and Delano (1998: 157) conclude that ethics for British journalists are 'somewhat blurred', with respondents showing a higher likelihood relative to other nationalities to condone subterfuge, distortion and paying sources.

2 Gartman (1991: 434), however, argues that Bourdieu fails to account for the dynamism and variability of capitalist societies in applying an essentially precapitalist model. See also Guillory (2000: 29).

3 Valorisations were coded as binary couples; hence, a negative ascription of 'egoism' has the same base coding as a positive ascription of 'selflessness'.

4 This sense of intimacy is also described in terms of parasocial interaction (Horton and Wohl, 1956).

5 See also Reay (2005) on the gendered aspects of emotiveness and its absence.

6 'The paradox of the imposition of legitimacy is that it makes it impossible ever to determine whether the dominant feature appears as distinguished or noble because it is dominant – i.e. because it has the privilege of defining, by its very existence, what is noble or distinguished as being exactly what itself is, a privilege which is expressed precisely in its self-assurance – or whether it is only because it is dominant that it appears as endowed with these qualities and uniquely entitled to define them' (Bourdieu, 1984: 92).

6

How do audiences live journalism?

I'll say this about Tibetans, at least they're not polar bears.
(Comment posted on guardian.co.uk's Comment is Free discussion forum)

Much has been written in the past 20 years about the representation of 'distant others' in the news media. It was seen in the previous chapter that for Silverstone the issue of a 'proper distance' between audiences and mediated others is crucial because it involves the representation of humans to other humans. I have argued that we can reject the idea of a natural moral aspect to this representation in order to assess the strategic functions of morality for war reporters. But Silverstone (2007) is also compelling in arguing that the Western news media's focus on spectacle and otherness fosters a problematic sense of 'comfort' for the consumer, one whose perceived naturalness masks a specific discourse of good and evil in US foreign policy at the beginning of the twenty-first century. Zelizer (2004) and Chouliaraki (2006) have also explored the dehumanising effects of reducing suffering to media spectacle, documenting the overloading of such representation by narrative forms dominant in media and popular culture (see also Thussu, 2003; Griffin, 2004; 2010). Moeller (1999), similarly, argues that however noble the intentions of journalists and concerned citizens, the sheer amount and repetitiveness of conflicts worldwide will inevitably lead to compassion fatigue. Boltanski (1999: 3–19), meanwhile, explores the relationship between mediated distant others in phenomenological terms, raising the question also tackled more recently by Taylor (1994) and Fraser and Honneth (2003) of what level and form of recognition of one's existence as a sentient and competent agent are necessary in order to sustain community or the sense of belonging to a shared world.[1] These are all important contributions to debates over media morality, but each is primarily concerned with the implications of mediated representation for those represented. Here I will turn to the other side of the equation and ask: what are audiences actually doing when they consume war reporting?[2]

As an opening gambit, the most obvious answer is that people have a natural curiosity about others and a natural sense of compassion to the suffering of others (Güney, 2010; Johnson and Fahmy, 2010). This could alternately be characterised as a socialised sense of duty to bear witness to suffering, contingent on the universalisation of cultural norms of respect for human rights, and I would argue that the end result is the same: a moral dimension to consuming war reporting which is experienced by audiences as natural. The charge of voyeurism made by Moeller does not necessarily undermine this position, since watching voyeuristically simply represents an immoral way of doing something whose teleological purpose is accepted as moral. However, the political phenomenological approach taken in this book rejects the possibility either of a natural grounding or unproblematic universalisation of morality: the consumption of war reporting is not intrinsically a moral practice, and if morality does characterise cultures of practice of consumption, then we should ask what functions this serves. This is not intended as a cynical move: while in what follows it will be seen that there are interests at stake in the consumption of mediated conflict, the motivations and rewards of such consumption can also be admirable.

While Putnam's *Bowling Alone* thesis, that media consumption (television in particular) actively weakens participation in civic and social organisations, remains compelling, there is also evidence that specific forms of media consumption – and increasingly production on the part of audiences – could either sustain or at least link to new forms of engagement, reversing the individualism and alienation which accompanied the decline of the traditional public sphere (Coleman, 2005; Butsch, 2007; Couldry et al., 2007). The research project Media Consumption and the Future of Public Connection set out to explore how connection and disconnection are experienced in everyday life, and what role the media play (or do not play) in relation to this. Unsurprisingly, the results revealed a complex picture, but some findings are specifically relevant here. Roughly speaking, participants divided into four groups. The largest groups were those who were publicly connected and experienced this as a positive thing, and those who were disconnected and experienced this negatively. However, while theorists tend to pathologise disengagement and valorise engagement (Fraser, 1997), there was also a minority who were unquestionably connected but felt oppressed by their news engagement, as well as those who were satisfied with being disconnected. A cultural practice which responds to a lack of recognition from or inter-action with the public sphere with a metaphorical shrug of the shoulders may be indicative of a deeper malaise, but the point here is that no simple normative mapping between connection to either the news or the public sphere and contentment can be assumed. And significantly, those who were disconnected were 'already turned away' (Couldry et al., 2007: 3): there was no evidence that the media could offer this group a route to connection, and for some such a route was not desired in any case. Having established that the positive value of news consumption cannot be assumed, we now turn to consider what else audiences might be doing when they pay attention to war reporting.

Addressing oneself to a humanitarian crisis is never only about the crisis itself: it is also, in part, a performance of identity, a public projection whose recognition contributes to one's becoming a subject. Whether the centrality of media consumption – and specifically moralised media consumption – to subjectification is increasing is an open question to which we return below, as is the question of whether we should resist or welcome the development. Writing about the Bosnian war, Hammond (2007b: 49–50) highlights Salman Rushdie's claim to be an 'imaginary citizen' of Sarajevo, where the city itself is more imaginary than real. Sarajevo in effect became a floating signifier into which Western commentators could project more or less any symbolic meaning, but chiefly what was projected was liberal humanitarianism. Hammond justifiably identifies this phenomenon as narcissistic, serving the interests of the West's need to find meaning in its own existence rather than anything to do with events on the ground, where in fact the 'fantasy' of multiculturalism was by no means welcomed by all. The upshot is that concern for distant suffering, and as Michael Ignatieff argues (Hammond, 2007b: 54–7), the policy of humanitarian interventionism, ultimately stem from an existential crisis in the post-Cold War Western world: lacking any coherent idea of what it is for, it identifies or creates simulacra of crises 'demanding' principled action and, thereby, the enactment of moral national identity.

Hammond's point is not just that such displays of compassion are self-interested, but that they will inevitably fail to give Western nations a sense of purpose because they are based on fiction, or at least fictionalised accounts of what is happening in the world beyond the West. Moral posturing around spectacles of suffering is, in short, no substitute for ideological struggles properly grounded in the history and politics of Western society. However, as we turn back to media audiences of war reporting, it makes sense to withhold such meta-judgement for the sake of analysis. It is certainly possible (and has been argued by Hartley (1999), Moores (2000) and Landow [1992] 2006, amongst others) that a sense of self founded increasingly upon attention and reaction to symbolic media forms is intrinsically less solid than identity forged through historically dominant modes such as class and religion. Likewise, the comments on connection and disconnection above suggest that media consumption offers no guaranteed solution to individualism and anomie. But even if mediated subjectifying practices are narcissistic (Bourdieu, 1993b; Rosen, 2007) – in the phenomenological sense of a short-circuited process of subjectification lacking adequately complex mediation[3] – this should not preclude a discussion of how it operates and how it is experienced. This means taking seriously the role media consumption plays in audiences' making sense of themselves. Suspending the question of whether media cause or solve disconnection, for example, we can ask whether media consumption helps audiences make sense of *either* of these states, and in the context of what symbolic economy of other actors.

In line with the reaction of the commentariat and political classes documented by Hammond, we might theorise that audiences too do not simply consume war reporting but make use of it to project an identity which is compassionate, tolerant and principled. Several media commentators (O'Neill, 2010) have written as much, arguing that the apparent preferential compassion amongst British (often 'middle class') media audiences for exotic rather than local suffering has more to do with the cultural cachet of distant suffering than its reality. This in turn raises the question of whether such a performance of identity needs an audience to achieve the sort of recognition identified by Hegel as essential to becoming a full subject, or whether it can sustain a stable sense of self in private (see below). The Public Connection project found that social contexts of media consumption – especially making use of news in social interactions – are important for some types of media user, but it is worth entertaining the possibility that, as lived, social or public recognition of one's media consumption and opinions about it is not integral to its being a subjectifying practice. That said, unpublicised media consumption is by definition invisible, and so for the purposes of getting an empirical perspective on the uses audiences make of conflict reporting, a discourse analysis was carried out into the comments left on a newspaper's online discussion forum about the riots in Tibet in 2008.

Strictly speaking, of course, these comments are evidence of media production as much as consumption (Örnebring, 2008; Bruns, 2008a; Fuchs, 2009); further, it is assumed that the technical format and broader discourse of discussion forums will have an influence on posts, and those posting are not representative of the newspaper's readers, let alone the broader population. But there is at least scope for exploring the motivations and functions of publicising opinions in this manner.

In order to test whether there is evidence that audiences use conflict reporting to project (whether to an audience or not) compassion or humanitarian credentials, it was decided to focus on the *Guardian*, a newspaper whose editorial line tends towards the liberal centre-left. The web forums selected housed responses to comment pieces by *Guardian* journalists and other commentators about the riots in Tibet. All but one of the 12 articles analysed were broadly pro-Tibet and critical of the Chinese government, with the remaining piece making the case against Western solipsism. The initial assumption was that posters on the *Guardian*'s Comment is Free website would be largely sympathetic to its comment and analysis, and based on the above reasoning there was a working hypothesis that the analysis would discern an economy of competitive (as opposed to collective) compassion, in which posters vied to position themselves as engaged, caring and concerned – all of which would be interpretable as social capital. It was also hypothesised that the currency of this compassion would be emotiveness – not because posters were expected to conform to the 'bleeding heart liberal' stereotype, but derived from MacIntyre's aforementioned contention about emotivism in moral discourse.

The analysis produced clear evidence of a symbolic economy in which posters presented themselves as authoritative: that is, not simply putting forward personal opinions but positioning themselves as valorised forms – as with war reporters in chapter 5, not just getting things right but being right, as individuals. Interestingly, however, the posts were predominantly opposed to the *Guardian*'s editorial line: approximately 60 per cent, compared with 30 per cent who were clearly 'pro-Tibet' and 10 per cent whose views were not discernible. That 60 per cent cannot be described as 'pro-China' as such: while some identified themselves as Chinese and used this to establish the authenticity of their views, other posters in this group coalesced around an opposition to what they saw as the sentimental romanticisation of ancient Tibetan culture and a moral injunction that it is hypocritical for Western commentators to criticise China given historical colonialism and contemporary foreign policy. Given our

focus here the substance of posters' opinions is of secondary importance to the way they are made, but it is significant that many
comments focused on romanticisation and specifically the allegation
that authors were deluded about events in Tibet and driven by the
need to demonstrate their liberal credentials. If Hammond is right and
there is a culture of moral positioning through attending compassion-
ately to overseas injustice, then, as with the war correspondent
interviews, it has to be admitted that there is a greater degree of
reflexivity about this 'game' than Bourdieusian phenomenology
concedes. Also in line with the war correspondent interviews, I would
argue that the opposition to perceived moral posturing on the
Guardian website is not a rejection of moral positioning per se, but an
alternative economy in which morality is rationalised and actively
decontested by overt recourse to realism and worldliness, in a similar
manner to that seen amongst war reporters.[4]

There was no shortage of claims to authority amongst the posts
based on purportedly factual evidence – sometimes from sources in
the region, but more commonly historical. But the way these and
other claims were made, evident especially in writing style and decontesting practices, supports the hypothesis that their content cannot be
separated from a symbolic economy in which authoritative status is
presented in terms of disposition. And this dispositional authority,
presented as something which just is rather than something which
needs to be explained, has four identifiable features. First, it is individual rather than institutional. Second, it is anti-elitist, with
distinctions made against both the political and media elite – indeed,
these were often conflated (see also Robinson, 2006). Third, it has an
alienated or overlooked quality: despite its nominal publicity through
appearing on a website, it was common to self-present as being
isolated from both elite and mainstream opinion (evidenced through
phrases like 'Why can no one see?' and claims about not hearing and
taking notice). Fourth, this authoritative disposition is distinctly
moral, with the morality of self and other cast in terms of personal
decency (in opposition to decency) and integrity (in opposition to
naivety) rather than following particular ethical principles or overt
moralising. Together, these features suggest an economy of moral
authority in which the authenticity of personal experience is valued
more highly than institutional, professional expertise. This authentic
artlessness is presented as naturalised selfhood, but is predicated on
specific linguistic practices, the most common of which were irony
('I'll say this about Tibetans, at least they're not polar bears'), rhetorical 'plain speaking' ('frankly', 'I'm sorry, but'), vitriol, self-deprecation,

playfulness and demotic cultural references (including British television programmes *Peep Show* and *Brass Eye*, and *Heat* magazine).
Finally, the evidence suggests that the plausible authenticity of this
disposition is primarily of significance to the poster rather than her
readers: while there are clearly collective practices of self-identification, there are very few posts (around 30) ascribing authority to other
posters or journalists, let alone evidence of collective mis-ascription to
others of authority as character, as Bourdieusian field theory would
have predicted.

Moral authority as authentic disposition

The most striking finding from the discussion board posts was that
those articulating the dominant view did so in a way that positioned
them in opposition to the presumed hegemonic discourse of Western
media, politics and, to an extent, culture. The pervasiveness of weary
cynicism as a speech style suggests that this positioning is experienced
not as a form of political activism or resistance (cf. Downing, 2001;
Kahn and Kellner, 2004; Levine and Lopez, 2004; Rauch, 2007), but
as a state of disconnection, an individual voice de-authorised and
unrecognised by the mainstream. Further, the communicative mode of
a clear majority of posts was either one-way or askew, with a widespread mutual misunderstanding of posters' opinions, wilful or
otherwise. This would suggest that such forums lack the kind of
cohesive structure which Goffman ([1959] 1971) identifies as central
to group solidarity, and whatever this says about discussion forums as
an alternative public space, it suggests once more that mutual recognition between audience members is not necessary to reflections on
media consumption being central to the presentation of self. Posters,
in particular those identifying themselves as British, remain highly
individualised – even if, as suggested here, their practices of individuation are at base collective. This is potentially significant. We saw in
chapter 2 that Bourdieu characterises all fields of cultural production
as pervaded by a systematic misrecognition of contingent practices
and quasi-arbitrary symbolic forms as personally innate and naturally
valuable. Here, though, there are collective practices of self-authorisation. Instead of the projection of these self-authorisations being met
by substantive recognition of the poster's status as an autonomous
subject, it is either ignored entirely or met by competing claims to
superior individuality. This is marked by distinction either against a
poster's lack of autonomy ('you're just another...', 'like everyone else
in the West you think...') or against their perceived inauthenticity,

through the charge of hypocrisy. In this there is a clear parallel to the symbolic economy of war reporting discussed in the previous chapter.

Positing a collective basis to individuation means that there is at least some stability to the practices and symbols through which it proceeds. If we look at the riots and their media coverage in strictly functional terms, we can say that they acted as a means of access to an established set of practices of position-taking, whose enactment has the dual purpose of establishing legitimate occupation of a position of authority, and reproducing those practices as dominant forms of distinction making. In other words, the appearance of Tibet on the news agenda provided a pretext for affirming and reaffirming (a longitudinal study across humanitarian crises could potentially establish the extent to which such affirmations are ritualised[5]) a poster's positions on Iraq, Palestine/Israel, colonial India, Ireland and indigenous Americans. It will be seen in the following chapter that this litany of signifiers parallels the way that the war reporters used different markers – conflicts, events, individuals, trends – as a way of positioning themselves discursively, each assumed by the speaker to act as collectively intelligible shorthand for a set of accepted truths, value judgements and means for *locating* the speaker dispositionally (see also Cenite et al., 2009). For the majority of comment posters this position taking is not only about having the 'correct' views on these issues, but how they relate to self-presented disposition: unsentimental, worldly, unpopular but right.[6] The importance of going 'against the grain' is predicted in Bourdieu's work (1991c; 2005) on cultural production: upon entering their professional field, journalists and academics alike will typically seek to overturn in a highly visible manner a few of each trade's sacred cows, while otherwise conforming increasingly over time to the more durable structures of the field. This is specifically manifest in the discussion forums in the frequent and often vituperative denunciation of the Dalai Lama as a dictator or CIA stooge, and criticism of his perceived beatification by the Western media. I do not aim here to judge the validity of their arguments one way or the other. Instead, as with the war reporter interviews, media practices are assumed not to be primarily determined by their object, and may be assessed strategically. Here, targeting a figure who has in many ways achieved the status of a mythic good in Western news discourse, and doing so in a polemical fashion, is an effective means of demonstrating autonomy, in the sense of being able to resist conventional wisdom and think what to others is unthinkable.

The analysis makes clear that interaction is not a significant aspect of the communicating done in the context of a comment forum (cf. Gillmor, 2004; Singer and Ashman, 2009). Users generally either post without regard to how their words might form part of a broader conversation, or if they do it is in an implicit way, with a reflecting-back from the world based on assumptions about what 'everyone else' thinks rather than actual valorisation or criticism. This is interesting in terms of what it tells us about how people participate online, but since it appears to be experienced as a private activity, it is reasonable to extrapolate from the analysis that it also tells us about news consumption. That is, the activity of posting doesn't appear overly to distort the manner in which people think about and reflect on what they read and watch. And since these practices of consumption are also practices of subjectification the broader question is this: if audiences make use of news about conflicts in order to make sense of themselves, what explains the centrality of media morality to selfhood? This in turn depends on whether subjectification as practised in the context of news consumption and reflection is competitive, peripheral to endogenous journalistic logics or ritualistic. Let us examine each possibility in turn.

From a Bourdieusian perspective we can hypothesise fields of consumption similar to those of production, since there is nothing teleologically unique about cultural production which sets it apart as uniquely politicised. Thus, a field of consumption could plausibly be characterised by a topography of positions of relative power and weakness, in which individuals act according to collective schemes of anticipation in pursuit of status as part of a broader 'game', the rules of which are simultaneously pervasive and misrecognised. While it may appear that there is a key difference here insofar as status is not explicitly accorded by others, in fact this is entirely consistent with the war-reporting study and works such as *Distinction*. Distinction makings are more often than not implicit, and making the rules of valorisation explicit is likely to be strategically disadvantageous – being at home in an environment means that its contingencies are too obvious to emerge to consciousness. What remains to be established is the extent to which there is a coherent, if unacknowledged, logic-structuring practices amongst posters, manifest in cultures of practice of subjectification. In the comment forums this took two forms. First, and less commonly, there was limited evidence of what might be called tribal subjectifying practices – claiming membership of a group as strategic self-positioning, opposed to official or elite power in the form of mainstream politics and media and thus evidently oriented towards the accumulation of the symbolic capital associated with authenticity and anti-elitism.

However, subjectification through group identification is easily outweighed by collective practices of competitive individuation: in line with the discussion above, positioning oneself as individually authoritative and authentic as a means of enacting one's status, whether or not it is recognised by others. This certainly fits the Bourdieusian claim that all communicative arenas are at base sites of struggle, and that competition takes place not so much at the level of the communicative content as embodied disposition. Here again, authority is a product not (only) of getting things right in comment posts, but being the right sort of poster, a disposition contingent on practices which signify such, and for the Bourdieusian analysis to hold then enacting a disposition which is individualised, anti-elitist, over-looked and moral must not simply be a dominant cultural norm but something by which individuals vie for position. The overlooked and anti-elitist dimensions are readily explicable in strategic terms, in that there is a strong precedent in the British press for them. While it is ostensibly a distinction against the supposed dominance of official power, each has been historically used by mid-market newspapers such as the *Daily Mail* and *Daily Express* in order to farm a particular brand of authority and credibility. This is an identity of 'noble alien-ation', of being a lone voice of reason and decency amid a sea of chaos and depravity. As regards comment posters, it is unclear whether they are mimicking professional journalistic practices when they engage in audience participation – this would be an interesting development, though the data here were inconclusive – or whether this is simply the way that they identify themselves in relation to media and other contexts anyway. The latter would suggest that these papers have successfully managed to echo their readers' voices; the former that when audiences participate they do so not simply using their 'authentic' voices but by using specific resources in order to appear authoritative – in this case using familiar news discourses in which the right way of speaking is well established. Either way, what is signifi-cant is that alienation (as opposed to the hypothesised humanitarianism) is properly characterisable as strategic – that is, a form of symbolic capital standing for the authority of the speaker. The principal drawback of the Bourdieusian account of competitive alienated subjectivities is its insistence that cultural producers are largely unaware of the game in which they are immersed. In fact, posters were quick to point out the strategies allegedly being disin-genuously employed by others – sentiment and guilt in reference to pro-Tibet posters, but also reflexive references to signifiers pervading the dominant symbolic economy described here: 'Oh look, another gratuitous and pointless mention of Iraq.... What were the odds?'). That said, there was no evidence of self-reflection about the role played by irony, 'plain speaking' or popular cultural references (see Liu, 2008) in their own performances. In any case, it is reasonable to presume that comment forums are a less immersive field than other Bourdieusian fields, and it is widely held that Bourdieu overstated the determining influence of even these on individual subjectivity.

A second possibility also sees practices of media consumption as acts of subjectification, but only as a by-product of a largely unac-knowledged competitive symbolic economy within professional journalism. This extension of the internal logic of the journalistic field to audiences is an instance of what Joel Best (1999) refers to as 'domain expansion', and is in line with Bourdieu's warning (1994c) that journalism's differentiating principles, dominated as they are by market forces, are colonising other spheres and compro-mising their autonomy. Unlike the first position, a shift towards the valorisation of individualised, anti-institutional authority should not be seen as a mass entry into the existing journalistic 'game' by actors who now have a stake in it, but the side effect of the competitive strategies of established journalistic sub-groups. In chapter 5 we saw that war reporters divide between those who claim overt moral authority and those who eschew moralising (itself a moral posi-tioning), and that the two, while vying at the macro level for supremacy, have co-existed historically in the US and UK for economic reasons – there is a market for each. However, the anti-moralising subfield has traditionally dominated war reporting and political journalism in these markets, with the implications that its internal logic for distribution of the symbolic capital of status – peer review, by and large – is dominant over other ways of 'doing' jour-nalism. This would explain the relatively low regard with which explicitly moral journalism is held amongst most war reporters. The performance and recognition of moral authority could be seen as a strategic advantage to the 'moralisers': a means of by-passing peer review and challenging prevailing rules by finding recourse to an alternate form of legitimisation – popularity or the perception of authenticity. This can be interpreted either as the dismantling of an elitist, exclusive economy of authority in journalism, or the displace-ment of professional values by populism or emotionalism. Either way, it is likely that such a shift is not the result of conscious strategis-ing on the part of crusading journalists of attachment, but a reflection of a broader cultural shift (towards authority as authen-ticity) of which particular journalistic sub-genres are beneficiaries.

The third possibility brings us to the ritualistic aspect of media consumption, interpreted in broadly Foucauldian terms (see for instance Andrejevic, 2008). By this account, posts on comment forums are characterised as a structured calling forth of expressive practices which functions as a disciplinary regime. Any shared orientation towards the performance of specific moral identities is ultimately a rationalisation of the process of becoming a subject. As in the Bourdieusian approach, audience participation is regarded only secondarily as expressive, its primary function being the reproduction of a media logic which is prior to the individuals who make sense of themselves in relation to it. This position can easily slide towards hyper-politicisation, with the inferable conclusion that all media consumption and production instantiates their cooption by the hegemonic forces of mainstream media and their complicity in the ongoing durability of the power relations which concretise their dominatedness. (In more practical terms, Stuart Allan (2006; see also Fuchs, 2009) argues that user-generated content amounts to the transformation of audiences into free labour for media multinationals.) Against this, there are undoubtedly non-professional blogs and online networks producing not only counter-hegemonic discourse but demonstrable political impact. But while it is conceivable that comment forum posts could initiate a snowball effect leading to substantive, coordinated action in a political arena, however defined, it remains the case that amateur media production usually requires uptake by mainstream media in order to wield effective influence (Singer, 2005; Allan, 2006; Carlson, 2007a; 2007b; Thurman, 2008).

Similarly, the current prevalence of 'Have Your Say' functionality on news websites is not in itself convincing evidence of new arenas for public engagement. At best this offers formal registration of audience views, rather than an active mediation reflecting a user's self-presentation as seen by other subjects. The lack of interlocution prevents such functions serving as an alternate communicative space, and the lack of articulation with action in other arenas prevents them providing the basis for an alternate public space (Bohman, 2007). At worst this could be argued to act as a pressure valve, allowing posters to let off steam in a manner that makes political action less likely. Or again, in Foucauldian terms, it could be seen as the summoning and thereby structuring of instinctive, unreflective views on events – views which, even if the default position is a knee-jerk anti-authority stance, are normalised and rationalised – ensuring the reinforcement if not of official policy then homogenised or oversimplified ways of seeing the world. The data from the forums show some (though not a lot of) evidence of structuredness and structuringness: the former refers to similarities in frames of reference (Iraq, Palestine etc.), the latter to affirmations (and it is significant that they were simple affirmations rather than step-by-step consensus building) of moral value systems which could reasonably be claimed to have ongoing regularising effects in the same way that discursive interaction between professionals regularises the norms and discourse of their worlds. Both Bourdieu and Foucault are instinctively inclined to view any new habits or shared cultures of practice simply as new and potentially more insidious forms of hegemonic reproduction. But this is a normative claim based on a questionable teleology of structuration – that is, relations of domination and dominatedness tend to be reproduced and progressively entrenched, because that is what they do. Such a belief is plausible, though ultimately unfalsifiable. More relevant to us is how news consumption can be understood in terms of recognition and narcissism. As before, this means looking to how consumption is lived, not as a means of accessing the authentic experience of audience, but because that experience is structured and structuring – a view which is compatible with the teleology of structural reproduction, but not limited by its narrow conception of power as domination and dominatedness.

Subjectification, recognition and its absence

While it makes sense to posit that the specific act of posting comments on a news website is not by its nature political (of course it may be by its particular content), is this an unreasonably exclusive yardstick by which to judge them (Bohman, 2007)? More widely, could we ask what other types of engagement, or belonging, or connection, are attached to shared practices of news consumption, and perhaps reflection? One possibility is that it is recognition that is central to fostering a conscious, lived relation to the society in which one lives, though this immediately raises several questions. Is it one's status as autonomous which needs to be recognised, one's citizenship, group membership or individual competence? If connection is conceived in opposition to alienation, to and from what – nation, neighbourhood, internet? And does it matter if the subject doing the recognising is an identifiable human being, or is seeing oneself represented in some form of public space – whether as a voter or an audience member – enough of a reflecting back from the world to constitute mediation of subjectivity? Hegel's original, phenomenological construction of the term emphasises recognition of one's professional competence, one's formal status as a citizen and recognition by family and friends as central to the dialectic by which one becomes a subject. In a now influential exchange between Nancy Fraser and Axel Honneth (2003), Honneth argues against Hegel's prioritisation of economic deprivation in defining the dominant barriers to selfhood. Instead, Honneth claims that lack of recognition (of any sort) is the essence of alienation, of which economic disadvantage should be seen as a subset. Fraser in response stresses the need not to define alienation so broadly as to render it meaningless, and indeed suggests that Hegel's taxonomy of alienation is not sufficiently differentiated. In this vein she argues that to Hegel's model in which the objects of recognition are formal citizenship and formal professionalism we need to add active participation in politics and recognition of one's professional autonomy – that is, not only the certificate that proves qualifications, but the ability to work independently.[7] This rightly puts the lived quality of recognition in the spotlight, though it bears clarifying that Hegel was keenly aware of the gap between formal and lived recognition.

These are important questions, but it is potentially fruitful at least to pose the question of what in the context of contemporary mass media would constitute recognition substantial enough to underpin not only formal inclusion in public discourse. Options include simply having maximal access to public information (however defined) and being formally authorised to comment on it, or alternatively evidence of active participation in public debates, or else evidence of subjects who are engaged and, in the phenomenological sense, complexly mediated – that is, having actively presented themselves to the world and consistently folded the resulting objectifications by others or the world into the ongoing dialectic of subjectification. For Hegel, as for Marx, we put ourselves out into the world primarily through labour, but it is worth considering media practices here – not only in terms of projecting opinions into public forums, but also, potentially, consumption. This is because consumption as a subjectifying practice is not only passive. It is an internalisation as much as an externalisation, both in the deterministic sense that all practices are the externalisation of previously internalised structures, and because the instinctive if latent question 'What does paying attention to this issue say about me?' is an act of self-presentation, a positioning act.

While the 'recognition' implied by such a question is undoubtedly presumptive and arguably fantastical, it is possible that it will be experienced by media consumers as real – a stepping outside of oneself which presents a form of the objectified self to consciousness. This may be delusional or it may be an accurate reflection of what others would perceive, perhaps confirmed by social interaction and perhaps not, but insofar as it is an established culture of practice it is worth asking, as with all forms of recognition, what qualities it would need to have in order to be successfully articulated with subjectification. The forums analysed here suggest three criteria, albeit ambiguously. The first is simply regularity or stability. While there was no evidence of a strong feedback mechanism (see Wilhelm, 2000), only fitful responses to posts easily outnumbered by posts which are not 'recognised' in the sense of generating responses at all, it is possible that regularity of posting, however non-interactional, lends a solidity to a poster's sense of position in the online world. Evidence of this comes chiefly through self-presentation as misunderstood outsider, and while it has been seen that this may be a strategic move, this does not preclude its being experienced as authentic. To be sure, this type of one-way projection of self may be interpreted as the opposite of a Habermasian ideal speech situation, which points to a second criterion on which both posts and reflexivity about one's own consumption largely fail to meet. This is recognition of the poster's authority to speak, which may fall short of an idealised form of communication ('mutual awareness', in Goffman's terms) which carries full cognisance of other consumers' status as autonomous, sentient beings. Responses to posts are selective and frequently misrepresentative of points made about Tibet – a pervasive misrecognition that goes well beyond the occasional failures of impression management that Goffman ([1959] 1971) regards as a normal state of affairs in interactional systems.

In this regard comment forums need not be seen as exceptional. For Bourdieu, all interactional systems are characterised by pervasive misrecognition: what Habermas calls the institutionalisation of the ideal speech situation, Bourdieu would interpret as the institutionalisation of symbolic violence (Markham, 2007). This is not to suggest that interaction is to be avoided, only that its absence as a central feature of the structure of a particular culture is not demonstratively a cause of alienation. Hypothetically, one could feel that one's authority to speak is recognised without actual interlocutors taking one's words seriously – if there were clearly established cultural norms about what counts as authoritative, for instance, though the literature suggests that this is decreasingly the case, if it ever was. But the authority to post opinions appears largely formal: those on the wrong side of the digital divide (Norris 2000, 2001; Lievrouw and Livingstone, 2002; Rice and Haythornthwaite, 2006; Zhao and Elesh,

2008) regard their lack of authority as natural ('not for the likes of us', in Bourdieu's famous words), while those who do post experience their authority as pre-given. This does not necessarily mean that such self-(de)authorisations do not involve externalisation and objectification of the self and thus do not amount to recognition. In Bourdieusian terms it could be said that objectification occurs all too readily: our sense of our place in the world is so hardwired as to be unremarkable, and our authority or otherwise to speak is indeed pre-given since our externalised selves are so thoroughly internalised (McNay, 2008). By this logic, the question of what we are doing when we consume news becomes a matter of what is naturalised as the sort of thing in which someone 'like me' would normally take an interest, rather than a voluntaristic strategy to present oneself in a particular way. This would suggest that active recognition over the quality of which individuals have some influence is impossible; it is always, already determined. But here Bourdieu (1993b) is at odds with the evidence which suggests that at least some audience members pay attention to mediated conflict in part because it says something about themselves and helps to make sense of their relation to the world. Examples of such codings include:

> I was (and continue to be) against the war in Iraq and Israel's actions in Gaza and the West Bank. You see, I like to be consistent.

> I've no confidence whatever our own spineless government will do anything.

> Oh, so I am accused of refusing to admit that I am Chinese? And yes indeed, I do refuse to admit that I am Chinese.

> Personally, I think life would be very sad without true diversity. The more the better.

> As an African I can also say to the Tibetans: In a way you are lucky – unlike us, at least your colonisers were/are not British for then you really would know what suffering is.

> I am a [sic] honourable Dutchman who hates commies. However, I am also sicken [sic] tired of our Media. Come on, deliberately or not, don't treat us as fools.

> I am a Chinese. Am I brain washed? Maybe, but at least my English ability allows me to read New York Times online, BBC, listen to NPR.

In short, even if in structural terms recognition or its absence is pre-reflexive, confirming rather than actively constituting an individual's orientation, it may be experienced – even in the context of private, passive media consumption – as substantively subjectifying.

The third criterion concerns group membership or imagined community (see for instance Anderson, 1983; Zelizer, 1993; Papacharissi, 2009). For both Fraser and Honneth (2003), recognition requires mutual awareness of commonality (sometimes called solidarity; see for instance Scheff, 2008) – recognition that other users are like us and are thus authorised to speak for us, rather than recognition of their singular, exceptional authority. What are we to make, then, of the evidence from the comment forums, in which what posters appear to have in common is the aforementioned sense of alienation from what is perceived as elite public life? ('But, intervention or no intervention, the people (that's us) are always expendable.') There were no indicators of recognition of common belonging to an alternate space to the mainstream media or political sphere, merely a sometimes shared sense of not belonging. This is clearly a recognition of sorts, but one entirely at odds with Hegel's ([1807] 1977) emphasis on universality, let alone the importance Fraser lends to active participation. This is by no means intended to characterise the intrinsic quality of communication in online media forums as a degraded version of face-to-face communication, which has often been idealised to the exclusion of other forms of interaction both in the internet age and historically (Williams, 1986). The medium is not the problem, and it is not hard to find examples online of communication characterised by feedback, solidarity and mutual respect. But at least in reflections on mainstream media coverage of international conflicts, the primary effect in subjectifying terms is confirmation of disconnection – shared for some, individualised for others – from the mainstream news media and politics. If this logic were transferable to private consumption then the implications would be considerable. We usually assume that attention paid to conflicts represents not only an individualised sense of duty to bear witness, but of self-identification as belonging to a group of civilised citizens who care about injustice and suffering. But the evidence presented here suggests three contrary conclusions: that attention is primarily motivated by distinction making rather than collectivity; distinction making is based not on competitive humanitarianism but competitive disillusion recognised as realism or maturity; and insofar as consumers do use conflict journalism in part to make sense of themselves, for some at least it is their disconnection that they are seeking, consciously or otherwise, to crystallise.

However, the point here is not to lambaste either conflict journalism or new media practices for failing to reconnect audiences to politics or the wider world. While it is common and normatively defensible to pathologise alienation, the aim here is instead to contextualise such practices in terms of their functionality, and in this regard there are two points to emphasise. The first is that, as we have seen, there can be an interest in disconnection: it appears here to operate as symbolic capital signifying authenticity and thus a certain form of authority. This may only be possible in the context of a broader cultural context which there is not space to investigate here, but might include historical trends such as the growth of individualism, declining trust in elite authority, and increasing emotionalism and populism. It is also worth stressing that if media consumption is used to make sense of people's disorientation in the world, that disorientation is real: there are sound reasons for experiencing disconnection, and making use of news media to understand this is at least as valid as expecting media to solve the problem of mass disaffection. Second, in phenomenological terms, for others lack of recognition – whether in public life, in online forums or as a private consumer – does not appear to be experienced as problematic in any way. For some comment posters, the act of expressing oneself appears more valorised than feedback or reaction. Seeing one's words on a website may for this group constitute sufficient recognition to be experienced as satisfactory subjectification.[8] By extension, private consumption will often be experienced in unproblematic terms, requiring neither validation of one's thoughts nor the implicit externalisation of reflexive media consumption. We could speculate that this is a manifestation of consumers' complicity in their own ongoing dominatedness, that the consequences of the short-circuiting of mediation of subjectivity through the absence of reflectings back means that the subject is inevitably less aware of their implicatedness in unequal power relations. However, we cannot presume that the lack of interaction of atomised passivity and the sporadic nature of online communication are lived as problematic, as much as we cannot presume that dutiful engagement with conflict reporting is satisfying.

While limited in its remit, the results of this survey of media consumption and non-professional media production appear to corroborate a significant contention relating to the social role of the war correspondent. Engagement with mediated conflict may not be motivated largely by genuine compassion for the suffering of others, but nor is it reduced to spectacle or entertainment (cf. Taylor, 1998; Burston, 2003; Thussu, 2003; Keeble, 2004; Stahl, 2009; Steuter and Wills, 2010). Instead, it is functional. It demands cultural competence and the internalisation of cultures of schemes of practice of orientation or positioning in relation to the objects of that culture. Whether the generally unacknowledged rules of engagement are at base competitive, ritualistic or narcissistic, war reporting is used to make sense of one's place as an audience member, if not citizen. None of this negates the possibility of compassion, but it does demonstrate that both compassion and distinctions against compassion are not neutral in relation to the stakes people have in news engagement. Let us now turn back to the other side of the screen to look at recent developments within the field of war reporting.

Notes

1 Cf. Benhabib (Wahl-Jorgensen, 2008), who makes the case for dignity rather than competence as the core condition of public recognition.
2 Cf. Carruthers (2008) and Bell (2008), both of whom argue that audiences for war reporting are in decline.
3 For Bourdieu (1993b), all self-reflexivity which lacks the double episte-mological break discussed in chapter 2 is narcissistic. See also Bourdieu (2004: 89–91); Pels (2000: 12). Bourdieu (Bourdieu and Wacquant, 1992: 72) distinguishes his epistemic reflexivity as 'fundamentally anti-narcissistic'. See also Maton (2003).
4 By contrast the pro-Tibet posts are mostly framed in terms of cultural self-determination and opposition to large power hegemony, though there was a significant minority within this category whose claims were contex-tualised with references to spirituality and environmental sustainability, framed in opposition to perceived Western materialism and consumerism.
5 See Savage et al. (2005) for a discussion of how such an analysis might proceed through examining various forms of capital, assets and other resources.
6 For the minority 'pro-Tibet' posters, by contrast, self-presented authority appears to consist in an authenticity of disposition predicated on the plausible (at least to self) performance of outrage and an affective rather than detached commitment to social justice.
7 Pateman (1989: 182) sets out the dilemma of enfranchisement by asking what the point is of giving workers the formal status of citizens if their day-to-day experience mocks that status?
8 After Dalton (2004), it could be argued that such representation is signif-icant since, while it may lack active recognition by others, it registers the user's creativity.

7

New developments in the field: brave new world or plus ça change?

Bourdieusian phenomenology is sometimes accused of being flatly deterministic (e.g. Eckstein, 1988; Minogue, 1992; Garnham, 1993; Bohman, 1997; Sayer, 1999; Noble and Watkins, 2003). Bourdieu in particular tends to work from the assumption that the structures of any field are naturally geared towards maintaining the status quo. The durable, transposable dispositions of habitus structure practice through instinctive anticipation of likely outcome, and are thus more or less naturally oriented towards reinstituting the material conditions which gave rise to their contingent existence. The fact that processes of structuration in fields are not monolithic but proceed at the microscopic level of instinct, intuition, spontaneity and so on is merely interpreted as evidence of the intractability of conservative reproduction. But there are two reasons why this need not be the case. First, structuring has a haphazard aspect (Bourdieu, 2000: 196–202; Fowler, 2003; Crossley, 2003). Determinations of practice may be logical expressions of the generative or 'genetic' structures of a field, but they are not linearly predictable. As Mauss ([1954] 2002) argued in relation to gift exchange, there is room in the gap between stimulus and response for negotiation, reversal and second guessing – even if individuals do not quite own these practices. Second, fields do not exist in a vacuum but in relation to other fields, all of which are part of a broader metafield of power. This means that a field such as journalism is subject to historical forces, shaped by and sometimes shaping the structure of that metafield. Journalism is being influenced by (and may also help to influence) shifting relations between the public and private spheres, and between the professional and personal aspects of everyday life. The rise of individualism and identity politics and the decline of traditional group allegiances such as class and religion have also transformed professional journalism and its audiences alike. Finally, technological developments over the past 20 years have had an immense impact on all cultural production, though the question remains open whether technological innovation causes or is an expression of cultural shifts (McChesney, 1998).

Likewise, war is not static.[1] The interviews on which this research is based were initially designed to ask reporters specifically about the 1990–91 Gulf War,[2] but it soon became apparent that wars did not exist as discrete units in their memory, instead forming part of a narrative that is part individual and part collective. This litany, depending on the correspondent's age, extends from the Bangladeshi war of independence through Vietnam, the Falklands, Grenada, the Gulf War, Bosnia and Kosovo to Afghanistan and finally the war in Iraq from 2003. While other conflicts were mentioned – Congo and Sierra Leone, for instance – these appeared as outliers, not forming part of the collective 'story' through which reporters described their own lives and the recent history of their profession. This is similar to the common referents used by audiences to position themselves in the previous chapter but, unexpectedly, amongst the war reporters interviewed there appears to be greater conformity to this discursive architecture. The ready availability of an established narrative framework, as well as reflecting the sequence of historical events (though usually limited to conflicts in which the US or UK played a part), means that there is a stable, collectively recognised chain of signifiers by which war reporters can make valorisations and enact their own professional dispositions. This culture of practice of self-positioning takes as read that every war is different, but for each there is a systematically, apparently pre-reflexively recognised symbolic economy by which distinctions are made and different forms of symbolic capital consecrated.

In this regard what is interesting about the prevalence of pooling (Tumber and Webster, 2006) during the Gulf War (used previously in Grenada, the Falklands and Panama but for different reasons and to a lesser extent) is how it influences dominant modes of positioning (in Bourdieu's term, position-taking). 'Independents' were lionised as in other conflicts,[3] but there was also scope for distinction in the absence of mobility and access, in the form of cynicism, irony and ambivalence. Reporters experienced their work as a constant battle with military media handlers, a kind of war of attrition of its own in which the journalistic object – information about the war – was thought of as being protected behind a military fortress, the defences of which it was the journalist's goal to breach, usually through cunning or 'working' sources. The nature of the Gulf War, in terms of there being consistent (and stage-managed) interactions between military and media, meant that relatively stable relations (and identifications) between correspondents and either senior military personnel or media managers were possible. We saw in chapter 4 that while there was an emphasis on penetrating the military 'machine' (mentioned by four), interviewees also spoke of enjoying relations of natural affinity or complicity with army officers, ranged against both junior military personnel and less experienced journalists. This does not preclude the idea of professional distance, but it does change the practices through which it is manifested; in particular, distance can consist in an amiable camaraderie coupled with an unspoken mutual respect for the other's professionalism.

Kosovo, on the other hand, and away from the bombing of Belgrade, was a war often fought from village to village in mountainous terrain that was not easy to navigate. While there were as ever journalists, much derided in the interviews, holed up in hotels and reliant on official press releases, much of the reporting recounted by interviewees was done in small groups travelling independently as far as was possible. As a result, the experience of the war, both in terms of following the events of the conflict and evading restrictions on mobility, was couched in terms of a cat-and-mouse game. Amongst those who did have the ability to report relatively freely, the way that values like authority and integrity were established – always, to an extent, competitively – consisted in how that autonomy was lived. This meant an emphasis on ingenuity and relishing chaos, and on the nature of relations with personnel on the ground: Serb warlords, for instance, were often described as eccentric 'characters' who could be bought or outwitted. The wider outcome is the same – a symbolic system in which the personal embodiment of guile, gall, cynicism/realism and ambivalence towards danger is strategically advantageous – but the particular forms that these significations take are dictated by local context. Likewise, whether the journalistic object is seen as something to be chased, or as something to be won through attrition in Iraq, or as something to be ambushed – another interviewee talked about 'Bangladashes', journalistic raids from across the border in India in 1971 – these are all particular expressions of a broader truth that events are experienced by journalists as something to be captured. This might seem an obvious statement, but the universalising of the trope of 'fact-gatherer' points to a broader, instrumentalist epistemological orientation to the world, and demonstrates the contingency of journalism's status as principal gatekeeper of contemporary knowledge.

Pooling, embedding and economies of journalistic authority

If it is difficult to speculate about the nature of future military conflicts and aspects of war reporting such as personal safety, media management and economic considerations, it is at first blush even harder to think about how the determinants of war reporters' experience of their field might change over time. This is particularly so if such a discussion revolves around the necessarily misrecognised logics of practice in the journalistic field which structure practice at a largely pre-reflexive level, determining that which is experienced as the given, natural frame of the journalistic lifeworld. The idea of the taken-for-granted applies even in a profession whose bread and butter is the extraordinary and abnormal: here too, there are aspects of the everyday that are forgotten as contingent practices or normalised as common sense – the professional identity of the ruggedly individual war reporter, the gathering and processing of facts as a normal thing to do, the unspoken rules by which journalists position themselves relative to each other and so on. But as much as they are the complex products and producers of history, field logics are also determined by concrete factors whose likely future trends are relatively straightforward to identify. The preceding remarks on Iraq and Kosovo, for instance, show the extent to which spatiality shapes how a conflict is experienced by reporters. But is the Bourdieusian model really saying that if you remove one important facet of journalists' work – their physical ability to move around – then they will simply find another, equally arbitrary, means of vying for status?

In fact it is more nuanced. Over time and from conflict to conflict, autonomy remains both a precondition of doing the job well and a means of establishing one's authority, but it is perceived and enacted in different ways in different contexts. When reporters are pooled, it is true that they tend to find other, often subtler linguistic ways to mark their professional distance and independence. But rather than seeing this as a compromised or degraded form of autonomy, autonomy itself should be understood as something which always exists in relation to constraints, in the same way that in phenomenology it makes no sense to think of idealised free agency – agency only has meaning in the context of the constraints which are its preconditions. Journalistic autonomy is always limited by factors beyond restrictions on access or censorship. Feelings of camaraderie, romanticisation of military life and a kind of Stockholm syndrome in relation to military censors and media handlers (see Tumber, 2004) were cited extensively in the interviews, usually as a means of distinguishing the speaker from those who have become too close to maintain professional perspective. But autonomy also depends on the extent to which journalists inhabit a relatively discrete symbolic world. The autonomy of such a world is maintained in part by professional norms, socialisation and the pervasiveness of a distinct journalistic cultural identity. However, if interaction between journalists is disrupted (whether through strategies of embedding reporters in military units or through more widespread communication with other external agents), or if spatial and temporal aspects of quotidian practice are shared with others, then an autonomous, stable journalistic subjectivity is less tenable.

The stabilisation of any symbolic forms, such as professional values and identities, is contingent on their patterned enactment and habituation in a given context, and this means that time is always an important factor (Couldry, 2003b). In the Gulf War, a system in which journalists were briefed (and fed) at regular intervals in hotels that acted as holding pens as much as safe havens imposed a highly structured temporal schedule on reporters whose professionalism is traditionally tied to adaptability and an affinity with chaos. As well as disrupting extant means for performing professional identity this introduces alternatives for routinisation and recognition of symbolic capital – structurings which are difficult to resist because they are in part constitutive of subjectivity. This is not to suggest that war reporting is normally characterised by regimented time schedules and hermetic spatial environments, but it does raise the possibility of comparing different conflicts and modes of war reporting according to their distinct rationalisations, as Foucault would have it, of the journalistic experience. The relative chaos or orderliness of conflicts and their reporting will inevitably have an impact on how journalists interpret events, recognise merit (or valorised symbolic forms) in practices, individuals and institutions, and make sense of their own identity as war reporter.

Comparing interviewees' comments on pooled and embedded journalism illustrates the point well. For pooled journalists, the imposition of a daily routine was vocally resisted, but it nonetheless seems to have effected a structuration of the perceived role of the reporter, which is best described in terms of the discourse which delimits the possibilities – what is ordinarily doable, sayable and potentially conceivable – of professional practice and identity (Foucault, 1981; Dent, 2008). This was manifest in a broad lowering of expectations accompanied by varying positioning strategies for expressing such, including cynicism and ambivalence towards restrictions on their professional practice – a reconception of what journalists were there to do which was (at least after the fact) effectively normalised as frustrating but uncontroversial. Temporal strictness and spatial sequestration were described as maddening and surreal – the unnaturalness of the experience saying much about what by implication counts as normal for the journalist – but it was also spoken about in terms suggesting quick normalisation: this is the way wars work these days, and government and military will always impose such constraints given the chance. Not recognising this new reality is to expose oneself as naive, rather than instinctively being thought of, as it appears to have been previously, as evidence that pooling is alien to the psyche of the war correspondent.

For embedded journalists, there is a similar loss of control over broad scheduling (several complained that the delays to which they were subjected meant their copy was no longer news by the time it was filed) and everyday routines (Brandenburg, 2007), along with a distinct means of signifying one's integrity as a journalist – through adapting easily to a world regarded by others as impenetrable while remaining objective. Another factor that emerges as significant is boredom (Mæland and Brunstad, 2009): lacking the usual means to kill time between conflict events, such as socialising with other journalists or locals, two interviewees found themselves ill-equipped to deal with the long stretches of downtime faced by soldiers and embedded reporters. Unsurprisingly, these reporters turned to soldiers' strategies for spending inactive time, and this temporal restructuration – new routines, alternate attitudes to time – raises the possibility of a limited intersubjectivity between soliders and the reporters assigned to them. Shared habits, particularly practices experienced as banal or corporeally natural (playing sports, for example), incite collective practices of subjectification, and it is on this level that journalistic autonomy may be compromised. It would be churlish to suggest that watching DVDs with soldiers undermines a journalist's independence, and both conscious distancing and the durability of journalistic culture militate against insidious rewiring of the journalistic mind. Further, I suggested earlier that the internal logic of journalism is often iniquitous (in terms of hierarchies and gatekeeping mechanisms), and in some respects a little disruption from without would be no bad thing. However, convergence of the practices which constitute the conscious experience, especially in an unfamiliar context (and embedding was a novel experience for those who spoke of it), can reasonably be expected to influence the way that war reporters inhabit their professional world as given. The precise nature of this influence will only become known over time if, as expected, embedding continues to be a key strategy of US and UK military media management.

New technologies and the phenomenology of war reporting

More than embedding, pooling and other strategies for managing journalists' access to and movement around war zones, however, it is technology which has transformed the journalist's experience of conflict most significantly (Matheson and Allan, 2009). In our context, what is particularly interesting is how new devices and formats for recording and communicating have been integrated into or have changed existing economies of distinction and professionalism (see Tumber, 2006). The interviews suggest two countervailing trends. On the one hand, some respondents perceive new technologies in the context of existing relations of power, allowing them to bypass barriers to information erected by military or political figures and mitigating the need to rely upon official information channels. Increasingly portable devices are thus merely a new resource in an economy of integrity and ingenuity the stakes of which are unchanged. One respondent recalled evading US military censorship in northern Iraq, first by trying to hire a satellite telephone (there were only 'two or three' in northern Iraq) so as to be able to wire his stories back to London independently, and then, on finding it more of a hindrance than a benefit (this was 1991, and the phone was described as needing a car to transport), negotiating directly with Jalal Talibani to use the Kurds' telegraph service. Another reporter described using more recently a smartphone to overcome the stonewalling tactics of his assigned military PR officer. In effect, though, this is no different from the Bangladashes described above: using whatever resources are available and waiting for the right moment to circumvent constraints; what is important is the effective use of guile, compatible with the underdog disposition, to get the better of those wielding official power over journalists. For others, especially more senior reporters, technology is used as an individuating resource (specifically individuation associated with professionalism), through its dismissal or their self-distancing from it. Several saw new communication technologies through the prism of substance or lack thereof, characterising devices as 'gadgets', 'gizmos' and 'toys', and their failing to fall for them as indicative of a personal straightforwardness immune to the vicissitudes of fashion. (Similarly, it was noted earlier that a reporter's stated aversion to clothing fashions, expressed not as a conscious rejection of superficiality but a personal incomprehension, helps to establish an unpretentious demeanour, essential in a field where showiness, self-indulgence and aspirationalism are all potent forms of negative capital.) This scepticism is in line with the economy of ambivalence, a naturalised performance of a dominant, no-nonsense journalistic disposition which is not easily impressed and quick to see through others' strategising, whether they be military personnel or advertisers.

The changes wrought by new technologies can also be understood in a specifically corporeal way. First, and most obviously, the mobility of journalistic hardware changes the manner in which war reporting is lived as a body: devices are worn, rather than the body addressing itself to larger pieces of equipment that are either immovable or transported mechanically. Instinctively this may be interpreted as liberating or at least convenient: an absence of physical constraint is to be welcomed in a field where constraints on professional practice are regarded as a bad thing. But what appear as destructurations should instead be seen as restructurations. Matheson (2003) wrote some time ago of war correspondents 'scowling at their notebooks', and in a similar vein I would offer the image of correspondents 'hunched over their laptops'. Matheson's point was not meant as caricature: it is the corporeal expression of an epistemological relation to the world in which facts have to be wrestled and fought into submission, and organising those facts into coherent journalistic language is conceived as a battle. More ethnographic research would need to be done into how posture and movement are associated with, say, collective recognition of professional identity, but it can be hypothesised that hunching over a laptop or recording on the fly is indicative of an epistemology in which facts are conceived as urgent, slippery and elusive.

Individuation, however, is only one set of practices affected by technological innovations, and it is important to assess the implications for other journalistic practices and universalised forms of valorised capital: in particular, witnessing and authenticity. Traditionally in journalism it is the eyewitness which is privileged above all other perspectives, though I would suggest that this is inextricable from an idealised im-mediacy which is simultaneously lionised and mythical. It is also inseparable from the proximity to danger which is a core element of the romanticism of war reporting. What, then, is the impact of increasingly convenient access to information and people by satellite or wireless network? It would at least be expected to lead to a reassessment of the importance of spatial and personal immediacy, encapsulated well by reporting of the initial phase of the war in Afghanistan in 2001, in which there was a consensus amongst all major broadcasters that having a correspondent inside (northern) Afghanistan was an indispensable indicator of institutional authority, notwithstanding that these correspondents were receiving the bulk of their information about (southern) Afghanistan from the wires and newsdesks of New York and London. It is difficult to know how to interpret this phenomenon. First-hand accounts have assumed an elevated, perhaps mystical status, but while they might appear purer than information hand-me-downs, they are still mediated – by the witness's culture, personal history, motivation, physiology and so on. That said, we should be uneasy about the findings of Nick Davies' *Flat Earth News* (2008), which documents how more and more journalistic work is done at a desk in front of a screen, with 'original' reporting increasingly left to the major news agencies. While an absence of mediation is a fantasy, overmediatisation remains a problem – not because all mediation is a corrupting influence, but because news produced largely through journalists talking to and reading each other tends to produce a homogeneous, stifling discourse which has more to do with simplistic historical and cultural narratives than the knotted, ambiguous series of events unfolding in reality.

An alternative future sees news organisations deploying more war correspondents, not fewer. But rather than emanating from a principled decision to dedicate ample resources to an expensive specialisation, this takes the form of employing 'local' foreign correspondents (Hamilton and Jenner, 2004; Palmer and Fontan, 2007). As well as ensuring that conflicts are witnessed, this could be argued in postcolonial terms to represent a more ethical way of doing war reporting than the traditional model of parachuting in a Westerner with potentially little knowledge of historical or cultural context to broadcast what will become the first draft of a conflict's history. However, there are at least two flaws in this argument. First, it relies on the assumption that a local reporter will be more authentic. I have emphasised in this book that authenticity is never pre-given and is always dependent on the mastery of a set of practices amounting to recognisable authenticity in a particular context. Being from a place does not guarantee authentic representation, but rather another form of authorisation to speak which is not naturally superior (or inferior) to any other. If local authenticity is a prized form of symbolic capital, it is so only in the context of a cultural shift from professional, institutional authority to the authority of personal experience. The relative merits of this shift are debatable; what should not be forgotten is that it is not a natural cultural evolution but the result of ongoing relations between social groups, each having a competing interest in which mode of cultural authority dominates. Second, it does not hold that the proliferation of sources, whether through local foreign correspondents or citizen journalism, is a good thing. Allan (2006) observes that it relies on a spurious epistemology that the 'highest' truth is that arrived at by combining a maximal number of perspectives, whereas in fact it leads as easily to homogenisation as diversification, and in Foucauldian terms can be argued to establish a more restrictive discourse through the increased abundance (and pervasiveness) of instruments of discursive reproduction.

More broadly, it is wide of the mark to suggest that the correspondent's experience of war is being inexorably transformed from a material to a virtual one. It is certainly true that an increasing proportion of the information gathered by war reporters comes in mediatised form – if not from an agency then through printed press release or briefing by military PR. But while it is tempting to argue that distance will be less of a hindrance to journalistic practice in the future, what is really happening is a re- rather than de-spatialisation. New technologies have undoubtedly disrupted what Heidegger refers to as 'thrownness' (Elliott, 2005: 125; Couldry and Markham, 2008), the sensation of being enveloped in the always-already existence of one's surroundings – it is less natural to experience as given the lifeworld that one physically inhabits when access to and interruptions from other worlds are common. However, this is not a simple opening up of the determination of the journalistic consciousness or a freeing of the journalistic mind from the considerable constraints of conflict situations. Instead, it should be seen as an alternate determination – it is not a matter of consecrating immediacy or multiplicity or fluidity in journalistic practice, but rather of understanding how new modes of communication and interaction structure the conscious experience of the journalist differently and what consequences this might have. The discourse analysis suggests four possibilities.

The first directs our attention to the internal power hierarchies of the journalistic field. It is widely accepted (see, for instance, Deuze, 2005) that autonomy is a key element of authority in journalism, whether it is the profession's independence from market or political forces or an individual journalist's autonomy from direct proprietorial interference or self-censorship. The latter is usually opposed on ethical grounds, though in reality we have to differentiate between types of self-censorship: that which ensues from job insecurity is rightly criticised, but whether a journalist is well served by autonomy from established journalistic cultures (see, for instance, Gillmor, 2004; Bruns, 2008b) or discourses is less obvious. In any case, autonomy in war reporting has historically assumed a particular importance in line with Fraser's elaboration, introduced in the previous chapter, of Hegel's emphasis on the recognition of one's work as a necessary grounding for human subjectivity. Simply put, this is a respect for reporters' professionalism which amounts to trusting them to get on with the job, to work in highly unpredictable situations without much in the way of supervision or management. Interviewees did not report that their editors were constantly calling to check up on them, and so the data cannot be interpreted to suggest that there has been a conscious wielding of new technologies to effect some kind of editorial power grab. However, there is more concrete evidence of two other trends. The first is that even if not filing a piece, correspondents are expected to provide more detailed and frequent information than previously, feeding in to an organisation's broader coverage of a conflict – forming the often unacknowledged basis for comment and analysis, for instance, for which there is increasing demand. Second, reporters are required to give increasingly detailed information about logistics and forward planning. This can be defended on grounds of duty of care and sensible risk management rather than characterised as an attempt to 'control' war reporters or impose dehumanising economic rationalisation on them (Tumber, 2006). Similarly, the first trend can be seen simply as the sort of 'job creep' that new communications technology has helped to foster across the cultural and service industries, rather than a Foucauldian disciplinary regime effected through the incitement of professional expression. It is worth, however, taking seriously the fact that war reporters' everyday lifeworld is less insulated from the editor's office and newsroom than previously, since it is in this isolation that much of their specific cultural symbolic consists. As with other constraints discussed here, there remains room for innovative distinction-making authority claims where traditional forms are eroded, with one respondent's description of the editorial team in London as worried parents properly describable as a strategic self-positioning in which he presents his self as relaxed and worldly, his humorous evocation of mild irritation an effective dismissal of editorial authority (Interviewee 5).

Second, and relatedly, both the war correspondent and the environment in which he works are subject to increasing media exposure through journalists' blogs and video diaries (Wall, 2005), and those posted by military personnel (Christensen, 2008; Andén-Papadopoulos, 2009). This raises the very real possibility that the experience of war (and war reporting) is no longer systematically mystified, mystification traditionally underpinning the valorised symbolic form of 'war reporter' in contemporary media culture. Of course it is also possible that increased visibility enhances rather than undermines the mystique of war reporting, with the rough-and-ready semiotic form of the conflict vlog conferring a kind of rarefied authenticity, and war reporters emphasise the unique perspective of 'being there' as much as ever. There was some evidence in interviews with other media professionals that war reporting is no longer considered the esoteric realm it once was (see also Tumber, 2006), though it is important to stress that as this was a snapshot study, it is also possible that such evaluations, as well as descriptions of war reporters as 'dinosaurs' and the like, are par for the course in ongoing competitive relations between different positions in the field of cultural production. The demystification of journalistic practice may be positive insofar as it exposes the often unjust principles by which authority is appropriated, but leaving journalism fully exposed to external principles of valorisation may be more of an expression of populist anti-professionalism than substantively democratic. But the literature suggests that, at least as of 2011, and while trust in journalism remains at a historic low, the rise of mass media production and citizen journalism (see below) has not decimated 'the journalist' as a stable cultural form (Paulussen and Ugille, 2008; Singer and Ashman, 2009; Hudson and Temple, 2010), and this stability is necessarily contingent upon the mystified embodiment of particular symbols and practices. It seems likely that the solidity of the cultural identity of the war correspondent will similarly survive the emergence of non-professional war reporting: mystification is not so much a matter of literal invisibility as the obscuring of cultures of practice, especially of personal disposition and professional identity. Cynical, reflexive comments about gravel voices and flak jackets, both in the interviews and in popular culture, indicate that there is a growing awareness of the charades underpinning the enduring cultural form of the war correspondent, but the alternative strategies enacted by those seeing through the 'game' suggest that journalistic habitus is adaptable enough to reorient practices, subjectifying and otherwise, towards new means of mystifying and thus decontesting the unique cultural position of the war reporter.

A third trend, and a significant one in terms of the conscious experience of the war correspondent, is that practices of journalistic production are increasingly interspersed with media consumption. The relatively easy availability of portable, wireless internet terminals means that reporters can consume news and other resources in the field, and – as is the case with many office workers – do so by dipping in and out throughout the day. Normalisation of such practices points towards an intimate embedding of media consumption cultures in everyday practices. It does not follow that they are simply more insidiously subject to the over-determining force of corporate and state media industries. The internalisation of social and cultural structures does shape subjectivities and it makes sense that if these cultures are commercial then their embedding in everyday routines will normalise the marketised aspects of production and consumption. However, while there are grounds for opposing the colonisation of the private realm by specifically corporate communication, or the incursion of the public sphere into the private more generally, there is no reason to assume that the pervasion of media practices is more nefarious than non-mediated practices – nor should it be supposed that subjectivity is somehow better in the absence of structured practices. Instead, we should look to the specific structuring effects that the intimate embedding of media consumption engenders. For audiences, the term 'ambient consumption' (McCarthy, 2001) captures well the phenomenon of regular but superficial news consumption motivated by the desire for confirmation rather than information, with implications for an individual's orientation to the outside world more broadly. For war reporters, the everyday temporal embedding of consuming practices suggests a mindset in which the conscious experiences of production and consumption do not simply collapse into each other, but produce a normalised grounding in 'home' news discourses and narratives, potentially with a more naturalised, instinctive awareness of peer and audience expectations. This does not suggest a new, coherent subjectivity common to producers and consumers alike, but an overlapping intersubjectivity in which certain subjectifying practices – the things it is normal to attend to as a matter of routine, and the relation between subject and object in practices of attending – become unremarkably universalised. While the separateness of journalistic subjectivity is in part strategic, a kind of cultural exceptionalism, it is possible that a growing intersubjective space shared by journalists and audiences will lead not to greater mutual understanding and accountability but an over-determination of news discourse by 'domestic' cultures from which no party has proper distance – notwithstanding that the alternative of news emerging from its object on the ground remains open to allegations of instrumentalist idealism. By extension, it might be assumed that if soldiers and journalists are not only consuming and producing the same sorts of media but doing so in similar ways then a space opens up for limited intersubjectivity in which the other does not appear as mutually incomprehensible. But if the basis of this intersubjectivity is the reflex incitement and reproduction of domestic norms then understanding of a conflict is more likely to be overloaded by historical narrative and cultural hegemonic forms.

Finally, Bourdieu is often accused of overstating the significance of professional fields, underplaying the fact that individuals are simultaneously immersed in several social spaces, professional and otherwise. New communication technologies provide evidence for an effective correction to this tendency, with contact with family and friends while on assignment no longer regarded as something either remarkable or particularly indulgent. This, though, is at odds with the misanthropy which appears to be associated with naturalised, personally embodied authority, along with the trope – sometimes described as cliché but more often than not as common sense – that natural war reporters, those who were born to it, are singularly unsuited to domestic family life. To suggest that there is such a natural war reporter profile is indefensibly essentialist, but the possibility remains that a naturalised culture of dispositional practices did emerge historically in war journalism, part fact and part myth, and that an extant economy which valorises rugged individualism may no longer be stable.

Citizen war reporting?

As well as the rise of the professional local-foreign correspondent, the past decade has also seen the emergence of non-professional local coverage of wars and political unrest. This predominantly takes the form of footage of violence recorded on mobile devices, blogs and briefer comments posted on social networking sites – all of which appears to match definitions of citizen journalism usually applied to Western audience participation in media production. It is often suggested that indigenous bloggers must be more representative, not only because they are local but also non-professional, untainted by an employment contract with a media multinational. However, if indigenousness is a problematic signifier of authentic representation, the same logic applies to amateurism: non-professional media production is not less determined by the power structures of the social or cultural spaces in which it emerges, but differently determined; it is not less contingent on mastery of practices enacting recognisable authenticity, but contingent on a different set of practices. This is not meant to undermine the contributions of local citizen journalists to our broader understanding of conflict, but it does raise interesting questions beyond those usually asked of bloggers in Iraq, Iran and Burma: are they too middle class, or politically implicated, or Westernised to be objective? Instead, we can ask what it means for an outsider to become a player in the Western journalistic field, and whether doing so shapes her experience of conflict where she lives.

Without wishing to attempt to get inside the heads of local citizen journalists, it is fair to say that the intention of their work is to document injustices and tragedies in a way that their local and national professional media do not, but also to get the attention of the world with an aim to influence events on the ground – whether through diplomatic pressure, humanitarian assistance, intervention or an end to intervention. It has been demonstrated elsewhere (see especially Allan, 2006) that, at present, for citizen journalism to have authority beyond its limited arena of production, then it must be taken up and republicised by mainstream media. Authority is never conferred simply because of the content of a citizen journalist's work: to be sure, it is often the case that local blogs are used because their authors have greater access to facts, but the value ascribed to their media production is not derived solely from that. For a piece of citizen journalism to become globally newsworthy, then not only it but its author has to conform to the symbolic economy of one or another international journalistic field. Globalisation has not led to a monolithic global media field with a single Murdoch-shaped centre surrounded by dominated peripheries (McNair, 2003a). There are relatively autonomous subfields which may compete but also co-exist fairly peaceably, defined either geographically, economically, ideologically or discursively. A citizen war reporter must therefore appeal personally to, which is to say embody symbolic forms valorised in, only one or other of these centres of power. What counts as globally newsworthy is not simply determined by the much demonised media multinationals, but also by an array of more or less dominant cultures of media production and consumption. Importantly, this does not mean that they have to play the same game as Western journalists, internalising the internal logic of their field and externalising it as disposition and instinct. Their authority may consist in a different permutation of symbolic capital: authenticity predicated on the fallacious conditions of amateurism and localism, their perceived exoticism or, more likely, and following on from the discussion in the previous chapter, their viability as empty signifiers into which Western foreign editors, reporters and audiences can project their democratising credentials.

By way of illustration, let us consider Salam Pax, the pseudonomous 'Baghdad Blogger' who rose to celebrity status in 2003–4 by blogging about the invasion of Iraq on his website and in the UK's *Guardian* newspaper. The status Salam Pax achieved is not reducible to the fact that he offered a unique perspective on a war in which censorship and violence had blocked off the normal channels of news gathering and dissemination. Nor was it because MSNBC or the BBC consecrated his work as authoritative. Instead, it appears that Salam Pax's international profile is explicable by his apparently natural fit with the symbolic economy endogenous to a specific subfield of the British press. This depiction of a (successful) engagement with a 'foreign' culture of practice is by no means intended to be a normative judgement on the blogs themselves, nor an ascription of cynical calculation to the blogger. In line with Hammond (2007b), the success of Salam Pax is as much about his own citizen journalism as the collective orientation of audiences in the West towards media consumption which signifies something about themselves, as well as the naturalised instinct amongst specific subfields of journalists and editors that this kind of perspective will 'go down well'. It is plausible that commissioning Salam Pax was an effective strategy in the context of the *Guardian*'s relations with competitors such as the *Independent* and the *Times*. What is less clear is the extent to which the move was seen by editors and journalists at the *Guardian* as a cynical means to sell a new commoditised form of liberalism to its readers, or as a natural thing for the *Guardian* to do, given its editorial line and audience profile. The interviews did not tackle this subject; the analysis would predict that cynicism would dominate the views of war reporters on this phenomenon – a cynicism which, beyond its specific object, enacts the speaker's ability to see through the way that journalism really works, to fail to be impressed by the latest must-have, and quietly to dismiss the authority of this potential competitor, not on the quality of their work but their unwitting cooption in a world they do not understand.

While it has been suggested that foreign bloggers do not have to become fully immersed in the Western journalistic game, does the situation of their practices in the international journalistic field influence the consciousness they have of the lifeworld they inhabit on a day-to-day basis? There is clearly a potential gap between the intention of the citizen journalist and the way their work is appraised and used, but there is a further possibility that local blogger subjectivity is partly structured by a dominant journalistic culture which eludes individual awareness, let alone control. And it is certainly consistent with Bourdieu's model to depict a citizen journalist's conscious intentions as, if not irrelevant, then less significant than their practically embodied dispositions to act. By this approach, on

encountering and over time becoming familiar with the world of
Western journalism, indigenous reporters will become increasingly
instinctively oriented towards producing valorised cultural forms (in
this case, particular journalistic products). Doing so will come to be
experienced as second nature, as it is not just a matter of learning
what sort of content is well received and how to produce it, but seeing
the world and oneself through an increasingly naturalised gaze in
which such practices of production and subjectification are pre-given
elements of the lifeworld. None of this means that indigenous
amateurs on becoming active in Western cultures of journalism will
automatically become hardwired to produce whatever Western
audiences demand, including content which primarily serves to flatter
those audiences. The likelihood is instead that the advantages of practising citizen journalism in a certain way and being a certain kind of
'authentic' voice will come to be felt instinctively. Such a structuring
of anticipation is not linear, and the diversity of dominant media
means that there are many 'best fits', some requiring more adaptation
than others, not only on the basis of cultural differences but of educational background, professional experience and so on. Salam Pax
aside, commentators have seen evidence of anticipation of newsworthiness in communications with Burmese citizens in the aftermath of
Cyclone Nargis (Leech, 2008), and Moeller (1999: 14) detected
similar phenomena as far back as Tiananmen Square in 1989. But
while Bourdieusian phenomenology stresses that such restructurings
of subjective experience occur at the pre-reflexive level, Bourdieu also
concedes that field outsiders are more able to see its machinations
than those for whom immersion overwhelms the subjective experience of it. This is not an exercise in lionising a romanticised other or
reifying the marginal (Ang, 1992: xvii). It seems more likely, however,
that citizen war reporters would consciously seek to step outside of
their own 'normal' way of seeing things and ask what they would look
like through Western eyes, than that their media production is simply
a field effect. Universalisations are in reality resisted, contested,
adapted and appropriated, pointing towards an international media
landscape characterised by what has been labelled 'glocalisation'
(Wasserman and Rao, 2008) and in line with Brian McNair's (2003a)
chaos paradigm, rather than global regimes of discipline effected
through the incitement of media production by non-professionals.

While plausible predictions have been made about conflicts over
resources and conflicts between non-state actors, it is impossible to
know what form war will take in the coming years. Likewise, the
future field of war reporting will be shaped by developments in media

management, technology and cultural shifts. However, the Bourdieusian model does not advocate extrapolating from generative structures to possible future cultural worlds – not only because they are not predictable, but because the worlds professionals inhabit are structured in ways which have little obvious connection to the object of their work. Underlying all experiences of the taken-for-granted in a field where individuals and groups have an interest in accumulating status and authority is a symbolic economy that is collectively misrecognised as such by those actors. As with all fields of professional cultural production, journalism is characterised by shared cultures of practice which are experienced as naturally emerging from the journalistic object, but which often accord status and authority according to principles which remain obscure – usually the contingent embodiment of particular forms of symbolic capital which comes to be perceived as disposition. To the extent that historical changes in a field disrupt such misrecognised symbolic economies, they may be welcomed as a force for good. However, I have argued here that what may appear as destructurations of the field of war reporting should instead be regarded as restructurations. Subsequently, we should remain alert to new cultures of practice which accord authority in ways that are not overt, and to the continuities underlying apparent shifts in the power relations that characterise all fields.

Notes

1 This is in line with Clausewitz's ([1832] 2005) dictum that war should not be seen as *sui generis* but rather as continuous with society and politics. For assessment of coverage of different conflicts, see Hammond (2004; 2007a); Hammond (2007); McNulty (1999); Sonwalkar (2004); Carruthers (2004); Atkinson (1999); Nohrstedt et al. (2000); Banks and Wolfe Murray (1999).
2 Bourdieu's own view of the first Gulf War was that it constituted 'drunken war-mongering' (Zamiti, 1996).
3 There was some disagreement about this, with one editor stating: 'there were some really good reporters out there, independents ... but that's not covering the war. It's not giving the public a good idea about what's going on, it's just good stories, interesting angles' (Interviewee 6).

8

Conclusion: implications for war reporting, journalism studies and political phenomenology

Introduction

This chapter considers the implications of an analytical perspective on journalism which focuses on the politics underlying the lived aspects of journalism that 'just are'. The approach taken in this book has asked what structures consciousness of the professional world as given, and what structuring effects normalisation of this consciousness might have – and in each case we are directed to look at forces both endogenous and exogenous to the journalistic field. While war reporting is more autonomous than most subfields of journalism, it remains part of a field which is weakly autonomous at best in the context of the wider field of cultural production. The upshot is that war reporting will inevitably reflect broader shifts such as that from institutional to individual authority and from the valorisation of professional to authentic knowledge. The question of whether an increasing normalisation of 'star' correspondents could contribute to the solidification of this shift remains open, but significant. Attention then turns to internal field logics, and the reflexive question of what the political phenomenological perspective allows us to say about war reporting and journalism generally. Does it simply add up to the claim that the processes by which news is gathered, processed and disseminated is structured in a way that, regardless of its content, is oriented towards the reproduction of unacknowledged power relations? The generative or genetic structuralist model proffered in this book is not an argument for wholesale relativism, though nor does it fall back on deontological categories of news values and journalistic ethics. Journalists do not inhabit a discrete symbolic world divorced from objective reality, and their news values, ethics and professional identities are not arbitrary – though nor are they deontological. Instead, they are particular (out of a range of possible) expressions of historical, economic and social context whose practical universalisation can and should be challenged. This Bachelardian injunction will be illustrated through two germane examples: employment insecurity and embedding journalists with military units. In the case of the latter, there is strong evidence that when faced with the physical restrictions of embedding, correspondents will simply find other ways to make distinctions against peers, for instance by reacting with irony or worldliness. It remains valid to defend endogenous journalistic principles such as autonomy against external forces – whether it be from military PR, political interference or the market – but we should also acknowledge the misrecognised interest reporters have in doing so, not as high-minded principle but the decontestation of position-takings achieved through engagement with unacknowledged economies of practice. The chapter then turns to a reflexive appraisal of Bourdieusian political phenomenology, setting out the defence against allegations of circumscription and relativism, and demonstrating how it makes a compelling case for professional expertise in an age when such a conception of authority is increasingly unpopular.

Implications for war reporting

As well as establishing a gatekeeping structure by which entry into the journalistic field is controlled by other journalists, not merely overtly but through domination of principles of legitimation, the mystification of the skills of the journalist has the effect of enhancing the symbolic value of journalism in the broader metafield of cultural production and, by extension, in the public sphere.[1] Journalists are accorded the authority to articulate how and why events have occurred, and to decide whether events are newsworthy and thus, in a sense, whether they have happened at all. There is little to be gained from problematising the social necessity of delegating and professionalising the task of recording, interpreting and disseminating phenomena. However, it is of considerable significance that the dominant principles which do not merely rule on legitimacy and authority but positively produce journalistic practice by way of structuring differentiation in the field are themselves structured according to a misrecognised symbolic economy which is productive of discernible effects (viz., the enshrining of hierarchies of power in the field). Further, the mystification of the journalistic trade allows it as a field to compete for symbolic capital (authority, legitimacy) with adjacent fields of cultural production, such as art, literature, the judiciary and science, a thesis which increasingly occupied Bourdieu in the last decade of his life. While it is impossible to demonstrate that a field reproducing itself through regulated practice structured according to the principles of a misrecognised symbolic economy will necessarily be politically nefarious, it is feasible to assert not only that the overt rules of the journalistic game do not fully determine journalistic practice, but that this overt economy renders another set of structured political effects unknowable. This is not the same as contending that it is impossible for the field to produce actors who are 'good' by the overt standards of journalism, nor that an actor has no meaningful capacity to pursue a strategy consciously constructed upon these overt principles. It does suggest, however, that legitimacy, as well as domination over what counts as legitimate, is occupied, embodied and wielded on the basis of a complex set of structured practices, a good deal of which are inconceivable to actors in the field.

But how far should we push this idea that journalism operates according to field logics that are largely unknown or misrecognised? The fundamental insolubility of the structure/agency debate (Markham, 2007: 63–9)[2] means that social theory tends to shift between determinism and voluntarism over time, and the Bourdieusian approach emphasises that we should see such movements in terms of the sociology of the academic field as much as the result of ongoing refinement in phenomenological, existentialist and feminist philosophy. Media research has tended towards a more agencial bent over the past two decades (see for instance Philo, 2008; van Dijck, 2009), from the broader sociological dominance of Habermas' theory of communicative action and Giddens' conception of social structures as resources and accomplishments (Livesay, 1985: 69), to Stuart Hall's (1973) encoding/decoding model and the rise of audience theory. As such, a more deterministic analysis of the journalistic field could be read in the same way that Bourdieu accounts for shifts both in twentieth-century neo-Kantian philosophy and journalism itself: a strategic claim to academic authority based on overthrowing some key tenet of the prevailing conventional wisdom (while presumably leaving much else unchallenged). But we have seen that interpreting journalists' behaviour in terms of structured, structuring strategy does not preclude their having valid things to say about the world they report. Similarly, the political phenomenological approach taken here is not an exercise in navel gazing: if it does promote reflexivity about the context in which it is carried out, it does not reduce academic research to a self-contained symbolic world incapable of apposite insights into the world it studies.[3]

This approach does tend towards the deterministic but, to restate an earlier point, there are many determinisms. There are valid reasons for rejecting brute economic reductionism (Lebaron, 2003) and political conspiratorialism (Bohman, 1997), and it is hoped that this book has demonstrated the viability of analysing the ways that the lived experience of journalism are structured and with what effects.

To be sure, to read Bourdieu's own writing about the media, intemperate as it often is, the logical starting point for a Bourdieusian analysis of journalism is that the way news is gathered, processed, disseminated, consumed and valued is structured in such a way that, regardless of its content, it is oriented towards the reproduction of unacknowledged power relations both within the journalistic field and in the broader field of cultural production. And to an extent this is the case: a key premise of this book is that the particular form of news values, media ethics and professional identity is secondary to their function. However, this does not render the substance of these categories arbitrary, nor does it mean that these symbolic forms shape journalists' conscious experience of their work in a way that is disarticulated from events on the ground and meaningful discourses of morality and objectivity. News values, ethics and journalistic dispositions do not emerge naturally out of the stuff of journalism, but they do have reason. They are a logical expression of the generative structures of the field, but one of many possible journalistic worlds which has, in a particular time and place, become universalised. And while it is true that this universalisation entails the reproduction of hierarchical and often unjust relations of power, it also dominates the lived experience of journalism in a way which is anything but superficial. To suggest that consciousness is a determination of dominant symbolic systems which are merely instances of the possible is not to undermine that conscious experience – this is not *The Matrix*. All conscious experience is determined by a variety of factors; the aim of political phenomenology is not to seek some idealised, purer, undetermined experience but rather one where the specificity of determination is acknowledged and, within bounds, contested.

At first blush it might seem as though the political phenomenological approach would be indifferent to the increasing prevalence of embedding and its impact on journalistic standards. After all, if conceived purely in functional or strategic terms, all that matters is how journalists, other actors and various institutions vie for power and status. If embedding disrupts the usual means by which journalists establish their authority, either through overt rivalry or an unacknowledged game of dispositions and significations, they will simply find other ways to compete. Here, the evidence suggests that when journalists are constrained both in the doing of their professional work and the normal performance of their professional identity, alternative distinctions are made around their reaction to embedding – namely ironic understatement and cynicism encoded in metaphors (tourism, babysitting) rather than vocal dissent. Further, the systemic facility amongst journalists to adopt and adapt to new economies of authority points to the continuity of underlying field structures (professional hierarchies and gatekeeping mechanisms) through changes to the lived experience of journalism.

However, this conclusion is compatible with normative critiques of the implications of embedding for journalistic autonomy, and indeed this approach pushes us to frame such critiques in a properly contextualised fashion. It compels us to ask not only who benefits and loses from embedding, but who has a stake in either opposing embedding policies or positioning themselves in relation to it in other ways. This in turn enables us to assess the impact of embedding on journalistic autonomy in a manner that does not romanticise the rugged individualism of the war correspondent, in which authority is invested in perceived disposition based on a mastery of practices not necessarily concomitant with overt professional principles. Similarly, if embedding is to be opposed according to the principle that good journalism relies on access by multiple journalists rather than one appointed by military media managers, then our approach here allows us to identify what epistemology has to be in place as unremarkably dominant in order for such a claim to seem naturally appropriate – and, again, who may benefit. Prioritising multiple sources over singular journalistic authority may laudably oppose the conditional individual embodiment of journalistic 'talent' or 'instinct', but it does so by making recourse to a worldview which prioritises the incremental accumulation, or averaging, of knowledge in the pursuit of objectivity. Whether valid or otherwise, in strategic terms this anti-individualistic position points to a more collective and consensual way of doing journalism – which could be a good or a bad thing,[4] but either way represents an alternative more beneficial to some than others.[5]

As well as the multi-perspectival critique, restrictions on journalistic access to war zones are opposed by journalists and media analysts on the grounds that eyewitness reporting of events is always preferable to second-hand accounts, relayed either through other (embedded) journalists or military press releases. This too is entirely valid, though here again we can identify the strategic aspect of such a claim: that is, the valorisation of the eyewitness report is predicated on a perceived (though phenomenologically impossible) im-mediacy which, as we saw in the previous chapter, constitutes not just journalistic authority per se, but a specific form of authority. Whatever the merits of the argument, some stand to benefit more than others. In each case, it is certainly valid to argue that journalistic authority needs to be defended against military or political public relations, but the form that authority takes, as well as how it is appropriated and embodied, can defensibly be questioned. There is no ideal form of journalistic authority or news values: that which is free from official control is still subject to market or industrial forces; that defined endogenously by peer review is open to allegations of self-serving insularity. A journalistic principle such as objectivity remains entirely defensible, though it has been seen here that it is not detachable from other principles such as the duty to sources and audiences, morality or its disavowal, in each of which there is a strategic interest, pursued through practices – news practices, but also practices of subjectification which perform a distinction-making, position-taking function which is little understood.

Job insecurity, while broadly and rightly seen as a threat to journalistic standards, can likewise be seen in terms of strategic positioning or distinction, as well as the broader commitments that have to be in place in order for critiques of insecurity to make intuitive sense. For one, opposition to growing job insecurity in journalism is predominantly framed in terms of self-censorship: if your position is uncertain you are less likely to rock the boat, especially in a context of increasing concentration of ownership where alternative employers are scarce (Accardo, 1998). This specific argument, while again entirely plausible, entails a claim about the cultural value of unfettered journalism, a noble profession holding power to account but now under threat from elite or corporate forces. It was noted in chapter 5 that establishing one's anti-establishment credentials, as well as one's endangeredness, is a standard authority-constituting move made both in the subjectifying practices of journalists and the overt strategies of tabloid and mid-market newspapers. In any case, while these specific claims to authority and cultural value may work to establish journalism as an exceptional field under unique threat, they are made against a wider backdrop in the cultural industries and beyond where the casualisation of labour is endemic.[6] There is certainly an argument to be made that good journalism relies on stable positions of authoritative production. But instead of conceiving of this need in terms of individual guardianship of a mythologised ideal of journalism, in which the individual making such a claim has a clear interest, we can disaggregate the role journalism can play in sustaining a robust public sphere, and the Hegelian imperative of professional autonomy which underpins full individual participation in that public sphere. True, this could be seen as the elevation of an idealised autonomy against the warnings made in this book that such autonomies are inevitably strategic, but it is at least an active, engaged autonomy rather than the defensive, self-enclosing autonomy constituted in claims to journalistic exceptionalism.

The Bourdieusian approach to studying journalism clearly has its uses. However, it inevitably runs the risk of appearing irredeemably self-referential (Verdès-Leroux, 2003) – a concern amplified by a lecture published posthumously in which Bourdieu (2005) seems to confirm the belief that academics and journalists can never really say anything about the world around them; instead everything academics and journalists write is an expression of the competitive interaction between the social scientific, journalistic and political fields. If this is the case, would we be better served by cleaving to existing theories of professionalism and journalistic discourse? The next section sets out the defence of the viable object and authoritative subject of cultural production: put simply, a defence of the ability of academic researchers and journalists alike to produce meaningful accounts of events and phenomena. The chapter then assesses what is distinctive about Bourdieu's contribution to journalism studies, before sketching some broader observations connecting the economies of authority identified in the discourse analysis to Bourdieu's more overtly, tradi-tionally political treatises on the crisis of liberalism in the post-1968 Western world.

The object and subject of Bourdieusian theory

The results of the analysis presented in chapters 4 and 5 detailed the symbolic economies underpinning the collective recognition of qualities such as authority as personal traits. In phenomenological terms this is equivalent to establishing the structures of subjectifica-tion in the journalistic field: namely which subjectivities are recognisable (by peers and the broader public audience) as war corre-spondents or other professionals, and how individuals embody those subjectivities in a way that seems to them and others a natural fit. But this throws up two related dilemmas. First, any conclusions drawn from this research entail constructing interviewees as analytic objects, while it is a key tenet of Bourdieusian theory that objectification is invariably complicit in the reproduction of differential relations of power in some form or other. Second, subjectivity is simultaneously unattainable and a normal part of our everyday lives. We act as though subjectivity is stable and 'ownable' while as phenomenologists we know that it is a conflicted process of forever becoming, a process which precedes and outlasts any individual association. Further, the theory tells us that where there are relatively stable structures providing the preconditions for collective recognition, what is actually enabled (or necessitated) is misrecognition – and all of this applies as much to academic as to journalistic work.

Bourdieu, like Foucault and many others,[7] is frequently preoccupied with the risk that the best-intended social theorist may inadvertently reinforce an unacknowledged coercive power relation. Further, it is argued that academic self-reflexivity is not infallible: the writing of political and sociological theory is always liable to be complicit with dominatory structures in ways which are to an extent unknowable. On first principles, the object of political theory (for academics) is that which is determined by academic practices recognised as legitimate within the field – in a sense, the object is whatever those with authority say it is. But while theorists from the post-structuralist, neo-colonial and ethnomethodological traditions emphasise the ethical commitment to avoid over-determining the analytic subject, Bourdieu argues instead that such objectification is unavoidable – and the only defensible methodological response is to make overt and defend the specific character of that objectification (Bourdieu, 1999: 8). The potential implication is that the 'object' is not equatable with a social group or individual as such; it is instead the product of multiple habitus, and nothing more. That is, the objects of Bourdieusian theory are the generative logics constructed in methodological practice, distinct from and not thickly representative of the 'things' or social groups themselves. Bourdieu thus distances himself from that theoretical position which aims to allow its discrete objects to 'speak for themselves' or to represent their experience 'authentically'. But likewise, to suggest that the objects of research are constituted by and indistinguishable from that research is a little wide of the mark. Bourdieu does not reject the idea of representationalism, at least not entirely. His response to the problem of over-determination of the focus of analysis, characteristic of neo-Marxist theorists from Adorno to Laclau, is the constant questioning of the conditions of particular forms of objectification – scientific, economic, psychological and so on. In so doing, the theorist inevitably posits other objectifications – for Adorno it is a dialectical doubly negated object, for Bourdieu it is the logic of generative structures – and the professional imperative is to make the particular assumptions and commitments of each approach explicit. The result is an approach which is less apologetic and circular than some of the post-structuralist literature with which Bourdieu is occasionally associated (Neveu, 2005) but it does invite the reflexive question (Maton, 2003) of who is recognised as an authority at responsible objectification.

It is by now clear that a key aim of any Bourdieusian analysis is to undermine the natural embodiment of a 'legitimate' subjectivity, and this applies self-reflexively to the social theorist as well as to the matter of his work. Rather than recognised repositories of knowledge, there are objective positions in the academic field, and there is competition over those positions from which the dominant principles of legitimation are practically stabilised.[8] This is distinct from conventional postmodernist (Barthes, 1973; Bourdieu, 1993a: 254–5) claims of the 'death' of the author, for while Bourdieu rejects the individualistic conflation of theorist and theory, he nonetheless defends professional expertise and authorial responsibility (Bourdieu, 2000: 1–8). The individual cannot be constructed as the embodiment of a certain knowledge without taking into account the social space and associated economy in which that individual operates and in which the knowledge is produced. But it should be possible to assess knowledge in terms other than how well a theorist's habitus is aligned to the particularities of the professional academic field. That is, *pace Homo Academicus*, we can rightly interpret academic legitimacy as the accretion of symbolic capital which is objectively meaningless; we can reconstruct legitimate knowledge as the mere recitation of practices mandated by an arbitrary social structure; but nonetheless we can critically assess different accounts as representations of the same material object, even though as objects of knowledge they are distinct. This may be seen as a normative injunction whereby Bourdieu defends the notions of authorial responsibility and 'critical spirit' (Bourdieu et al., 1996), in contradistinction to the 'consensualism' which he argues has accompanied the rise of relativism in social theory.[9] This consensualism is given to consist in the universalisation of 'liberalist' values,[10] to the extent that their material finitude and the specific context of their emergence have become obscured.[11] As specifically regards the contemporary state of academic research, he emphasises in particular three themes. First, 'radical' political theory dealing with 'properly' material sociohistorical change has been replaced by identity politics and managerialism (Wilcken, 1995: 42–3). Second, the centrality of individualism to contemporary political thought and practice has gone uncontested.[12] Third, the principle of avoiding over-determination of the objects of research has its own practical implications: namely the silencing of the academic voice through a thoroughgoing suspicion of elitism.[13] Bourdieu's response is to make overt that which has in his view become excluded, and whose exclusion is now perceived as natural, from academic discourse, and to construct an epistemological subject which is professional, institutionalised, elite and defensible.

I noted at the beginning of this book that the scientific field operates in such a way as to obscure the conditionality of the principles of legitimacy upon which success in the field is judged, by restricting access to positions of scientific knowledge production. However, it is precisely that restricted locus which allows for the production of 'practical' (if not absolute) universals whose claims to legitimacy may be mystified by professional practice, but whose effects can be publicly assessed (Lowrey, 2006). Bourdieu argues against the inherent advantage of having a maximal variety of knowledges produced according to different principles of legitimation (restricted and unrestricted), since it does not logically hold that 'more is better' when it comes to knowledge; such a move entails a conflation of choice and freedom (Lloyd, 1999: 205; Allan, 2006; Thorsen, 2008).[14] Bourdieu argues that while there is nothing naturally valuable about academic knowledge, anti-elitist arguments to open academia to the principles of legitimation which govern the field of cultural production and the metafield of power more broadly are themselves politically implicated. What is held to be democratising is in fact an advocacy of heteronomy, and for Bourdieu the case for defending the autonomy of a subspace of a field against heteronomous forces is always valid on normative grounds.[15] Bourdieu attaches the caveat that the fruits of restricted cultural production should be accessible to all, but despite this it is clear that the defence of authoritative, institutionalised academic knowledge does amount to a defence of what would on sociological principles be incompatible with Bourdieusian theory: monopoly of the principles of differentiation by those who possess the symbolic capital to enter the academic field and negotiate its quasi-arbitrary rules.[16]

There are at least three problems with this position. First, and perhaps most obviously, it looks like a post-hoc rationalisation of the position that social scientists already occupy. Second, it does not follow that those taking up positions at the autonomous pole of a field, sheltered from the demands of the heterogeneous pole, engage only in transparent, productive competition. Finally, the Bourdieusian model requires that we accept autonomy deontologically, as a political good which does not need to be contextualised and disaggregated. I would suggest that the first and second problems can be addressed fairly simply, by encouraging critical engagement within and without the field: as with war reporters, the call for autonomy does not equate to living in a professional vacuum. And the final point is entirely concessible. The commitment to autonomy is a normative one, as is Bourdieu's belief that those realms of existence beyond the reaches of knowability are politically implicated. I have suggested that Bourdieu's politics cannot be inferred from his philosophy of social science (Costa, 2006) and vice versa. Transparency regarding the political motivations of Bourdieu's and Bourdieusian research invites contestation, obviates the need to pursue self-reflexivity endlessly (Bourdieu and Wacquant, 1992: 72; Bourdieu, 1993b, 2004: 89–91; Pels, 2000: 12; Maton, 2003), and thus allows for the limited stabilisation of an authoritative subject.

In more general terms, the political loading of the determination of practice necessitates conceptions of domination and transformation whose precise form and conditionality are occluded.[17] This occlusion, which succeeds in positing transformative politics as a transcendental category, in turn rests upon Bourdieu's conception of practice. Practice for Bourdieu is, in some limited but crucial respect, mystified: it is the location of the invisible action of coercive political power and simultaneously the indefinable, intangible site of political resistance and subversion. Methodologically, it follows that every observed and observable social phenomenon is to be interpreted as an instance of domination or autonomy (or both). Not only does this preclude a differentiation of power effects, it rules out any limits to the political at all, since there is no phenomenological category which is not characterised by determination, and determination is inherently, inescapably political. This extension not just of power effects but of violence to every conceivable action, rather than generating a more incisive, calibrated account of the operation of power, in fact results in the opposite. There remain no means by which to distinguish the determined and determining aspects of practice from the merely observed, since the scope of what counts as practice is limited to the points of inscription. Further, if there is determination, there are no means by which to differentiate the significantly political from the trivial, since to exclude any manifestation of power from the (meaningfully) political is to commit precisely the fallacy that Bourdieusian theory seeks to expose in other theories as well as in culturally accepted normative frameworks and in common sense. Such judgements can only be made on normative grounds by an authoritative subject whose authority consists in making such judgements.

What does a Bourdieusian perspective tell us about journalism that others do not?

Bourdieu is frequently categorised as adjacent to post-structuralist theory.[18] This is a debatable claim which depends on how we define post-structuralism, a question which is beyond our scope here. But Bourdieu does share the post-structuralist and structuralist prioritisation of *parole* over *langue*: speech expresses the entire relation structure of language, or in Foucault's more politicised terms, speaking tells us more about the totality of power relations in a professional or social hierarchy than any authentically held belief. But is it really the case that the primary function of language is structural reproduction? Expressed in these words, it can sound too functionalist, glossing over the fractured way that structuring in fact occurs. But the interviews show that there are regularities in the way that people talk – not in terms of journalists all being the same sort of person, but in common frames of reference, a shared epistemological relation to the world and shared practices of self-positioning in relation to the objects of journalistic work. Such regularities are both political and unacknowledged, in the sense of reinforcing collective pre-reflexive schemes of recognition. However, while there are demonstrably unspoken rules that govern what is experienced as instinct, there is also evidence of a level of critical insight which cannot be squared with Bourdieu's outright dismissal of reflexivity in his comments about journalists (Hamel, 1998). An answer to this apparent impasse can be found within Bourdieu's work, in his insistence on a dual rejection of the linear determination of language (on the part of functionalist structuralism) and the fundamental elusiveness of language in the work of Derrida or Deleuze.

First, let us look at analyses of journalism where there is a precedent for interpreting journalistic practices of differentiation and, particularly, self-reflection, not merely on its own terms but as strategic in the Bourdieusian sense. Drawing primarily on *Language and Symbolic Power* (Bourdieu, 1991b), Matheson (2003) puts forward the Bourdieusian contention that reflection by journalists on their professional practice serves a political function. The first part of this function is, to be sure, at the more conspiratorial end of the interpretative spectrum: if we look empirically at existing evidence of journalists' reflections, we can conclude that the particular forms it takes actually prevent real reflexivity – where 'real' refers to a level of insight capable of leading to objective changes in the structures of the journalistic field. The second part of the political function is that this political determination of reflection, which amounts to censorship, closes down any contestation of journalistic symbolic capital and thereby helps to reproduce the power relations of the field. The result is not simply the circumscription of debate over what constitutes good journalism and the concomitant mystification of journalistic practice, but also the occlusion of the political impact these phenomena have: cementing the gatekeeping and specialisation hierarchy which ensure that those in dominating positions in the field – successful individual journalists in this case, but also editors, advertisers and owners associated with media outlets occupying positions in either the cultural or economic elite (or both) – maintain their positions.

Matheson takes as his analytic object a discursive form of reflection quite distinct from the case study: journalists' memoirs (Matheson, 2003: 171). The language observed in these publications is broadly news-like, written either in the mood of the 'thrill of the chase' or else seeking to be as accurate a mirror as possible to reality. It is precisely because the language is performative or generic that it ceases functioning as the 'real', everyday, unreflexive discourse which is most revealing of the pervasive but forgotten norms of the field, and thus can tell us nothing about the political implications that such decontestation will have. We have seen that the language observed in the interviews is both more subtle and more fertile in terms of what it can tell us about the journalistic field, especially as regards the use of understatement and irony. It is certainly less obviously generic: while many of the journalists spoke or behaved similarly, at no point did this amount to the deterministic reading of Bourdieu that one cannot do otherwise than perform a pre-existing disposition. The observed language of reflections on war correspondence could best be described not as over-determined but structured: that is, it is not uniformly categorisable, and it is spontaneous and occasionally chaotic, but it does exhibit sufficient regularity to suggest that structural reasons for its particular articulations can be posited. Bourdieusian analysis allows us to examine first the symbolic criteria according to which individuals compete for, occupy and defend the relative positions of a field. Second, it allows us to see the political effect that euphemism, linguistic shorthand and stylistic mannerisms have. In combination, we can see not only the distorted (though not arbitrary) relation between success or power in the field and any set of essential journalistic values, but also the silencing, normalising effect that particular modes of reflection have. The discourse analysis confirms Matheson's argument to a point, in that reflections by interviewees about how journalism is and should be done were structured in such a way as to obscure the politics underpinning what it takes to be 'a natural' (Zelizer, 1993: 219). Matheson conceives of the determination of reflection on journalistic values as somewhat monolithic, such that euphemism produces a closed system with a single strategic function (Matheson, 2003: 171). The case study demonstrates that while there is linguistic determination – language which has the clear effect of depoliticising something contestable, or naturalising an existing hierarchy – there is also slippage,[19] and insights that exceed whatever function it might serve. As noted in chapter 2, these amount not to 'deep' ontological insight into the structures of a field, but reflections on how the field could be changed according to normative commitments.

Cameron, similarly, writes that the theory of political determination and efficacy of language amounts to regarding people not as talking the way they do because of who they are, but 'as who they are because of (among other things) the way they talk' (Cameron, 1999: 444). The interviews reveal the practical, methodological limitations of the plausible but sweeping claim, and the possibility of avoiding both the over-determination of language and the post-structuralist linguistic conjecture that language is necessarily elusive. Instead, where statements appear patterned there are likely reasons for their structured emergence, but one cannot posit a generative structure which necessitates the occurrence of any given speech act. This position also implies that some observed statements will not be reasonable, in the sense of being particular instances of the discursive possibilities of a professional field. Interpreting all utterances as performances of identity and status is in fact a decontesting move, precluding debate over the distinction between the politically meaningful and insignificant. However, it remains salient that the language journalists use when reflecting on journalism plays a significant role in the struggle for status in that field. The import of this qualification of linguistic determination in the journalistic field is threefold.

First, it demonstrates that a strict interpretation of Bourdieu's field model is impracticable and politically counter-productive (Hartsock, 1990: 171–2; Grimshaw, 1993). That is, proceeding from the premise that journalistic ethics is entirely strategic, and is a wholly symbolic world with no correspondence to the objective world, itself has the effect of reproducing existing hierarchical political structures, by fostering fatalism about the possibility of a better journalism (Garnham, 1990: 85). I have argued that it is erroneous to depict the relationship between the symbolic and material in Bourdieu's work as wholly arbitrary (Bourdieu, 2000: 200). While there is distortion and dislocation between the two, there is also mutual constitutivity. This does not suggest that the material only exists as an object of symbolic knowledge, since the symbolic system in which it emerges is only a particular permutation of a range of possible systems associated with 'real' objective context.

Second, there is the question of how, in phenomenological terms, journalists experience and make sense of their own identity. On one level it has been established above that Bourdieu is too narrowly deterministic on this point. Spoken evidence of identity does not only reveal the politically complicit practices of identification embedded in the journalistic field, because social agents in that field are many things besides journalists. As well as producing variety amongst journalists beyond the natural variability generated by class habitus, it also allows journalists to retain, to a degree, an outsider's view on their trade. The 'furrowed brow' comment by Interviewee 5 (p. 61) is a good example of the kind of perspective supposedly unavailable to insiders.

Third, journalistic language is determined not only by the economies of the journalistic field, or by the other fields which journalists simultaneously inhabit, but also by journalism's position within the metafield of cultural production (Bourdieu, 2005). The characteristics of this determining aspect are difficult to ascertain, but if we accept Bourdieu's claim that journalism occupies a dominated position in the field of cultural production then it may be expected that journalists' language will reflect this inferiority. There is inconclusive evidence of this in the interview data – self-deprecation, ambivalence and references to popular culture – but an alternative analysis can be constructed: namely that this language is used reflexively, with the effect of solidifying an agent's claim to other marketable forms of symbolic capital, such as autonomy, anti-elitism, authenticity and integrity.

I suggested above that in any investigation into journalism (or any other cultural space), it becomes necessary at some point to bracket out the question of how deep the originary determinism of a field's generative structures runs. The approach to unacknowledged symbolic economies in this work reflects the political phenomenological focus on the structuration of the very means by which individuals experience their professional lives. A less stringent threshold, however, points to a position closer to the branches of journalism studies which interpret the field through theories of professional identity and discourse. While there are varying accounts of professionalisation in journalism (Gjelten, 1998; Boudana, 2010), the core theme of each is that journalistic self-identity is held together by a professional identity which journalists project, articulate to each other and operationalise in work practices. Deuze begins with a delineation of overt principles which is equatable to the construction of the first-order symbolic economy detailed in chapter 4 (Deuze, 2005: 442–64). Further, as with this study, Deuze advocates moving beyond this first economy to another locus of ideological meaning. However, his conception of ideology is not posited as Marxist false consciousness, such that the true nature of the relation between journalistic practice and the world could be objectively discovered. Nor is it a generative structuralist or Gramscian hegemonic interpretation in which the dominant culture of journalism exists mainly to reinforce hierarchical political structures. Rather, for Deuze there is a 'meaning' of journalism which can be understood in deontological terms (Deuze, 2005: 445). This meaning may change over time or from place to place, but the social scientist's aim is to describe whatever meaning to the profession there is beyond 'telling people what they want to know' (Deuze, 2005: 442). For this professionalisation model, professional meaning can be found in the conscious reflections of journalists; for instance, professional identity may consist in an inflated sense of social importance. I would argue that this narrows the scope for interpretation in a similar, if obverse, fashion to the pervasively determinist approach.

If theories of professionalisation construct journalistic identity as an ideology by which it attains special status in society as a whole, they do not effectively explain how this ideology is internalised and naturalised, nor do they account for how it changes over time (cf. Bourdieu, 1991b: 240–2). They do offer a different level of interpretation from analytic frameworks which seek to understand journalism primarily as an industry, literary genre, culture or social system, in that they look at how journalists make sense of their own work. Professionalisation theory does not question, however, the structural determination underpinning the process of individuation. Instead, it takes a more 'horizontal' approach, seeing journalistic ideology as reproduced between journalists, through the continuous refinement of the consensus about who is a 'real' journalist and what constitutes 'real' news (Zelizer, 1993). This was the object of the early stages of analysis here, in which each speech act referring to good or bad journalistic practice (or journalists) was coded and structured. This preliminary analysis confirms that there is a consensus of sorts, but it is bifurcated. In accordance with the traditional divide in journalistic principles discussed since the late nineteenth century, there are two models of good practice, based on the conception of the task of journalism as reporting the facts or performing a moral service (Schudson, 2003: 64–89). While there is, unsurprisingly, considerable derision between the two camps, there is also a general consensus within each (especially within the 'reporting' subfield), and also evidence of continual refinement and negotiation.

The discourse analysis also confirmed another trend noted in professionalisation studies: the mystification of professional practice to outsiders. However, while the analytic categories of mystification or esotericisation are widely used in the professionalisation literature (Johnson, 1972), specifically applying the Bourdieusian model allows us a level of insight available neither to professionalisation's ideological approach nor to the structurally over-determining approach detailed above. With regard to the former, Bourdieu is able to show not only that mystification occurs but also *how*, in the form of subjectification and distinction (or self-positioning). Professional identity is not simply a functional myth into which individuals buy, fooling themselves and each other. It is inextricably linked with the political process of individuation: that is, professional identity is implicated in the process by which individual consciousness emerges. By this account, the political necessity for distinction at the field level precedes individual identity. Mystification operates as a strategy for achieving distinction, and also precedes selfhood. Thus, not only the form but the fact of self-reflection is necessitated by structural demands – which also shape its particular form.

Theories of professionalism make reference to the ideologies or discourses that govern norms and values in the trade, although the precise nature of these terms is often ambiguous (Deuze, 2005). Schlesinger (1978) and Golding and Elliott (1979) mention a journalistic 'occupational identity', while Soloski (1990) names an 'ideology of professionalism' without detailing what this is in practice. It was seen above that for Deuze this ideology is not precisely Gramscian, in that although it does reproduce relations of hegemony it does not exist solely as an instrument of structural reproduction (see also Eckstein, 1988). The analysis presented here supports this position, for two reasons. First, as suggested above, while there are discursive patterns which do give rise to the inferability of the staticisation of arguably arbitrary symbolic capital configurations, many observed speech acts clearly have no such function, because they can reasonably be interpreted as being inconsequential. Second, it is often difficult to pin down which determinations are effected specifically in the context of the journalistic field, as opposed to other fields in which an agent is active. One could theoretically make the case that all reflections by an individual effect hegemonic reproduction at some level – the wider field of cultural production, for example – this is essentially unfalsifiable. To modify Deuze, in this context a journalistic ideology is best defined, after Freeden (1996: 3), as a coherent set of ideas by which individuals interpret their world and engage with it. To follow Giddens, some of these practices will have political implications and all are at least partly determined by an ideology internalised as normal (Giddens, 1976: 121). Journalistic professionalism is thus an ideology in that it is the product of political structures and is generally oriented towards the political function of structural reproduction – but it is not exhausted by this function.

If journalistic ideology is conceived as a partially politically complicit way of interpreting one's own practice and journalism's relation to society, what is its content? For McMane (1993) it consists largely in a collective identity of 'class spirit'. This identity is explained in part by the historic overrepresentation of journalists of working-class backgrounds, but is at odds with the contemporary world in which journalism recruits are increasingly middle class (a shift that could either be due to status, in that journalism is arguably increasingly perceived as a profession (Deuze, 2005), or more simply the fact that entry-level positions are unpaid, and thus dependent on parental support). In fact it is plausible that a working-class ideology can easily co-exist with a predominantly middle-class demographic. It is common to hear journalists say that you wouldn't go into the trade for the money, or to mention the gap between average levels of prosperity amongst journalists and in the more elite circles they encounter professionally. For some, including the former international editor of a British broadsheet, a senior columnist from a broadsheet and the news editor of a major US quality newspaper, this gap is palpably untrue. However, it does serve to reinforce pervasive journalistic self-deprecation, in both the fields of power and cultural production. The journalistic ideology, then, is not tied to personal economic capital, but to a form of symbolic capital manifest in self- and collective identity, characterised by an anti-establishment outlook (Carpentier, 2005). This serves the dual purpose of obscuring the elitism which indubitably pervades journalism internally and emphasises the functional myth of journalists defending the interests of the masses, speaking truth to power. That it frequently takes the form of a roguish, adventurous anti-elitism also invests journalistic identity, and that of war reporting in particular, with a certain romantic appeal. While it could be argued that this is offset by the negative conventionally received tropes of journalistic identity, it does help to secure journalism's place within the field of cultural production, a place which is by no means naturally its own.

Where journalistic identity is romanticised or valorised, it serves a gatekeeping function as well as reinforcing power relations within the field. The number of speech acts in which participants talk about a good journalist's innate 'feel' for the demands of the profession thus support the theories of professionalism put forward by Johnson and Deuze. In fact, this argument applies equally to negative mythologies of journalistic identity. Public trust in journalists may be at a historic low,[20] but this could in itself help to reinforce an ideology within the field, and the relative positions of individual journalists. That is, whether a journalist is perceived as good because of an instinctive sense of journalistic ethics or because he possesses the lack of scruples needed to succeed in a cynical world, there is a set of traits the performance and internalisation of which have the political effect of stabilising relative positions of legitimacy. Schudson nominates a definition of professional ideology which could feasibly incorporate both negative and positive identification: put simply, the knowledge of what constitutes news, deeply rooted in the communicators' consciousness (Schudson, 2001: 153). This is entirely consistent with the mystification thesis which emerged from the interviews. The literature, however, lacks a discussion of the degree to which this sense is dislocated from the material represented in news, the extent to which it is defined by a quasi-autonomous symbolic system. We have seen that any of these characterisations of journalistic identity – whether they be ethical, ruthless or having an innate nose for news – are partially constructed according to the power relations of the field, and broadly operate in such a way that dominant actors or institutions can maintain their positions of status (as well as potentially reinforce the dominance of competitive individualism in the broader field of cultural production). However, there is also a case to be made on phenomenological and normative grounds for bracketing out the question of whether ethics or professional principles can be debated uncynically. While Bourdieu's own work on journalism sees it as a pointless exercise (Bourdieu, 1998b: 70–7), the working through of Bourdieusian theory presented here validates the discussion continued by Schudson and Dahlgren (Dahlgren and Sparks, 1992:

1–23; Dahlgren, 1996: 59–72) on the basis of a reflexive consideration of the political consequences of not discussing journalistic
principles in deontological terms, and in terms of the phenomenological contention that the fundamental priority of dominatory political
structures cannot be known.

A distinction needs to be drawn between a putative ideology,
identity and culture of journalism. A 'culture' of journalism is in fact
closer to Schudson's definition of an ideology of professionalism and
journalism: a collection of values, strategies and codes characterising
professional journalism and shared most widely by its members
(Pedelty, 1995; Kögler, 1997: 145; Carey, 1999: 53; Deuze, 2005:
445; Hanitzsch, 2007; Kunelius and Ruusunoksa, 2008). An ideology
of journalism in the context of this discussion is such a culture as it
reinforces the structures of the field or, putting it into Foucauldian
terms as Dahlgren (1996) does, reinforcing the 'dominant discourses'
of journalism. Identity is not constituted simply in terms of identity
politics – that is, in a manner in which identity is prima facie meaningful – but rather in light of the role that field power relations play
in the emergence of individual self-consciousness. Identity is thus a
narrower category than disposition. Journalistic disposition here
refers not to personality characteristics, but the adaptive alignment of
individual practices to the demands of the journalistic game. Practices
of selfhood form a subset of this field of practices, though others – for
Bourdieu, the more effective ones, politically – are those which
function outside of consciousness, as instinctive, practical memory.

Three broad dispositional characteristics were sketched in chapter 4
in terms of individualistic misanthropy, tenacity and moral authority.
It was emphasised that these are necessarily heterogeneous and
sometimes conflicting, but I would suggest that they are the compli-
cated, uneven counterparts of more simplistic tropes of journalistic
identity: the journalist as cynic, reporter and campaigner. These are
stereotypes to be sure, but also functional myths operative in the
public perception of journalism (in the case of the first two) and
amongst peers (for the third). Does it make sense to assume that journalistic identity can be reduced to a handful of categories which apply,
if not universally, then at least across the Western world? Bourdieu,
certainly, is criticised for positing such a monolithic model of the journalistic field (Benson, 2005). However, this criticism is baseless if the
analytic position Bourdieu sets out in *Outline of a Theory of Practice* is
taken seriously. For Bourdieu it is only the objective structural origins
of symbolic capital, identity and so on which are monolithic. The
observable permutations generated by these conditions of possibility

need share little resemblance in order for commonality of generative structures to be viable. Weaver goes further and suggests, by way of an international comparative analysis, that in terms of newsworthiness and news values, journalistic identity actually is substantially uniform (Weaver, 1998: 456). The present interviews, while more limited in their international scope, reveal substantially more contestability than Weaver suggests, though it has been seen that some common core norms were in evidence.

In Bourdieusian terms, what is important is not the presence or absence of contestability or diversity of journalistic values and subjectivities, but rather the effects of each. In this sense, more important than the fact that there is much debate over journalistic values are the other discourses which are thereby reinforced (van Dijk, 1988; 1997). Thus, while I have suggested here that debates on the nature of journalism are defensible even if only on deontological grounds, it remains important for the social scientist to be aware that even apparently radical debates usually have the conservative effect of enshrining some or other principle of differentiation. In his influential work on the role of the media in the Vietnam War, Hallin (1986) posits two interconnected factors which shaped journalistic discourse. The first of these is more bluntly political: government control of the news agenda and its influence over the specific framing of international news. A Bourdieusian analysis does not contribute substantially to this argument since, while Bourdieu does not disagree that holders of official power use overt control, influence and censorship to preserve their positions of domination, his focus is aimed not at disciplinary regimes but at power relations reproduced with the complicity of its victims. In this regard, Bourdieu's potential contribution to journalism studies aligns more closely with Hallin's second factor influencing journalistic discourse: the Cold War consensus (Bourdieu and Wacquant, 1999). Of course, Bourdieu does not tackle the conceptual framework underpinning foreign relations in the US, but he does write of the tendency of both the media and official discourse to reduce political issues to binaries of us/them, liberal/authoritarian and democratic/communist (Bourdieu, 1994c). Since journalists in specific professional contexts are already invested with these oppositions, there is no need for the use of overt political coercion to reinforce them. For Bourdieu the consensus in the field of cultural production after 1968 (noted above) was not a monolithic but a binary one. That is, journalists, academics and other cultural producers were not coerced into reproducing a single ideology, but rather into conforming to a continuum – left to right, or liberal to conservative, or, in the case of the French left, social democratic to socialist. The consensus Bourdieu refers to, then, is over the terms of political debate rather than a political programme as such, and those terms concern specifically the management of the market in social democratic capitalist societies.

In more specific terms, it is possible to flesh out how this consensus leads to conformism and exclusions in journalistic practice. First, political reporting may oppose one political position or another, but is incapable of challenging (or being cognisant of) the conditions of possibility of the political landscape itself. Financial journalism may support or oppose fiscal or monetary policies, but will unthinkingly conform to sustained economic growth through market development as the overarching goal of economic policy. Foreign affairs coverage may support or oppose nationalism, interventionism or humanitarianism, but will instinctively reinforce an exclusionary, us-and-them categorisation, usually determined hierarchically. And arts journalism may champion the avant-garde over traditional cultural producers, but only in such a way that preserves certain principles of differentiation and the elites who consecrate them.[21] Bourdieusianism augments contemporary journalism studies by suggesting that even a good journalist can only hope to have autonomy from a particular dominant journalistic or cultural ideology, not from ideology as such. A journalist cannot reliably reflect critically on the paradigm from without, since she is herself a product of a discourse defined in oppositional terms. Applying this argument to academics, writers and artists, while an individual may set out any position on cultural production from elitist to populist, according to Bourdieusian logic it is unthinkable to an individual implicated in the game of cultural production to question why culture matters, politically, at all. The culturalist allegations against Bourdieu are well known (Garnham, 1993): like Marcuse, he is criticised for assuming that the category of 'culture' is politically meaningful before analysing the politics of the specific forms it takes. However, it can be countered that Bourdieu is not using culture deontologically, but rather seeking to make sense of the political structures which produce not only the forms culture takes but also the means of their apprehension and differentiation. In journalism studies, specifically, the Bourdieusian approach can describe those conceptual categories which become practically unthinkable in a particular sociohistorical context. These are the metafields within which not only the particular dominant forms but the categorical validity of concepts such as culture attain political meaningfulness.

In a later work Hallin (1992) articulates a position closer to this Bourdieusian account. Instead of speaking of the dominance of US liberalism or conservatism or of a nationalist or patriotic consensus in international news, Hallin points to a broader historical trend in which ebbs and flows in political predominance as well as journalistic principles should be located. This is a period of 'high modernism', in which norms such as 'seamlessness' and 'wholeness' dominate the working journalist's view of her profession. It is only on the basis of this meta-concept of the journalist's relation to the world that more concrete principles can become operative. Commenting on the work of Golding and Elliott (1979), Merritt (1995) and Kovach and Rosenstiel (2001), Hallin groups the dominant principles of the high modernist period in journalism (roughly identified as 1960–90) as public service, objectivity, autonomy, immediacy and ethics. The interviews demonstrate that if there is seamlessness, then it is beyond even these meta-concepts, about which there is a fair amount of contestation – if only about content rather than the fact that they should be active categories at all. And this is the seamlessness of an orientation to the world which experiences as pre-reflexive the suitability or otherwise of individuals to the journalistic field, an orientation which incorporates a specific epistemology as well as misrecognised economies of authority and authenticity.

As with professionalism, it is useful to assess what a Bourdieusian account of journalism tells us that new institutionalism does not.[22] It has been a recurring theme that Bourdieu conceptualises journalists not as individuals as such, but as journalists who differ. That is, it is cultural and class distinctions which characterise the journalistic field, rather than some collective professional identity. This depiction of the journalistic field (like any other) as an arena of struggle does give a more variegated account than new institutionalism could generate. However, Benson (2005) argues that new institutionalism, for its part, has greater scope for explaining what he terms the 'cultural inertia of professional traditions' (Benson, 2006). It is certainly the case that institutionalism stresses the role of historical practices in explaining a professional or institutional culture which exceeds the sum of its practices. However, I would argue that Bourdieu's use of habitus as 'double historicity' is also capable of explaining the role that traditions play in shaping present practice. Moreover, Bourdieu adds two significant elements to the institutionalist account: first, he describes how the historicity of habitus is forgotten as history (Bourdieu, 1990a: 56); second, he gives cogent explanation of why there is cultural inertia – in short, that it preserves the status quo which benefits certain groups of actors in the field. Bourdieu writes:

> The stakes of the struggle between dominants and pretenders, the issues
> they dispute ... depend on the state of the legitimate problematic, that
> is, the space of the possibilities bequeathed by previous struggles, a
> space which tends to give direction to the search for solutions and,
> consequently, influences the present and future of production.
> (Bourdieu, 1996: 206, cited in Benson, 2006: 188)

However, what new institutionalism does address in a way which
Bourdieu does not is the influence on field practices of other fields.
Bourdieu writes that 'if I want to find out what one or another journalist
is going to say or write, or will find obvious or unthinkable, normal or
worthless, I have to know the position that journalist occupies in this
space. I need to know, as well, the specific power of the news medium in
question' (Bourdieu, 1998b: 41). Bourdieu does allow that the journalistic field varies according to medium, but does not adequately develop
the possibility that it also varies by country, or that the unique economic
and political fields in different countries will influence agents in their
respective journalistic fields in distinct ways. Duval, for instance,
attempts to measure both internal and external capital in the French
business press (Duval, 2005). The results are tentative, highlighting not
the inadequacy of the research but the difficulty of constructing
accurate measures of metacapital in the metafield of power within
which the journalistic field interacts with others, but does suggest the
potential benefit of including extra-field influences in any analysis of
professional behaviour. Bourdieu does embrace this approach in later
works (e.g. Bourdieu, 2005), but continues to stress the tendency of one
field's dominant principles of differentiation to supplant another's,
rather than exploring the idea that an agent's habitus may be simultaneously aligned to several fields.

Concluding remarks

While Bourdieu does not give full consideration to simultaneous field
immersion (McNay, 1999: 107), he places emphasis on another set of
extra-field factors explaining agents' behaviour: namely their personal
histories before becoming professionals.[23] This is by no means to
suggest that Bourdieu invokes a discrete, voluntarist individual whose
personality resists professional normalisation. Rather, an individual's
habitus will have been active in various fields throughout the agent's
lifetime, and as such her sense of selfhood – including professional
selfhood – will have been multiply determined. The interviews did not
run to detailed life histories, but they did seek to establish why
entering the journalistic field made sense to a respondent, why it

seemed a logical or natural step to take. The responses – in the majority of cases along the lines of 'I'm just that sort of person' – bear out the contention that for each individual a combination of experiences and position-takings with regard to location, class and so on will make certain life choices more or less automatic and others unthinkable. The advantage of this approach is that, instead of viewing a journalist's output or behaviour as an unequivocal structural determination, they should be seen as manifestations of a finite range of possibilities. The social scientific construction of habitus does not allow for the prediction of behaviour, but it does point towards the mechanisms which make particular acts unremarkable and felicitous.

While diverging significantly on emphasis, the authors included in this discussion of journalistic ideology, professionalism and discourse all confirm the notion that professional journalistic principles are not universal, but historically and socially specific. This context may be determined variously, from the dominance of a particular capitalist economic mode, or of liberalism, or of a teleological shift towards or away from rationalism or relativism, for example. The literature demonstrates that it is nothing new to interpret trends in journalism as reflective of historic shifts (Schudson, 1995; McNair, 1998, 2003b; Conboy, 2004, 2007). Nor is it a radical departure to contend that such shifts represent not simply journalism adapting to what economic or social forces require of it, but to an extent a quasi-autonomous development whose meaning is impossible to assess apart from internally – that is, in terms of the symbolic system which characterises journalism at any particular juncture. While Bourdieu tends to stress continuity to the detriment of an account of historic change, shifts can be accounted for in his model, and explained both according to endemic and extrinsic forces. The primary political function of journalistic principles in any particular context is as a means of differentiating dominated and dominating positions within the journalistic field, and journalism's position in society more broadly. If struggle is the defining characteristic of a field of cultural production, then a dominant set of professional principles can be understood as the means by which individuals and institutions compete. This competition is not so much for ownership of whatever the dominant principles of the day are, but for the ability to determine what counts as a recognisably dominant principle of differentiation in future.

In practical terms, this means that we can look both at what constitutes journalistic subjectivity, as well as more traditional categories such as codes of conduct, ethics and journalism's role in society. Against the professionalisation model, this does not proceed from an assumption of homogeneity in journalistic dispositions; it was seen above that journalistic identities are diverse and often conflicting. What a Bourdieusian perspective allows for, which professionalism does not, is the contention that oppositional or conflicting identities – between generations, specialisations, or between 'reporters' and 'moral authorities' – rather than transforming the field through struggle, actually serve to reinforce hierarchical power structures in the field. Carpentier's (2005: 199–202) evocation of Laclau and Mouffe's theory of discourse is appropriate here, insofar as it empha-sises that while there are significant stakes in the struggles between sub-groups in a field, the continuation of those struggles will cement the terms of reference for future struggles, thus effecting a reproduc-tion not of who dominates and who is dominated, but of the principle of differentiation between the two. Ultimately, both the content of intrafield struggles as articulated by agents, and the underlying polit-ically structured space which is obscured by those overt struggles, are politically salient and methodologically defensible.

Finally, having focused most of our attention on the internal logics of the field of journalism and the subfield of war reporting, let us consider the extent to which journalism is the expression of broader cultural factors. Edgar (2000), for instance, presents a means of describing the political context of journalistic reflection in terms which transcend the traditional structuralist argument that discourse helps to preserve the status quo of dominatory relations. One aspect is the overriding influence of liberalism, a theme which Bourdieu and Wacquant (1999) tackle in 'On the cunning of imperialist reason'. Bourdieu and Wacquant argue that the effective universalisation of a particular, neo-Kantian form of liberalism after 1968 precludes reflec-tion on its key tenets and implications. It has been normalised to the extent that it *is* liberalism, rather than one manifestation of it, and to the extent that liberalism exhausts progressive politics. In the broader sense, this hegemony means that it becomes increasingly unthinkable (rather than simply unfashionable) to question that which should be questioned if reflexivity remains a political aim. There is not space here to address the defensibility of the 1960s cultural turn in social theory and methodology (see for instance Jones and Collins, 2006), but we can at least set out what it means, in Bourdieusian terms, for journalists and academics. Bourdieu's point is, first, that liberal hegemony means that cultural producers and academics alike have developed a collective amnesia about how contested, and resisted, this turn had been previously (Bourdieu, 1998c: 29–44). Second, the naturalisation of a specific form of liberalism also makes natural the ideal of the absence of conflict in both politics and political theory, such that, it can be argued, the default mindset in the field of cultural production sees conflict as something to be resolved, rather than as formative or definitive. Journalism trades on conflict, needless to say, but with the rise of peace journalism (Lynch and McGoldrick, 2005) there is a detectable shift towards conceiving of journalism as a potential tool for conflict resolution rather than a lens on a world where violence is a given. The import here is not proving which model of conflict is correct, but rather to point out that there appears to be a decontestation in process of the cultural meaning of conflict, manifest in what is experienced as common sense (Rahkonen, 1999). Third, this form of liberalism, dominant in the journalistic field (McNair, 1998: 84), sets itself against one form of elitism – traditional political authority – while implicitly enshrining a cultural elite.[24] I have argued that certain elitisms can under certain circumstances (and qualified by finite contestation) be defended, but others remain unacknowledged, undefended and unopposed.

Fourth, Bourdieu contends that the dominant contemporary mode of liberalism consecrates a culture of individualism, extending from identity politics to social scientific methodology (Bourdieu, 2000: 155). According to Bourdieu's philosophy of social science, method-ological individualism is fallacious in the same way that Weber's (and Simmel's) analytic framework has been criticised (Heartfield, 1996). That is, by starting from the individual as the basic analytic unit, methodological individualists err in assuming that large macroscopic social behaviour can be explained by extrapolating from interactions within small groups. For Bourdieu, individuals are not discrete entities in functional possession of their attributes and actions, but rather the active determinants of processes of individuation; and to begin from an unproblematised individual ignores how collective (and political) a process individuation inevitably is. It is thus a matter of beginning from broader structures which generate collective attributes and action, which – to reiterate – are to be considered particular cases of the possible. This is not presented as a merely theoretical argument: for Bourdieu, the internalisation and naturalisation of the idea that social meaning derives from the deontological individual is at the heart of the atomisation of western societies witnessed over the past 40 years (Bourdieu, 2000: 155, 227; Bourdieu and Wacquant, 1999). It is for Bourdieu this specific incarnation of liberalism, built around the rights of the competitive individual, conceived largely in terms of personal economic gain, which underpins the widely documented phenomena of class disintegration, the fragmentation of identity and collective narcissism (Lasch, 1978; Bourdieu and Wacquant, 1999: 43; Furedi, 2003; Kilminster, 2008). In the present context, this individualism is perhaps best encapsulated by the ruggedly individual star war reporter. It could be posited that the individual as the dominant form of authority in this subfield makes intuitive sense given the nature of the work. But it can also be seen as reflecting a broader trend in which cultural institutions are increasingly challenged by individuals as the default point of orientation to society, and the catalyst of that orientation is authenticity and identification rather than professional expertise.

Notes

1 Hodgson (2005), for instance, introduces Judith Butler's concept of performativity to an analysis of professionalism in the context of project management, and draws similar conclusions to the present analysis on the interests vested in both conformity and non-conformity in professional practice.
2 See, for instance, Hays (1994: 57); Sayer (1999). Berard (2005: 204–5) argues that Bourdieu, amongst others, has failed to overcome the dualism of structure on the one hand and agency or practice on the other. A similar critique is presented in Dreyfus and Rabinow (1993). It is, however, more common to find in the literature (e.g. Anderson, 2004) arguments about structure and agency in Bourdieu's work in spite of his rejection of the terms.
3 Pels (1995: 80) argues that Bourdieu's account of intellectual authority amounts to the invocation of an 'anarchist utopia'.
4 It is worth noting that while media scholars (including Bourdieu in *On Television*) tend to see journalistic interaction as a homogenising force, the war reporters interviewed were more likely to describe it as a self-correcting mechanism.
5 Keen (2007) identifies those having the most to gain from this as 'the mob'.
6 While usually deemed a negative phenomenon, precarity is also seen in some readings of Marxism as a model for individual creativity and autonomy (Gill and Pratt, 2008; Ross, 2008).
7 The academic over-determination of the analytic object is a particularly recurrent preoccupation in postcolonial theory. See, for example, Bhabha (1994: 245–82); Spivak (1985). Bourdieu largely opposed postcolonial theory, as Richard Nice (1985: 38) notes: 'He argues with Franz Fanon. He's unable to subscribe to the romantic idea of the Third World revolution, precisely because he is too aware of the conditions for what he calls a rational project, and he is rewriting those ideas in *Algeria 1960*.' See also Jenkins (1992: 29).

8 As well as considering the stratified nature of particular disciplines, this
   entails an examination of the relational positions of those disciplines with
   respect to each other. For example, Bourdieu notes that to become a sociologist at the time he graduated from the École normale supérieure
   amounted to joining 'France's intellectual outcaste' (Wacquant, 2004:
   388). The academic field is also determined by gendered and class-based
   principles of differentiation (Reay, 2004).
9 This echoes arguments set out by Edward Said (1994).
10 'Un entretien avec Pierre Bourdieu', *Le Monde*, 14 January 1992.
11 See, for instance, Bourdieu and Wacquant (1999). By contrast, Wilcken
   (1995) argues that the principal cause of post-1968 intellectual malaise
   in France is not consensus but the pluralisation of social theory effected
   by the rise of 'anti-humanist' doctrines such as post-structuralism, which
   masquerade as democratising.
12 See especially the collections of polemics published by the *Raison d'agir*
   'researcher activist' group which Bourdieu cofounded, *Contre-feux*
   (1998d) (published in English by Polity as *Acts of Resistance: Against the
   new myths of our time*) (1998c) and *Contre-feux 2* (2001a) (published in
   English (2003) by the New Press as *Firing Back: Against the tyranny of the
   market 2)*. While it is valid to speak of a generalised theoretical consensus
   over liberal individualism, it is not difficult to find dissenting scholars.
   See for example Lasch (1978); Sennett (1977).
13 See especially Bourdieu (1998b). On the role of intellectuals in resisting
   neoliberalism, see Bourdieu's (1998e) *New Left Review* essay on utopi-
   anism and fatalism.
14 Similarly, Adkins (2005: 9) argues that there is an 'elision of reflexivity
   and freedom'.
15 Bourdieu details the limits of democratisation of higher education in *The
   Inheritors*, making the broader point that what appears to be progressive
   or democratising will also entail the reproduction of stratified, coercive
   norms at some level (Lane, 2000: 61–3).
16 Arguments against the esotericising trends in contemporary social theory
   are widespread. See, for instance, Chomsky et al. (1979); Wilcken (1995:
   48–9).
17 See, for example, Calhoun and Wacquant (2002); Crowley (2002);
   Schudson (2005).
18 See, for instance, Robbins (2005). Bourdieu occasionally used the term
   'constructivist structuralism' (Bourdieu and Wacquant, 1992: 11).
   Bourdieu has also been variously labelled 'modernist' (Bennett, 2005),
   'relativist' (Smith, 1988) and 'postmodernist' (Miles, 1996; Lash, 1990).
19 In the Derridean sense of a sign failing to signify that which structural
   determination would predict.
20 See Committee on Standards in Public Life (2008).
21 For a Bourdieusian analysis of arts journalism see, for instance, Harries
   and Wahl-Jorgensen (2007).

22 This section refers in particular to the reworking of Weber by DiMaggio and Powell (1983).

23 Writing about the gendering of journalism, Van Zoonen (1998: 39, 45) notes that: 'men's professional identities are much less fragmented and problematic than those of women in journalism ... Female journalists working in traditional news journalism therefore have a much more frag- mented and contradictory professional identity than men.' This adds another dimension to the discussion over whether Bourdieu overstates the disposition-determining aspect of professional fields, suggesting that the extent to which professional identities are determined intra-field varies according to demographic variables. De Bruin (2000: 233) argues that globalisation is another factor leading to increasing fragmentation of disposition.

24 In more general terms, Edgar (2000) argues that the ethical emphasis on facticity in liberal theory renders journalism incapable of understanding its own cultural influence.

Appendix: interviewee profiles

	Age	Gender	Years in journalism	Nationality	Current location	Current position	Former position
1	65	Male	N/A	US	Washington DC, US	Think-tank senior adviser	US army general
2	Late 50s	Male	~30 yrs	UK	London, UK	Columnist, UK broadsheet	War correspondent, various newspapers (broadsheet/tabloid)
3	50s	Male	N/A	US	Washington DC, US	Think-tank president	Political scientist
4	38	Female	~15 yrs	Australian	Oxford, UK	Broadcast journalist and producer, BBC	Broadcast journalist and war correspondent, Australia
5	58	Male	~35 yrs	UK	London, UK	Broadcast journalist, non-BBC	War correspondent, broadcast and press (broadsheet)
6	50s	Male	~25 yrs	US	Washington DC, US	Senior editor (quality newspaper)	International editor (quality newspaper)

7	Late 40s	Female	N/A	US	Washington DC, US	US State Department press official	Government adviser
8	40s	Female	~20 yrs	US	London, UK	Broadcast journalist, non-BBC	War correspondent, US Television
9	50s	Male	~20 yrs	US	Baltimore, US	Senior academic	Broadcast journalist/editor, US public radio
10	28	Male	3 yrs	US	Washington DC, US	War correspondent, US weekly news magazine	N/A
11	63	Male	~40 yrs	UK	Washington DC, US	Journalist, US newspaper (quality)	Journalist, various US and UK newspapers (broadsheet/tabloid)
12	62	Male	~40 yrs	UK	London, UK	Senior editor, UK broadsheet	War correspondent, international editor, UK broadsheets
13	Late 30s	Male	10 yrs	UK	London, UK	War correspondent, UK broadsheet	War correspondent, UK tabloid
14	50s	Male	~30 yrs	UK	Washington DC, US	Columnist, UK broadsheet	Journalist/war correspondent, UK tabloids/broadsheets

Bibliography

Accardo, A. (1998), *Journalistes précaires, journalistes au quotidian*. Bordeaux: Le Mascaret.

Adkins, L. (2003), 'Reflexivity: Freedom or habit of gender?', *Theory, Culture and Society*, 20:6, 21–42.

Adkins, L. (2005), 'Introduction: Feminism, Bourdieu and after', in L. Adkins and B. Skeggs (eds), *Feminism After Bourdieu*. Oxford: Blackheath, pp. 3–18.

Adorno, T. W. (1973), *Negative Dialectics*. London: Routledge & Kegan Paul.

Adorno, T. W. and B. P. O'Connor (2000), *The Adorno Reader*. Oxford: Blackwell.

Alexander, J. (2004), 'Cultural pragmatics: Social performance between ritual and strategy', *Sociological Theory*, 22:4, 527–73.

Allan, S. (2006), *Online News: Journalism and the Internet*. Maidenhead: Open University Press.

Almond, G. A. and A. Verba (1963), *The Civic Culture: Political attitudes and democracy in five nations*. Princeton: Princeton University Press.

Altheide, D. (2002), *Creating Fear: News and the construction of crisis*. Hawthorne, NY: Aldine de Gruyter.

Andén-Papadopoulos, K. (2009), 'Body horror on the Internet: US soldiers recording the war in Iraq and Afghanistan', *Media, Culture and Society*, 31:6, 921–38.

Anderson, B. (1983), *Imagined Communities: Reflections on the origin and spread of nationalism*. London: Verso.

Anderson, D. (2004), 'Questioning the motives of habituated action: Burke and Bourdieu on practice', *Philosophy and Rhetoric*, 37:3, 255–74.

Anderson, P. (2007), 'Competing models of journalism and democracy', in P. Anderson and G. Ward (eds), *The Future of Journalism in the Advanced Democracies*. Aldershot: Ashgate, pp. 39–50.

Andrejevic, M. (2008), 'Power, knowledge and governance: Foucault's relevance to journalism studies', *Journalism Studies*, 9:4, 605–14.

Ang, I. (1992), 'Questioning "cultural studies"?', *Cultural Studies*, 6:3, xi–xx.

Anheier, H. K. and J. Gerhards (1995), 'Forms of capital and social-structure in cultural fields: Examining Bourdieu's Social Topography', *American*

Journal of Sociology, 100:4, 859–903.

Atkinson, P. (1999), 'Deconstucting media mythologies of ethnic war in Liberia", in T. Allen and J. Seaton (eds), *The Media of Conflict: War reporting and representations of ethnic violence*. London: Zed, pp. 192–218.

Austin, J. L. (1962), *How to Do Things with Words: The William James lectures delivered at Harvard University in 1955*. Oxford: Clarendon Press.

Bachelard, G. (1940), *La Philosophie du non: Essai d'une philosophie du nouvel esprit scientifique*. Paris: Presses universitaires de France.

Bachelard, G. (1946), *Le Nouvel esprit scientifique*, 4th ed. Paris: Presses universitaires de France.

Bachrach, P. (1969), *The Theory of Democratic Elitism: A critique*. London: University of London Press.

Banks, M. and M. Wolfe Murray (1999), 'Ethnicity and reports of the 1992–95 Bosnian conflict', in T. Allen and J. Seaton (eds), *The Media of Conflict: War reporting and representations of ethnic violence*. London: Zed, pp. 147–61.

Barthes, R. (1973), *Mythologies*, trans. A. Lavers. St Albans: Paladin.

Baudrillard, J. (1995), *The Gulf War Did Not Take Place*. Sydney: Power Publications.

Beasley-Murray, J. (2000), 'Value and capital in Bourdieu and Marx', in N. Brown and I. Szeman (eds), *Bourdieu: Fieldwork in culture*. Oxford: Rowman & Littlefield Publishers, pp. 100–21.

Beaugrande, R. (1996), 'The story of discourse analysis', in T. van Dijk (ed.), *Introduction to Discourse Analysis*. London: Sage, pp. 35–62.

Beck, U. (1992), *Risk Society: Towards a new modernity*. London: Sage.

Behr, E. (1982), *Anyone Here Been Raped and Speaks English?* London: Penguin.

Bell, D. (1990), *Husserl*. London: Routledge.

Bell, M. (1995), *In Harm's Way: Reflections of a war zone thug*. London: Hamish Hamilton.

Bell, M. (1997), 'TV news: How far should we go?', *British Journalism Review*, 8:1, 7–16.

Bell, M. (1998), 'The truth is our currency', *The Harvard International Journal of Press/Politics*, 3:1, 102–9.

Bell, M. (2008), 'The death of news', *Media, War and Conflict*, 1:2, 221–31.

Bennett, T. (2005), 'The historical universal: The role of cultural value in the historical sociology of Pierre Bourdieu', *British Journal of Sociology*, 56:1, 141–64.

Bennett, W. L. and D. L. Paletz (1994), *Taken by Storm: The media, public opinion, and U.S. foreign policy in the Gulf War*. Chicago: University of Chicago Press.

Benson, R. (2005), 'Mapping field variation: Journalism in France and the United States', in R. Benson and E. Neveu (eds), *Bourdieu and the Journalistic Field*. Cambridge: Polity, pp. 85–112.

Benson, R. (2006), 'News media as a "journalistic field": What Bourdieu adds to new institutionalism, and vice versa', *Political Communication*, 23:2, 187–202.

Bentivegna, S. (2002), 'Politics and new media', in L. Lievrouw and S. Livingstone (eds), *Handbook of New Media*. London: Sage, pp. 50–61.

Berard, T. (1999), 'Dada between Nietzsche's birth of tragedy and Bourdieu's distinction: Existenz and conflict in cultural analysis', *Theory, Culture and Society*, 16:1, 141–66.

Berard, T. (2005), 'Rethinking practices and structures', *Philosophy of the Social Sciences*, 35:2, 196–230.

Berger, P. L. and T. Luckmann (1966), *The Social Construction of Reality: A treatise in the sociology of knowledge*. Garden City, NY: Doubleday.

Best, J. (1999), *Random Violence: How we talk about new crimes and new victims*. Berkeley, CA: University of California Press.

Bhabha, H. K. (1994), *The Location of Culture*. London: Routledge.

Blewitt, J. (1993), 'Film, ideology and Bourdieu's critique of public taste', *British Journal of Aesthetics*, 33:4, 367–74.

Bohman, J. (1997), 'Reflexivity, agency and constraint: The paradoxes of Bourdieu's sociology of knowledge', *Social Epistemology*, 11:2, 171–86.

Bohman, J. (2007), 'Political communication and the epistemic value of diversity: Deliberation and legitimation in media societies', *Communication Theory*, 17:4, 348–55.

Boltanski, L. (1999), *Distant Suffering: Morality, media and politics*. Cambridge: Cambridge University Press.

Boudana, S. (2010), 'On the values guiding the French practice of journalism: Interviews with thirteen war correspondents', *Journalism*, 11:3, 293–310.

Bourdieu, P. (1958), *Sociologie de l'Algérie*. Paris: Presses universitaires de France.

Bourdieu, P. (1961), *The Algerians*. New York: Beacon Press.

Bourdieu, P. (1972), *Esquisse d'une Théorie de la Pratique: Précédé de trois etudes d'ethnologie Kabyle*. Geneva: Droz.

Bourdieu, P. (1975), 'The specificity of the scientific field and the social conditions of the progress of reason', *Social Science Information*, 14:6, 19–47.

Bourdieu, P. (1977), *Outline of a Theory of Practice*. Cambridge: Cambridge University Press.

Bourdieu, P. (1980), *Questions de Sociologie*. Paris: Éditions de minuit.

Bourdieu, P. (1984), *Distinction: A social critique of the judgement of taste*. London: Routledge & Kegan Paul.

Bourdieu, P. (1985), 'The social space and the genesis of groups', *Theory and Society*, 14:6, 723–44.

Bourdieu, P. (1986), 'The forms of capital', in J. G. Richardson (ed.), *Handbook of Theory and Research for the Sociology of Education*. Westport, CN: Greenwood Press, pp. 241–58.

Bourdieu, P. (1987), *Choses Dites*. Paris: Éditions de minuit.

Bourdieu, P. (1989), *The State Nobility: Elite schools in the field of power*. Stanford: Stanford University Press.

Bourdieu, P. (1990a), *The Logic of Practice*. Cambridge: Polity Press.

Bourdieu, P. (1990b), *In Other Words: Essays towards a reflexive sociology*.

Oxford: Basil Blackwell.

Bourdieu, P. (1991a), 'On the possibility of a field of world sociology', in P. Bourdieu and J. Coleman (eds), *Social Theory for a Changing Society*. Boulder, CO: Westview, Russell Sage Foundation, pp. 373–88.

Bourdieu, P. (1991b), *Language and Symbolic Power*. Cambridge: Polity Press.

Bourdieu, P. (1991c), *The Political Ontology of Martin Heidegger*. Cambridge: Polity Press.

Bourdieu, P. (1991d), 'The peculiar history of scientific reason', *Sociological Forum*, 6:1, 3–26.

Bourdieu, P. (1992), 'Commentary on the commentaries', *Contemporary Sociology*, 21:2, 158–61.

Bourdieu, P. (1993a), *The Field of Cultural Production: Essays on art and literature*. Cambridge: Polity Press.

Bourdieu, P. (1993b), 'Narzisstische Reflexivität und Wissenschaftliche Reflexivität', in E. Berg and M. Fuchs (eds), *Kultur, Soziale Praxis, Text*. Berlin: Suhrkamp Verlag KG.

Bourdieu, P. (1994a), 'Rethinking the state: Genesis and structure of the bureaucratic field', *Sociological Theory*, 12:1, 1–18.

Bourdieu, P. (1994b), 'Libé vingt ans après', *Actes de la recherche en sciences sociales,* 101–2, 39.

Bourdieu, P. (1994c), 'L'Emprise du journalisme', *Actes de la recherche en sciences sociales*, 101–02, 3–9.

Bourdieu, P. (1996), *The Rules of Art: Genesis and structure of the literary field*. Cambridge: Polity Press.

Bourdieu, P. (1997), 'Passport to Duke (text read on behalf of the author at the Duke-University conference honoring his work, April 1995)', *Metaphilosophy*, 28:44, 449–55.

Bourdieu, P. (1998a), *Practical Reason: On the theory of action*. Cambridge: Polity Press.

Bourdieu, P. (1998b), *On Television and Journalism*. London: Pluto Press.

Bourdieu, P. (1998c), *Acts of Resistance: Against the new myths of our time*. Cambridge: Polity Press.

Bourdieu, P. (1998d), *Contre-Feux: Propos pour servir à la résistance contre l'invasion néo-libérale*. Paris: Editions liber.

Bourdieu, P. (1998e), 'A reasoned utopia and economic fatalism', *New Left Review*, 227, 125–30.

Bourdieu, P. (1999), *The Weight of the World: Social suffering in contemporary society*. Cambridge: Polity Press.

Bourdieu, P. (2000), *Pascalian Meditations*. Cambridge: Polity Press.

Bourdieu, P. (2001a), *Contre-feux 2: Pour un mouvement social européen*. Paris: Raisons d'agir editions.

Bourdieu, P. (2001b), *Masculine Domination*. Cambridge: Polity Press.

Bourdieu, P. (2002), *Si le monde social m'est supportable, c'est parce que je peux m'indigner*. La Tour d'Aigues: Editions de l'aube.

Bourdieu, P. (2003), *Firing Back: Against the tyranny of the market 2*. New York, London: The New Press.

Bourdieu, P. (2004), *Science of Science and Reflexivity*. Cambridge: Polity Press.

Bourdieu, P. (2005), 'The political field, the social science field and the journalistic field', in R. Benson and E. Neveu (eds), *Bourdieu and the Journalistic Field*. Cambridge: Polity Press, pp. 29–47.

Bourdieu, P. (2008), *The Bachelors' Ball*. Cambridge: Polity Press.

Bourdieu, P. and L. Wacquant (1992), *An Invitation to Reflexive Sociology*. Cambridge: Polity Press.

Bourdieu, P. and L. Wacquant, (1999), 'On the cunning of imperialist reason', *Theory, Culture and Society*, 16:1, 41–58.

Bourdieu, P., J.-C. Chamboredon, J.-C. Passeron and B. Krais (1991), *The Craft of Sociology: Epistemological preliminaries*. Berlin: Walter de Gruyter.

Bourdieu, P., J.-C. Passeron and M. de Saint Martin (1996), *Academic Discourse: Linguistic misunderstanding and professorial power*. Stanford: Stanford University Press.

Bouveresse, J. (1999), 'Rules, dispositions and the habitus', in R. Shusterman (ed.), *Bourdieu: A critical reader*. Oxford: Blackwell, pp. 45–63.

Bouveresse, J. (2004), *Bourdieu: Savant et politique*. Marseille: Agone.

Bowman, L. (2006), 'Reformulating "objectivity": Charting the possibilities for proactive journalism in the modern era', *Journalism Studies*, 7:4, 628–43.

Boyd-Barrett, O. (2004), 'Understanding: The second casualty', in W. Allan and B. Zeliger (eds), *Reporting War: Journalism in wartime*. Oxford: Routledge, pp. 25–42.

Brandenburg, H. (2007), 'Security at the source: Embedding journalists as a superior strategy to military censorship', *Journalism Studies*, 8:6, 948–63.

Brown, N. and I. Szeman (2000), 'Introduction: Fieldwork in culture', in N. Brown and I. Szeman (eds), *Pierre Bourdieu: Fieldwork in culture*. Oxford: Rowman & Littlefield Publishers, pp. 1–17.

Brown, R. (2003), 'Spinning the war: Political communication, information operations and public diplomacy in the war on terror', in D. Thussu and D. Freedman (eds), *War and the Media: Reporting conflict 24/7*. London: Sage, pp. 87–100.

Bruns, A. (2007), '"Anyone can edit": Understanding the produser'. Paper presented at the Mojtaba Saminejad Lecture series September, SUNY Buffalo.

Bruns, A. (2008a), *Blogs, Wikipedia, Second Life and Beyond: From production to produsage*. New York: Peter Lang.

Bruns, A. (2008b), 'Gatewatching, gatecrashing: Futures for tactical news media', in M. Boler (ed.), *Digital Media and Democracy: Tactics in hard times*. London: MIT Press, pp. 247–70.

Burston, J. (2003), 'War and the entertainment industries: New research priorities in an era of cyber-patriotism', in D. Thussu and D. Freedman (eds), *War and the Media: Reporting conflict 24/7*. London: Sage, pp. 163–75.

Butler, J. (1990), *Gender Trouble: Feminism and the subversion of identity*.

New York, London: Routledge.

Butler, J. (1997), *Excitable Speech: A politics of the performative*. London: Routledge.

Butsch, R. (2007), 'Introduction', in R. Butsch (ed.), *Media and Public Spheres*. London: Palgrave Macmillan.

Calhoun, C. J., E. LiPuma and M. Postone (eds) (1993), *Bourdieu: Critical perspectives*. Cambridge: Polity Press.

Calhoun, C. and L. Wacquant (2002), '"Social science with conscience": Remembering Pierre Bourdieu (1930–2002)', *Thesis Eleven*, 70, 1–14.

Cameron, D. (1999), 'Performing gender identity: Young men's talk and the construction of heterosexual masculinity', in A. Jaworksi and N. Coupland (eds), *The Discourse Reader*. London: Routledge, pp. 442–58.

Carey, J. (1999), 'In defense of public journalism', in T. Glasser (ed.), *The Idea of Public Journalism*. New York: Guildford Press, pp. 49–66.

Carles, P. (director) (2001), *La Sociologie est un sport de combat* [film].

Carlson, M. (2007a), 'Blogs and journalistic authority: The role of blogs in US election day 2004 coverage', *Journalism Studies*, 8:2, 264–79.

Carlson, M. (2007b), 'Order versus access: News search engines and the challenge to traditional journalistic roles', *Media, Culture and Society*, 29:6, 1014–30.

Carpentier, N. (2005), 'Identity, contingency and rigidity: The (counter-) hegemonic constructions of the identity of the media professional', *Journalism*, 6:2, 199–219.

Carruthers, S. (2004), 'Tribalism and tribulation: Media constructions of "African savagery" and "Western humanitarianism" in the 1990s', in S. Allan and B. Zeliger (eds), *Reporting War: Journalism in wartime*. Oxford: Routledge, pp. 155–73.

Carruthers, S. (2008), 'No one's looking: The disappearing audience for war', *Media, War and Conflict*, 1:1, 70–6.

Carvalho, A. (2008), 'Media(ted) discourse and society: Rethinking the framework of critical discourse analysis', *Journalism Studies*, 9:2, 161–77.

Cenite, M., B. H. Detenber, A. W. K. Koh, A. L. H. Lim and N. E. Soon (2009), 'Doing the right thing online: A survey of bloggers' ethical beliefs and practices', *New Media and Society*, 11:4, 575–97.

Chambers, D., L. Steiner and C. Fleming (2004), *Women and Journalism*. London: Routledge.

Champagne, P. (1994), 'The law of numbers: Measurement of audience and political representation of the public', *Actes de la recherche en sciences sociales*, 101–2, 10–22.

Champagne, P. (2005a), 'The "double dependency": The journalistic field between politics and markets', in R. Benson and E. Neveu (eds), *Bourdieu and the Journalistic Field*. Cambridge: Polity Press, pp. 48–63.

Champagne, P. (2005b), '"Making the people speak": On the social uses of and reactions to public opinion polls', in L. Wacquant (ed.), *Pierre Bourdieu and Democratic Politics: The Mystery of ministry*. Cambridge: Polity Press, pp. 111–32.

Chomsky, N., M. Ronat and J. Viertel (1979), *Language and Responsibility*. Brighton: Harvester Press.

Chouliaraki, L. (2000), 'Political discourse in the news: Democratizing responsibility or aestheticizing politics?', *Discourse and Society*, 11:3, 293–314.

Chouliaraki, L. (2006), *The Spectatorship of Suffering*. London: Sage.

Chouliaraki, L. (2008), 'The media as moral education: Mediation and action', *Media, Culture and Society*, 30:6, 831–52.

Christensen, C. (2008), 'Uploading dissonance: YouTube and the US occupation of Iraq', *Media, War and Conflict*, 1:2, 155–75.

Clark, T. (2005), *The Poetics of Singularity: The counter-culturalist turn in Heidegger, Derrida, Blanchot and the later Gadamer*. Edinburgh: Edinburgh University Press.

Clausewitz, C. [1832] (2005), *On the Nature of War*. London: Penguin.

Coleman, S. (2005), 'The lonely citizen: Indirect representation in an age of networks', *Political Communication*, 22:2, 197–214.

Committee on Standards in Public Life (2008), *Survey of Public Attitudes towards Conduct in Public Life 2008*, accessed from www.public-standards.org.uk/Library/SOPA_bookmarked.pdf (3 January 2009).

Conboy, M. (2004), *Journalism: A critical history*. London: Sage.

Conboy, M. (2006), *Tabloid Britain: Constructing a community through language*. London: Routledge.

Conboy, M. (2007), 'Permeation and profusion: Popular journalism in the new millennium', *Journalism Studies*, 8:1, 1–12.

Cook, R. (2000), 'The mediated manufacture of an "avant-garde": A Bourdieusian analysis of the field of contemporary art in London, 1997–9', in B. Fowler (ed.), *Reading Bourdieu on Society and Culture*. Oxford: Blackwell, pp. 164–85.

Corner, J. and D. Pels (2003), *Media and the Restyling of Politics*. Thousand Oaks, CA: Sage.

Costa, R. (2006), 'The logic of practices in Pierre Bourdieu', *Current Sociology*, 54:6, 873–95.

Couldry, N. (2003a), 'Media meta-capital: Extending the range of Bourdieu's field theory', *Theory and Society*, 32:5–6, 653–77.

Couldry, N. (2003b), *Media Rituals: A critical approach*. London: Routledge.

Couldry, N. (2008), 'Mediatization or mediation? Alternative understandings of the emergent space of digital storytelling', *New Media and Society*, 10:3, 373–91.

Couldry, N. and T. Markham (2008), 'Troubled closeness or satisfied distance? Researching media consumption and public orientation', *Media, Culture and Society*, 30:1, 5–21.

Couldry, N., S. Livingstone and T. Markham (2007), *Media Consumption and Public Engagement: Beyond the presumption of attention*. Basingstoke: Palgrave Macmillan.

Crossley, N. (1994), *The Politics of Subjectivity: Between Foucault and Merleau-Ponty*. Aldershot: Avebury.

Crossley, N. (2003), 'From reproduction to transformation: Social movement fields and the radical habitus', *Theory, Culture and Society*, 20:6, 43–68.

Crowley, J. (2002), 'Pierre Bourdieu's anti-politics of transparency', *Innovation: The European Journal of Social Sciences*, 15:2, 149–66.

Curry, M. R. (2002), 'Discursive displacement and the seminal ambiguity of space and place', in L. Lievrouw and S. Livingstone (eds), *The Handbook of New Media*. London: Sage, pp. 502–17.

Dahlgren, P. (1996), 'Media logics in cyberspace: Repositioning journalism and its publics', *Javnost/The Public*, 3:3, 59–71.

Dahlgren, P. and C. Sparks (eds) (1992), *Journalism and Popular Culture*. Thousand Oaks, CA: Sage.

Dalton, B. (2004), 'Creativity, habit, and the social products of creative action: Revising Joas, incorporating Bourdieu', *Sociological Theory*, 22:4, 603–22.

Davies, N. (2008), *Flat Earth News*. London: Chatto & Windus.

Davis, J. N. (2005), 'Power, politics, and pecking order: Technological innovation as a site of collaboration, resistance, and accommodation', *Modern Language Journal*, 89:2, 161–76.

De Albuquerque, A. (2005), 'Another "fourth branch": Press and political culture in Brazil', *Journalism*, 6:4, 486–504.

De Bruin, M. (2000), 'Gender, organizational and professional identities in journalism', *Journalism*, 1:2, 217–38.

Debray, R. and D. Macey (1981), *Teachers, Writers, Celebrities: The intellectuals of modern France*. London: NLB.

Deleuze, G. (1988), *Foucault*. London: Athlone.

Delli Carpini, M. and B. Williams (2001), 'Let us infotain you', in L. Bennett and R. Entman (eds), *Mediated Politics*. Cambridge: Cambridge University Press, pp. 160–81.

Dent, C. (2008), '"Journalists are the confessors of the public" says one Foucaultian', *Journalism*, 9:2, 200–19.

Derrida, J. (1973), *Speech and Phenomena, and Other Essays on Husserl's Theory of Signs*. Evanston, IL: Northwestern University Press.

Derrida, J. (1991), 'From "Différance"', in P. Kamuf (ed.), *A Derrida Reader: Between the blinds*. New York: Columbia University Press, pp. 59–79.

Deuze, M. (2005), 'What is journalism?', *Journalism*, 6:4, 442–64.

Deuze, M., A. Bruns and C. Neuberger (2007), 'Preparing for an age of participatory news', *Journalism Practice*, 1:3, 322–38.

DiMaggio, J. Paul and W. W. Powell (1983), 'The iron cage revisited: Institutional isomorphism and collective rationality in organizational fields', *American Sociological Review*, 48, 147–60.

Domingo, D. (2008), 'Interactivity in the daily routines of online newsrooms: Dealing with an uncomfortable myth', *Journal of Computer-Mediated Communication*, 13, 680–704.

Downing, J. (2001), *Radical Media: Rebellious communication and social movements*. Thousand Oaks, CA: Sage.

Dreyfus, H. and P. Rabinow (1993), 'Can there be a science of existential structure and social meaning?', in C. Calhoun, E. LiPuma and M. Postone (eds), *Bourdieu: Critical perspectives*. Cambridge: Polity Press, pp. 35–44.

Duval, J. (2005), 'Economic journalism in France', in R. Benson and E. Neveu (eds), *Bourdieu and the Journalistic Field*. Cambridge: Polity Press, pp. 135–55.

Eagleton, T. and P. Bourdieu [interview] (1992), 'Doxa and common life', *New Left Review*, 191, 111–21.

Eckstein, H. (1988), 'A culturalist theory of political change', *American Political Science Review*, 82:3, 789–804.

Eder, K. (1993), *The New Politics of Class: Social movements and cultural dynamics in advanced societies*, London: Sage.

Edgar, A. (2000), 'The "fourth estate" and moral responsibilities', in D. Barry (ed.), *Ethics and Media Culture: Practices and representations*. Oxford: Focal Press, pp. 73–88.

Ekelund, P. (2000), 'Space, time and John Gardner', in N. Brown and I. Szeman (eds), *Pierre Bourdieu: Fieldwork in culture*. Oxford: Rowman & Littlefield Publishers, pp. 215–40.

Elliott, B. (2005), *Phenomenology and Imagination in Husserl and Heidegger*. London: Routledge.

Emirbayer, M. (1997), 'Manifesto for a relational sociology', *American Journal of Sociology*, 103:2, 281–317.

Evans, H. (2003), *War Stories: Reporting in the time of conflict from the Crimea to Iraq*. Hawkhurst, Kent: Bunker Hill.

Evans, T. M. S. (1999), 'Bourdieu and the logic of practice: Is all giving Indian giving or is "generalized materialism" not enough?', *Sociological Theory*, 17:1, 3–31.

Everitt, D. and S. Mills (2009), 'Cultural Anxiety 2.0', *Media, Culture and Society*, 31:5, 749–68.

Fahmy, S. and T. J. Johnson (2005), '"How we performed": Embedded journalists' attitudes and perceptions towards covering the Iraq War', *Journalism and Mass Communication Quarterly*, 82:2, 301–17.

Fairclough, N. (1995), *Media Discourse*. London: Arnold.

Fairclough, N. (2003), *Analysing Discourse: Textual analysis for social research*. London: Routledge.

Faris, D. (2010), '(Amplified) voices for the voiceless', *Arab Media and Society*, 11, accessed from www.arabmediasociety.com (20 September 2010).

Feinstein, A. (2003), *Dangerous Lives: War and the men and women who report it*. Toronto: Thomas Allen.

Fengler, S. and S. Ruß-Mohl (2008), 'Journalists and the information-attention markets: Towards an economic theory of journalism', *Journalism*, 9:6, 667–90.

Fenton, F. (2010), 'Drowning or waving? New media, journalism and democracy', in N. Fenton (ed.), *New Media, Old News*. London: Sage, pp. 3–16.

Fiske, J. (1992a), 'Popularity and the politics of information', in P. Dahlgren and C. Sparks (eds), *Journalism and Popular Culture*. London: Sage, pp. 45–63.

Fiske, J. (1992b), 'Cultural studies and the culture of everyday life', in L. Grossberg, C. Nelson and P. Treichler (eds), *Cultural Studies*. New York: Routledge, pp. 154–73.

Flynn, T. R. (1985), 'Truth and subjectivation in the later Foucault', *Journal of Philosophy*, 82:10, 531–40.

Foucault, M. (1981), 'The order of discourse', in R. Young (ed.), *Unifying the Text: A post-structuralist reader*. Boston: Routledge & Kegan Paul, pp. 44–77.

Foucault, M. (1982), *The Archaeology of Knowledge, and The Discourse on Language*, 1st Pantheon pbk. ed. New York: Pantheon.

Foucault, M. and C. Gordon (1980), *Power/Knowledge: Selected interviews and other writings, 1972–1977*. Brighton: Harvester.

Foucault, M. and P. Rabinow (1984), *The Foucault Reader*, 1st ed. New York: Pantheon Books.

Fowler, B. (2000), *Reading Bourdieu on Society and Culture*. Oxford: Blackwell/The Sociological Review.

Fowler, B. (2003), 'Reading Pierre Bourdieu's *Masculine Domination*: Notes towards an intersectional analysis of gender, culture and class', *Cultural Studies*, 17:3–4, 468–94.

Fowler, B. (2009), 'The recognition/redistribution debate and Bourdieu's theory of practice: Problems of interpretation', *Theory, Culture and Society*, 26:1, 144–56.

Fox, N. (2003), *The New Sartre: Explorations in postmodernism*, New York, London: Continuum.

Fraser, N. (1997), *Justice Interruptus*. New York: Routledge.

Fraser, N. and A. Honneth (2003), *Redistribution or Recognition: A politico-philosophical exchange*. London: Verso.

Freeden, M. (1996), *Ideologies and Political Theory: A conceptual approach*. Oxford: Clarendon Press.

Frère, B. (2004), 'Genetic structuralism, psychological sociology and pragmatic social actor theory: Proposals for a convergence of French sociologies', *Theory, Culture and Society*, 21:3, 85–99.

Frith, S. and P. Meech (2007), 'Becoming a journalist', *Journalism*, 8:2, 137–64.

Fuchs, C. (2009), 'Information and communication technologies and society: A contribution to the critique of the political economy of the Internet', *European Journal of Communication*, 24:1, 69–87.

Furedi, F. (1997), *Culture of Fear: Risk-taking and the morality of low expectation*. London: Cassell.

Furedi, F. (2003), *Therapy Culture: Cultivating vulnerability in an uncertain age*. London: Routledge.

Garnham, N. (1986), 'Contribution to a political economy of mass-communication', in R. Collins, J. Curran, N. Garnham, P. Scannell, P. Schlesinger and C. Sparks (eds), *Media, Culture and Society: A critical reader*. London: Sage, pp. 9–32.

Garnham, N. (1990), *Capitalism and Communication: Global culture and the economics of information.* London: Sage.

Garnham, N. (1993), 'Bourdieu, the cultural arbitrary, and television', in C. Calhoun, E. LiPuma and M. Postone (eds), *Bourdieu: Critical Perspectives.* Cambridge: Polity Press, pp. 178–92.

Garnham, N. (2005), 'A personal intellectual memoir', *Media, Culture and Society*, 27:4, 469–93.

Garnham, N. and R. Williams (1980), 'Pierre Bourdieu and the sociology of culture: An introduction', *Media, Culture and Society*, 2, 209–23.

Gartman, D. (1991), 'Culture as class symbolization or mass reification? A critique of Bourdieu's *Distinction*', *American Journal of Sociology*, 97:2, 421–47.

Gaston, S. (2005), *Derrida and Disinterest.* London: Continuum.

Giddens, A. (1976), *New Rules of Sociological Method: A positive critique of interpretative sociologies.* New York: Basic Books.

Giddens, A. (1979), *Central Problems in Social Theory: Action, structure and contradiction in social analysis.* Basingstoke: Macmillan.

Gilbert, G. N. and M. Mulkay (1984), *Opening Pandora's Box: A sociological analysis of scientists' discourse.* Cambridge: Cambridge University Press.

Gill, R. and A. Pratt (2008), 'In the social factory? Immaterial labour, precariousness and cultural work', *Theory, Culture and Society*, 25:7–8, 1–30.

Gillmor, D. (2004), *We the Media: Grassroots journalism by the people, for the people.* Sebastopol, CA: O'Reilly.

Gjelten, T. (1998), *Professionalism in War Reporting: A correspondent's view.* New York: Carnegie Corporation of New York.

Glasser, T. (1996), 'Journalism's glassy essence', *Journalism and Mass Communication Quarterly*, 73, 784–6.

Goffman, E. [1959] (1971), *The Presentation of Self in Everyday Life.* London: Penguin.

Goffman, E. (1972), *Interaction Ritual: Essays on face-to-face behaviour.* London: Allen Lane.

Goffman, E. (1981), *Forms of Talk.* Philadelphia, PA: University of Pennsylvania Press.

Golding, P. and P. Elliott (1979), *Making the News*, 1st ed. London: Longman.

Gouldner, A. W. (1971), *The Coming Crisis of Western Sociology.* London: Heinemann.

Grenfell, M. and C. Hardy (2003), 'Field Manoeuvres: Bourdieu and the Young British Artists', *Space and Culture*, 6:1, 19–34.

Griffin, M. (2004), 'Picturing America's "war on terrorism" in Afghanistan and Iraq', *Journalism*, 5:4, 381–402.

Griffin, M. (2010), 'Media images of war', *Media, War and Conflict*, 3:1, 7–41.

Grimshaw, J. (1993), 'Practices of freedom', in C. Ramazanoglu (ed.), *Up Against Foucault: Explorations of some tensions between Foucault and feminism.* London: Routledge, pp. 51–72.

Guillory, J. (2000), 'Bourdieu's refusal', in N. Brown and I. Szeman (eds), *Pierre Bourdieu: Fieldwork in culture.* Oxford: Roman & Littlefield, pp. 19–43.

Güney, Ü. (2010), '"We see our people suffering": The war, the mass media and the reproduction of Muslim identity among youth', *Media, War and Conflict*, 3:2, 168–81.

Hafez, K. (2002), 'Journalism ethics revisited: A comparison of ethics codes in Europe, North Africa, the Middle East, and Muslim Asia', *Political Communication*, 19:2, 225–50.

Hall, S. (1973), *Encoding and Decoding in Television Discourse*. Birmingham: CCCS Occasional Paper.

Hallin, C. (1986), *The 'Uncensored War': The media and Vietnam*. Oxford: Oxford University Press.

Hallin, C. (1992), 'The passing of the "high modernism" of American journalism', *Journal of Communication*, 42:3, 14–25.

Hamel, J. (1998), 'The positions of Pierre Bourdieu and Alain Touraine respecting qualitative methods', *British Journal of Sociology*, 49:1, 1–19.

Hamilton, J. and E. Jenner (2004), 'Redefining foreign correspondence', *Journalism*, 5:3, 301–21.

Hammersley, M. (1997), 'On the foundations of critical discourse analysis', *Language and Communication*, 17:3, 237–48.

Hammersley, M. (2002), 'Discourse analysis: A bibliographical guide', accessed from www.tlrp.org/rcbn/capacity/Activities/Themes/In-depth /guide.pdf (20 June 2009).

Hammond, P. (2004), 'Humanizing war: The Balkans and beyond', in S. Allan and B. Zeliger (eds), *Reporting War: Journalism in wartime*. Oxford: Routledge, pp. 174–89.

Hammond, P. (2007a), *Framing Post-Cold War Conflicts*. Manchester: Manchester University Press.

Hammond, P. (2007b), *Media, War and Postmodernity*. London: Routledge.

Hanitzsch, T. (2007), 'Deconstructing journalism culture: Toward a universal theory', *Communication Theory*, 17:4, 367–85.

Hardt, M. (1993), *Gilles Deleuze: An apprenticeship in philosophy*. London: UCL Press.

Harland, R. (1991), *Superstructuralism: The philosophy of structuralism and post-structuralism*. London: Routledge.

Harries, G. and K. Wahl-Jorgensen (2007), 'The culture of arts journalists: Elitists, saviors or manic depressives?', *Journalism*, 8:6, 619–39.

Hartley, J. (1999), *Uses of Television*. London: Routledge.

Hartsock, N. (1990), 'Foucault on power: A theory for women?', in L. Nicholson (ed.), *Feminism/Postmodernism*. London: Routledge, pp. 157–75.

Haugaard, M. (2008), 'Power and habitus', *Journal of Power*, 1:2, 189–206.

Hays, S. (1994), 'Structure and agency and the sticky problem of culture', *Sociological Theory*, 12:1, 57–72.

Heartfield, J. (1996), 'Marxism and social construction', in S. Wolton (ed.), *Marxism, Mysticism and Modern Theory*. Basingstoke: Palgrave Macmillan, pp. 7–27.

Hegel, G. W. F. [1807] (1977), *The Phenomenology of Spirit*, trans. A. Miller.

Oxford: Oxford University Press.

Henningham, J. and A. Delano (1998), 'British journalists', in D. Weaver (ed.), *The Global Journalist: News people around the world*. Creskill, NJ: Hampton Press, pp. 143–60.

Herman, E. S. and N. Chomsky (1988), *Manufacturing Consent: The political economy of the mass media*. New York: Pantheon.

Herscovitz, H. (2004), 'Brazilian journalists' perceptions of media roles, ethics and foreign influence on Brazilian journalism', *Journalism Studies*, 5:1, 71–86.

Himelboim, I. and Y. Limor (2008), 'Media perception of freedom of the press: A comparative international analysis of 242 codes of ethics', *Journalism*, 9:3, 235–65.

Hodgson, D. (2005), '"Putting on a professional performance": Performativity, subversion and project management', *Organization*, 12:1, 51–68.

Höijer, B. (2008), 'Ontological assumptions and generalizations in qualitative (audience) research', *European Journal of Communication*, 23:3, 275–94.

Horton, D. and R. R. Wohl (1956), 'Mass communication and para-social interaction: Observations on intimacy at a distance', *Psychiatry*, 19, 215–29.

Hudson, G. and M. Temple (2010), 'We are *not* all journalists now', in S. Tunney and C. Monaghan (eds), *Web Journalism: A new form of citizenship?*. Brighton: Sussex Academic Press, pp. 63–76.

Hull, C. (1997), 'The need in thinking: Materiality in Theodor W. Adorno and Judith Butler', *Radical Philosophy*, 84, 22–35.

Hulteng, J. L. and R. P. Nelson (1971), *The Fourth Estate: An informal appraisal of the news and opinion media*. New York: Harper & Row.

Husserl, E. (1931), *Ideas: General introduction to pure phenomenology*, trans. W. R. Boyce Gibson. London: George Allen & Unwin Ltd.

Husserl, E. (1970), *The Crisis of European Sciences and Transcendental Phenomenology: An introduction to phenomenological philosophy*. Evanston, IL: Northwestern University Press.

Husserl, E. (1982), *Ideas Pertaining to a Pure Phenomenology and to a Phenomenological Philosophy*. Boston: Kluwer.

International Federation of Journalists (2009), *Perilous Assignments: Journalists and media staff killed in 2008*. Brussels: International Federation of Journalists.

Jenkins, R. (1982), 'Bourdieu, Pierre and the reproduction of determinism', *Sociology: The Journal of the British Sociological Association*, 16:2, 270–81.

Jenkins, R. (1992), *Pierre Bourdieu*. London: Taylor & Francis.

Jenkins, R. (2008), 'Erving Goffman: A major theorist of power?', *Journal of Power*, 1:2, 157–68.

Johnson, S. (2007), '"They just make sense": Tabloid newspapers as an alternative public sphere', in R. Butsch (ed.), *Media and Public Spheres*. Basingstoke: Palgrave Macmillan, pp. 83–95.

Johnson, T. (1972), *Professions and Power*. London: Macmillan.

Johnson, T. and S. Fahmy (2010), '"When blood becomes cheaper than a bottle of water": How viewers of Al-Jazeera's English language website judge graphic images of conflict', *Media, War and Conflict*, 3:1, 43–66.

Johnson-Cartee, K. (2005), *News Narratives and News Framing: Constructing political reality*. Oxford: Rowman & Littlefield.

Johnston, G. and J. Percy-Smith (2003), 'In search of social capital', *Policy and Politics*, 31:3, 321–34.

Jones, P. and C. Collins (2006), 'Political analysis versus critical discourse analysis in the treatment of ideology: Some implications for the study of communication', *Atlantic Journal of Communication*, 14:1–2, 28–50.

Jung, H. Y. (1988), 'Being, praxis, and truth: Toward a dialogue between phenomenology and Marxism', *Dialectical Anthropology*, 12:3, 307–28.

Kahn, R. and D. Kellner (2004), 'New media and Internet activism: From the "Battle of Seattle" to blogging', *New Media and Society*, 6:1, 87–95.

Karakayali, N. (2004), 'Reading Bourdieu with Adorno: The limits of critical theory and reflexive sociology', *Sociology: The Journal of the British Sociological Association*, 38:2, 351–68.

Kauppi, N. (1996), *French Intellectual Nobility: Institutional and symbolic transformations in the post-Sartrian Era*. Albany, NY: State University of New York Press.

Keeble, R. (2004), 'Information warfare in an age of hyper-militarism', in S. Allan and B. Zeliger (eds), *Reporting War: Journalism in wartime*. Oxford: Routledge, pp. 43–58.

Keen, A. (2007), *The Cult of the Amateur: How today's Internet is killing our culture*. New York: Doubleday.

Kelly, S. D. (2002), 'Merleau-Ponty on the body', *Ratio-New Series*, 15:4, 376–91.

Kilminster, R. (2008), 'Narcissism or informalization? Christopher Lasch, Norbert Elias and social diagnosis', *Theory, Culture and Society*, 25:3, 131–51.

King, A. (2000), 'Thinking with Bourdieu against Bourdieu: A "practical" critique of the habitus', *Sociological Theory*, 18:3, 417–33.

Kingston, P. (2001), 'The unfulfilled promise of cultural capital theory', *Sociology of Education*, 74 (extra issue), 88–99.

Klinenberg, E. (2005), 'Convergence: News production in a digital age', *Annals of the American Academy of Political and Social Science*, 597, 48–64.

Knightley, P. (2003), *The First Casualty: The war correspondent as hero, propagandist and myth-maker from the Crimea to Iraq*. London: Andre Deutsch.

Kögler, H.-H. (1997), 'Alienation as epistemological source: Reflexivity and social background after Mannheim and Bourdieu', *Social Epistemology*, 11:2, 141–65.

Kovach, B. and T. Rosenstiel (2001), *The Elements of Journalism*. New York: Crown Publishers.

Krais, B. (1993), 'Gender and symbolic violence: Female oppression in the light of Pierre Bourdieu's theory of social practice', in C. Calhoun, E. LiPuma and M. Postone (eds), *Bourdieu: Critical perspectives*. Cambridge: Polity Press.

Kuhn, T. S. (1962), *The Structure of Scientific Revolutions*. Chicago: University of Chicago Press.

Kunelius, R. and L. Ruusunoksa (2008), 'Mapping professional imagination', *Journalism Studies*, 9:5, 662–78.

Lacey, N. (1998), *Unspeakable Subjects: Feminist essays in legal and social theory*. Oxford: Hart.

Laclau, E. (2000), 'Identity and hegemony: The role of universality in the constitution of political logics', in J. Butler, E. Laclau and S. Zizek, *Contingency, Hegemony, Universality: Contemporary dialogues on the left*. London, New York: Verso, pp. 44–89.

Lahire, B. (2002), 'How to keep a critical tradition alive: A tribute to Pierre Bourdieu', *Review of International Political Economy*, 9:4, 595–600.

Landow, G. [1992] (2006), *Hypertext 3.0: Critical theory and new media in an era of globalisation*. Baltimore: Johns Hopkins University Press.

Lane, J. F. (2000), *Pierre Bourdieu: A critical introduction*. London: Pluto Press.

Lasch, C. (1978), *The Culture of Narcissism: American life in an age of diminishing expectations*. New York: Norton.

Lash, S. (1990), *The Sociology of Postmodernism*. London: Routledge.

Lau, R. W. K. (2004), 'Habitus and the practical logic of practice: An interpretation', *Sociology*, 38:2, 369–87.

Lebaron, F. (2003), 'Pierre Bourdieu: Economic models against economism', *Theory and Society*, 32:5–6, 551–65.

Leech, K. (2008), 'Burma: A deluge of moral posturing', accessed from www.spiked-online.com/index.php?/site/article/5133/ (12 February 2009).

Lemert, C. C. (1994), 'Post-structuralism and sociology', in S. Seidman (ed.), *The Postmodern Turn: New perspectives on social theory*. Cambridge: Cambridge University Press, pp. 265–81.

Levine, P. and M. Lopez (2004), *Young People and Political Campaigning on the Internet*. Baltimore: CIRCLE, University of Maryland.

Liebes, T. and Z. Kampf (2004), 'The PR of terror: How new style wars give voice to terrorists', in S. Allan and B. Zeliger (eds), *Reporting War: Journalism in wartime*. Oxford: Routledge, pp. 77–95.

Lievrouw, L. and S. Livingstone (2002), 'The social shaping and consequences of ICTs', in L. Lievrouw and S. Livingstone (eds), *Handbook of New Media*. London: Sage, pp. 1–15.

Lievrouw, L. and S. Livingstone (2006), 'Introduction to the updated student edition' in L. Lievrouw and S. Livingstone (eds), *Handbook of New Media: Updated student edition*. London: Sage, pp. 1–14.

Lingard, B. and S. Rawolle (2004), 'Mediatizing educational policy: The journalistic field, science policy, and cross-field effects', *Journal of Education Policy*, 19:3, 361–80.

Lisosky, J. and J. Henrichsen (2009), 'Don't shoot the messenger: Prospects for protecting journalists in conflict situations', *Media, War and Conflict*, 2:2, 129–48.

Liu, H. (2008), 'Social network profiles as taste performances', *Journal of*

Computer-Mediated Communication, 13:1, 252–75.

Livesay, J. (1985), 'Normative grounding and praxis: Habermas, Giddens, and a contradiction within critical theory', *Sociological Theory*, 3:2, 66–76.

Livingstone, S. (1998), *Making Sense of Television: The psychology of audience interpretation*, 2nd ed. Oxford: Butterworth-Heinemann.

Lizardo, O. (2004), 'The cognitive origins of Bourdieu's habitus', *Journal for the Theory of Social Behaviour*, 34:4, 375–401.

Lloyd, M. (1999), 'Performativity, parody, politics', *Theory, Culture and Society*, 16:2, 195–213.

Lovell, T. (2000), 'Thinking feminism with and against Bourdieu', in B. Fowler (ed.), *Reading Bourdieu on Society and Culture*. Oxford: Blackwell, pp. 27–48.

Lowrey, W. (2006), 'Mapping the journalism–blogging relationship', *Journalism*, 7:4, 477–500.

Luft, S. (1998), 'Husserl's phenomenological discovery of the natural attitude', *Continental Philosophy Review*, 31:2, 153–70.

Lukes, S. (1973), *Power: A radical view*. Oxford: Basil Blackwell.

Lynch, J. and A. McGoldrick (2005), *Peace Journalism*. Stroud: Hawthorn Press.

Macann, C. E. (1993), *Four Phenomenological Philosophers: Husserl, Heidegger, Sartre, Merleau-Ponty*. London: Routledge.

MacIntyre, A. (1981), *After Virtue: A study in moral theory*. London: Duckworth.

Mæland, B. and P. Brunstad (2009), *Enduring Military Boredom: From 1750 to the present*. Basingstoke: Palgrave Macmillan.

Mannheim, K. [1936] (1998), *Ideology and Utopia: Collected works of Karl Mannheim, vol. 1*. London: Routledge.

Marchetti, D. (2005), 'Subfields of specialized journalism', in R. Benson and E. Neveu (eds), *Bourdieu and the Journalistic Field*. Cambridge: Polity Press, pp. 64–82.

Marcoulatos, I. (2001), 'Merleau-Ponty and Bourdieu on embodied significance', *Journal for the Theory of Social Behaviour*, 31:1, 1–28.

Markham, T. (2007), *Bourdieusian Political Theory and Social Science: The field of war correspondence 1990–2003*. Unpublished doctoral thesis, University of Oxford.

Markham, T. (2010), 'The case against the democratic influence of the Internet on journalism', in S. Tunney and G. Monaghan (eds), *Web Journalism: A new form of citizenship?'* Brighton: Sussex Academic Press, pp. 77–96.

Marlière, P. (1998), 'The rules of the journalistic field: Pierre Bourdieu's contribution to the sociology of the media', *European Journal of Communication*, 13:2, 219–34.

Marlière, P. (2000), 'The impact of market journalism: Pierre Bourdieu on the media', in B. Fowler (ed.), *Reading Bourdieu on Society and Culture*. Oxford: Blackwell, pp. 199–211.

Martin, B. and I. Szelenyi [1987] (2000), 'Beyond cultural capital: Toward a theory of symbolic domination', in D. Robbins (ed.), *Pierre Bourdieu, vol. 1*. London: Sage, pp. 278–302.

Marx, K. and F. Engels (1998), *The German Ideology: Including theses on Feuerbach and introduction to the critique of political economy*. Amherst, NY: Prometheus Books.

Matheson, D. (2003), '"Scowling at their notebooks": How British journalists understand their writing', *Journalism*, 4:2, 165–83.

Matheson, D. and S. Allan (2009), *Digital War Reporting*. Cambridge: Polity Press.

Maton, K. (2003), 'Reflexivity, relationism, and research: Pierre Bourdieu and the epistemic conditions of social scientific knowledge', *Space and Culture*, 6:1, 52–65.

Mauss, M. [1954] (2002), The Gift: The form and reason of exchange in archaic societies. Oxford: Routledge.

Mauss, M. (1979), *Sociology and Psychology: Essays*. London: Routledge & Kegan Paul.

Mayer, N. (1995), 'The interview according to Pierre Bourdieu: Critical analysis of *La Misère du monde*', *Revue Française De Sociologie*, 36:2, 355–70.

McCarthy, A. (2001), *Ambient Television: Visual culture and public space*. Durham, NC: Duke University Press.

McChesney, R. (1998), 'The political economy of global communication', in R. McChesney, E. Wood and J. Foster (eds), *Capitalism and the Information Age: The political economy of the global communication revolution*. New York: Monthly Review Press, pp. 1–26.

McGuigan, J. (1996), *Culture and the Public Sphere*. London: Routledge.

McLaughlin, G. (2002), *The War Correspondent*. London: Pluto.

McMane, A. (1993), 'A comparative analysis of standards of reporting among French and US newspaper journalists', *Journalism Quarterly*, 79:1, 87–100.

McNair, B. (1998), *The Sociology of Journalism*. London: Arnold.

McNair, B. (2000), *Journalism and Democracy: An evaluation of the political public sphere*. London: Routledge.

McNair, B. (2003a), 'From control to chaos: Towards a new sociology of journalism', *Media, Culture and Society*, 25:4, 547–55.

McNair, B. (2003b), *News and Journalism in the UK*. London: Routledge.

McNay, L. (1999), 'Gender, habitus and the field: Pierre Bourdieu and the limits of reflexivity', *Theory, Culture and Society*, 16:1, 95–118.

McNay, L. (2000), *Gender and Agency: Reconfiguring the subject in feminist and social theory*. Cambridge: Polity Press.

McNay, L. (2008), *Against Recognition*. Cambridge: Polity Press.

McNulty, M. (1999), 'Media ethnicization and the international response to war and genocide in Rwanda', in T. Allen and J. Seaton (eds), *The Media of Conflict: War reporting and representations of ethnic violence*. London: Zed, pp. 268–86.

McRobbie, A. (2002), 'A mixed bag of misfortunes? Bourdieu's *Weight of the World*', *Theory, Culture and Society*, 19:3, 129–38.

Merleau-Ponty, M. (1962), *Phenomenology of Perception*. London: Routledge & Kegan Paul.

Merquior, J. G. (1986), *From Prague to Paris: A critique of structuralist and post-structuralist thought*. London: Verso.

Merritt, D. (1995), 'Public journalism: Defining a democratic art', *Media Studies Journal*, 9:3, 125–32.

Mesny, A. (2002), 'A view on Bourdieu's legacy: *Sens pratique* v. hysteresis', *Canadian Journal of Sociology–Cahiers Canadiens De Sociologie*, 27:1, 59–67.

Miles, S. (1996), 'The cultural capital of consumption: Understanding "postmodern" identities in a cultural context', *Culture and Psychology*, 2:2, 139–58.

Mill, J. S. [1872] (1987), *The Logic of the Moral Sciences*. London: Duckworth.

Minogue, K. (1992), 'Language and domination in some latter-day Marxists', *Government and Opposition*, 27:3, 397–404.

Moeller, S. (2004), 'A moral imagination: The media's response to the war on terrorism', in S. Allan and B. Zeliger (eds), *Reporting War: Journalism in wartime*. Oxford: Routledge, pp. 59–76.

Moeller, S. D. (1999), *Compassion Fatigue: How the media sell misery, war, and death*. London: Routledge.

Moi, T. (1991), 'Appropriating Bourdieu: Feminist theory and Pierre Bourdieu's sociology of culture', *New Literary History*, 22:4, 1017–49.

Moore, R. (2004), 'Cultural capital: Objective probability and the cultural arbitrary', *British Journal of Sociology of Education*, 25:4, 445–56.

Moores, S. (2000), *Media and Everyday Life in Modern Society*. Edinburgh: Edinburgh University Press.

MORI (2003), *Trust in Public Institutions*. London: MORI Social Research Institute.

Murrell, C. (2010), 'Baghdad bureaux: An exploration of the interconnected world of fixers and correspondents at the BBC and CNN', *Media, War and Conflict*, 3:2, 125–37.

Neilson, B. and N. Rossiter (2008), 'Precarity as a political concept, or, Fordism as exception', *Theory, Culture and Society*, 25:7–8, 51–72.

Neveu, E. (2005), 'Bourdieu, the Frankfurt School and cultural studies: On some misunderstandings', in R. Benson and E. Neveu (eds), *Bourdieu and the Journalistic Field*. Cambridge: Polity Press, pp. 195–213.

Nice, R. (1985), 'Interview with C. Mahar', unpublished interview cited in R. Harker, C. Mahar and C. Wilkes (eds), *An Introduction to the Work of Pierre Bourdieu*. London: Macmillan.

Noble, G. and M. Watkins (2003), 'So, how did Bourdieu learn to play tennis? Habitus, consciousness and habituation', *Cultural Studies*, 17:3–4, 520–39.

Nohrstedt, S., S. Kaitatzi-Witlock, R. Ottosen and K. Riegert (2000), 'From the Persian Gulf to Kosovo: War journalism and propaganda', *European Journal of Communication*, 15:3, 383–404.

Nolan, D. (2008), 'Journalism, education and the formation of "public subjects"', *Journalism*, 9:6, 733–49.

Norris, C. (1992), *Uncritical Theory: Postmodernism, intellectuals and the Gulf War*. London: Lawrence & Wishart.

Norris, P. (2000), *A Virtuous Circle*. Cambridge: Cambridge University Press.

Norris, P. (2001), *Digital Divide*. Cambridge: Cambridge University Press.

O'Neill, B. (2010), 'Après le deluge, the ghoulish opportunists', accessed from www.spiked-online.com/index.php/site/article/9468/ (27 August 2010).

Örnebring, H. (2008), 'The consumer as producer – of what? User-generated tabloid content in *The Sun* (UK) and *Aftonblat* (Sweden)', *Journalism Studies*, 9:5, 771–85.

Örnebring, H. and A. Jönsson (2004), 'Tabloid journalism and the public sphere: A historical perspective on tabloid journalism', *Journalism Studies*, 5:3, 283–95.

Ortner, S. (1996), *Making Gender: The politics and erotics of culture*. Boston, MA: Beacon.

Ortner, S. (1999), *The Fate of 'Culture': Geertz and beyond*. Berkeley, CA: University of California Press.

Palmer, J. and V. Fontan (2007), 'Our ears and our eyes: Journalists and fixers in Iraq', *Journalism*, 8:1, 5–24.

Papacharissi, Z. (2009), 'The virtual geographies of social networks: A comparative analysis of Facebook, LinkedIn and AsmallWorld', *New Media and Society*, 11:1–2, 199–220.

Pateman, C. (1989), *The Disorder of Women*. Cambridge: Polity Press.

Paulussen, S. and P. Ugille (2008), 'User-generated content in the newsroom: Professional and organizational constraints on participatory journalism', *Westminster Papers in Communication and Culture*, 5:2, 24–41.

Pedelty, M. (1995), *War Stories: The culture of foreign correspondents*. London: Routledge.

Pellerin, L. A. and E. Stearns (2001), 'Status honor and the valuing of cultural and material capital', *Poetics*, 29:1, 1–24.

Pels, D. (1995), 'Knowledge politics and anti-politics: Toward a critical appraisal of Bourdieu's concept of intellectual autonomy', *Theory and Society*, 24:1, 79–104.

Pels, D. (2000), 'Reflexivity: One step up', *Theory, Culture and Society*, 17:3, 1–25.

Philo, G. (2007), 'Can discourse analysis successfully explain the content of media and journalistic practice?', *Journalism Studies*, 8:2, 175–96.

Philo, G. (2008), 'Active audiences and the construction of public knowledge', *Journalism Studies*, 9:4, 535–44.

Philo, G. and G. McLaughlin (1993), *The British Media and the Gulf War*. Glasgow: Glasgow University Media Group.

Pickard, V. (2008), 'Cooptation and cooperation: Institutional exemplars of democratic Internet technology', *New Media and Society*, 10:4, 625–45.

Pintak, L. and J. Ginges (2009), 'Inside the Arab newsroom: Arab journalists evaluate themselves and the competition', *Journalism Studies*, 10:2, 157–77.

Pinto, L. (1994), 'Le Journalisme philosophique', *Actes de la recherche en sciences sociales*, 101–2, 25–38.

Pinto, L. (1999), 'A militant sociology: The political commitment of Pierre Bourdieu', in B. Fowler (ed.), *Reading Bourdieu on Society and Culture*. Oxford: Blackwell, pp. 88–104.

Pires, P. and P. Bourdieu (1998), 'Return to television' [interview], in P. Bourdieu, *Acts of Resistance*. Cambridge: Polity Press, pp. 70–7.

Plaisance, P. (2002), 'The journalist as moral witness: Michael Ignatieff's pluralistic philosophy for a global media culture', *Journalism*, 3:2, 205–22.

Platon, S. and M. Deuze (2003), 'Indymedia journalism: A radical way of making, selecting and sharing news?', *Journalism*, 4:3, 336–55.

Pöttker, H. (2004), 'Objectivity as (self-)censorship: Against the dogmatisation of professional ethics in journalism', *Javnost: The Public*, 11:2, 83–94.

Poupeau, F. (2000), 'Reasons for domination, Bourdieu versus Habermas', in B. Fowler (ed.), *Reading Bourdieu on Society and Culture*. Oxford: Blackwell, pp. 69–87.

Power, E. M. (2004), 'Toward understanding in postmodern interview analysis: Interpreting the contradictory remarks of a research participant', *Qualitative Health Research*, 14:6, 858–65.

Proust, M. [1919] (1970), 'Sentiments filiaux d'un parricide', *Pastiches et mélanges*. Paris: Gallimard.

Putnam, R. D. (2000), *Bowling Alone: The collapse and revival of American community*. New York: Simon & Schuster.

Rahkonen, K. (1999), *Not Class, but Struggle: Critical ouvertures to Pierre Bourdieu's sociology*. Unpublished PhD thesis, University of Helsinki.

Rauch, J. (2007), 'Activists as interpretative communities: Rituals of consumption and interaction in an alternative media audience', *Media, Culture and Society*, 29:6, 994–1013.

Reay, D. (2004), 'Cultural capitalists and academic habitus: Classed and gendered labour in UK higher education', *Women's Studies International Forum*, 27:1, 31–9.

Reay, D. (2005), 'Gendering Bourdieu's concept of capitals? Emotional capital, women and social class', in L. Adkins and B. Skeggs (eds), *Feminism After Bourdieu*. Cambridge: Polity Press, pp. 57–74.

Reckwitz, A. (2002), 'The status of the "material" in theories of culture: From "social structure" to "artefacts"', *Journal for the Theory of Social Behaviour*, 32:2, 195–217.

Rice, R. and C. Haythornthwaite (2006), 'Perspectives on Internet use: Access, involvement and interaction', in L. Lievrouw and S. Livingstone (eds), *Handbook of New Media: Updated student edition*. London: Sage, pp. 92–113.

Richardson, J. (2008), 'Language and journalism: An expanding research agenda', *Journalism Studies*, 9:2, 152–60.

Ricoeur, P. (1967), *Husserl: An analysis of his phenomenology*. Evanston, IL: Northwestern University Press.

Robbins, D. (ed.) (2000), *Pierre Bourdieu*. London: Sage.

Robbins, D. (2005), 'The origins, early development and status of Bourdieu's concept of "cultural capital"', *British Journal of Sociology*, 56:1, 13–30.

Robinson, S. (2006), 'The mission of the j-blog: Recapturing journalistic authority online', *Journalism*, 7:1, 65–83.

Rorty, R. (1986), 'Method, social-science and social hope: Dewey and Foucault', *Critique*, 42, 873–97.

Rose, G. (1984), *Dialectic of Nihilism: Post-structuralism and law*. Oxford: Basil Blackwell.

Rosen, C. (2007), 'Virtual friendship and the new narcissism', *The New Atlantis*, 17: Summer, 15–31.

Ross, A. (2008), 'The new geography of work: Power to the precarious?', *Theory, Culture and Society*, 25:7–8, 31–49.

Runciman, D. (2008), *Political Hypocrisy: The mask of power, from Hobbes to Orwell and beyond*. Princeton, NJ: Princeton University Press.

Said, E. W. (1994), *Representations of the Intellectual: The 1993 Reith Lectures*. London: Vintage.

Savage, M., A. Warde and F. Devine (2005), 'Capitals, assets, and resources: Some critical issues', *British Journal of Sociology*, 56:1, 31–47.

Sayer, A. (1999), 'Bourdieu, Smith and disinterested judgement', *Sociological Review*, 47:3, 403–31.

Schatzki, T. (1997), 'Practices and actions: A Wittgensteinian critique of Bourdieu and Giddens', *Philosophy of the Social Sciences*, 27:3, 283–308.

Schatzki, T. (2001), 'Introduction: Practice theory', in T. Schatzki, K. Knorr-Cetina and E. von Savigny (eds), *The Practice Turn in Contemporary Theory*. London: Routledge, pp. 1–14.

Scheff, T. (2008), 'Awareness structures: Defining alienation/solidarity', *Journal of Power*, 1:3, 237–50.

Scheuer, J. (2003), 'Habitus as the principle for social practice: A proposal for critical discourse analysis', *Language in Society*, 32:2, 143–75.

Schinkel, W. (2003), 'Pierre Bourdieu's political turn?', *Theory, Culture and Society*, 20:6, 69–93.

Schinkel, W. and J. Tacq (2004), 'The Saussurean influence in Pierre Bourdieu's relational sociology', *International Sociology*, 19:1, 51–70.

Schlesinger, P. (1978), *Putting 'Reality' Together: BBC News*. London: Constable.

Schmidt, J. (1985), *Maurice Merleau-Ponty: Between phenomenology and structuralism*. London: Macmillan.

Schrøder, K. and L. Phillips (2007), 'Complexifying media power: A study of the interplay between media and audience discourses on politics', *Media, Culture and Society*, 29:6, 890–915.

Schudson, M. (1995), *The Power of News*. Cambridge, MA: Harvard University Press.

Schudson, M. (2001), 'The objectivity norm in American journalism', *Journalism*, 2:2, 149–70.

Schudson, M. (2003), *The Sociology of News*. New York: W. W. Norton & Company.

Schudson, M. (2005), 'Autonomy from what?', in R. Benson and E. Neveu (eds), *Bourdieu and the Journalistic Field*. Cambridge: Polity Press, pp. 214–23.

Schudson, M. and C. Anderson (2009), 'Objectivity, professionalism and truth seeking in journalism', in K. Wahl-Jorgensen and T. Hanitzsch (eds), *The Handbook of Journalism Studies*. Oxford: Routledge, pp. 88–101.

Schultz, I. (2007) 'The journalistic gut feeling', *Journalism Practice*, 1:2, 190–207.

Schutz, A. (1972), *The Phenomenology of the Social World*. London: Heinemann Educational.

Schutz, A. (1973), 'Problems of interpretive sociology', in A. Ryan (ed.), *The Philosophy of Social Explanation*. Oxford: Oxford University Press.

Seib, P. (2002), *The Global Journalist: News and consciousness in a world of conflict*. Oxford: Rowman & Littlefield.

Sennett, R. (1977), *The Fall of Public Man*. Cambridge: Cambridge University Press.

Shilling, C. (2004), 'Physical capital and situated action: A new direction for corporeal sociology', *British Journal of Sociology of Education*, 25:4, 473–87.

Shoemaker, P., T. P. Vos and S. D. Reese (2009), 'Journalists as gatekeepers', in K. Wahl-Jorgensen and T. Hanitzsch (eds), *The Handbook of Journalism Studies*. Oxford: Routledge, pp. 73–87.

Shusterman, R. (1999), 'Bourdieu and Anglo-American philosophy', in R. Shusterman (ed.), *Bourdieu: A critical reader*. Oxford: Blackwell, pp. 14–28.

Silverstone, R. (1994), *Television and Everyday Life*. London: Routledge.

Silverstone, R. (2007), *Media and Morality: On the rise of the Mediapolis*. Cambridge: Polity Press.

Simons, J. (1995), *Foucault and the Political*. London: Routledge.

Singer, J. (2005), 'The political j-blogger', *Journalism*, 6:2, 173–98.

Singer, J. and I. Ashman (2009), '"Comment is free, but facts are sacred": User-generated content and ethical constructs at the *Guardian*', *Journal of Mass Media Ethics*, 24:1, 3–21.

Slattery, J. (2004), '"We've become poor relations"', *Press Gazette*, 4 November, p. 1.

Smith, B. (1995), 'Common sense', in B. Smith and D. W. Smith (eds), *The Cambridge Companion to Husserl*. Cambridge: Cambridge University Press, pp. 394–432.

Smith, B. (1988), *Contingencies of Value: Alternative perspectives for critical theory*. Cambridge, MA: Harvard University Press.

Smith, B. and D. W. Smith (eds) (1995), *The Cambridge Companion to Husserl*. Cambridge: Cambridge University Press.

Smith, D. W. (2007), *Husserl*. London: Routledge.

Soloski, J. (1990), 'News reporting and professionalism: Some constraints on the reporting of the news', *Media, Culture and Society*, 11:4, 207–28.

Sonwalkar, P. (2004), 'Out of sight, out of mind? The non-reporting of small wars and insurgencies', in S. Allan and B. Zeliger (eds), *Reporting War: Journalism in wartime*. Oxford: Routledge, pp. 206–23.

Sparks, C. (2000), 'Introduction', in C. Sparks and J. Tulloch (eds), *Tabloid Tales: Global debates over media standards*. Oxford: Rowman & Littlefield, pp. 1–39.

Sparrow, A. (1999), *Uncertain Guardians: The news media as a political institution*. Baltimore, MD: Johns Hopkins University Press.

Spivak, G. C. (1985), 'Can the subaltern speak? Speculations on widow-sacrifice', *Wedge*, 7:8, 120–31.

Stahl, R. (2009), *Militainment, Inc: War, media and popular culture*. London: Routledge.

Ståhlberg, P. (2006), 'On the journalist beat in India: Encounters with the near familiar', *Ethnography*, 7:1, 47–67.

Steuter, E. and D. Wills (2010), '"The vermin have struck again": Dehumanizing the enemy in post 9/11 media representations', *Media, War and Conflict*, 3:2, 152–67.

Streeck, J. and J. Scott Jordan (2009), 'Projection and anticipation: The forward-looking nature of embodied communication', *Discourse Processes*, 46:2, 93–102.

Sutton Trust (2006), *The Educational Backgrounds of Leading Journalists*. London: Sutton Trust.

Swain, N. (2003), 'Social capital and its uses', *Archives européennes de sociologie*, 44:2, 185–212.

Swartz, D. (2003), 'From critical sociology to public intellectual: Pierre Bourdieu and politics', *Theory and Society*, 32:5–6, 791–823.

Sweetman, P. (2003), 'Twenty-first century dis-ease? Habitual reflexivity or the reflexive habitus', *Sociological Review*, 51:4, 528–49.

Swingewood, A. (1999), 'Sociological theory', in S. Taylor (ed.), *Sociology: Issues and debates*. London: Macmillan, pp. 50–72.

Taylor, C. (1994), *Multiculturalism: Examining the politics of recognition*. Princeton, NJ: Princeton University Press.

Taylor, C. (1999), 'To follow a rule', in R. Shusterman (ed.), *Bourdieu: A critical reader*. Oxford: Blackwell, pp. 29–44.

Taylor, J. (1998), *Body Horror: Photojournalism, catastrophe and war*. Manchester: Manchester University Press.

Thierry, Y. (1995), *Conscience et humanite selon Husserl: Essai sur le sujet politique*. Paris: Presses Universitaires de France.

Thomson, A., P. White and P. Kitley (2008), '"Objectivity" and "hard news" reporting across cultures', *Journalism Studies*, 9:2, 212–28.

Thorsen, E. (2008), 'Journalistic objectivity redefined? Wikinews and the neutral point of view', *New Media and Society*, 10:6, 935–54.

Throop, C. J. and K. M. Murphy (2002), 'Bourdieu and phenomenology: A critical assessment', *Anthropological Theory*, 2:2, 185–208.

Thurman, N. (2008), 'Forums for citizen journalists? Adoption of user-generated content initiatives by online news media', *New Media and Society*, 10:1, 139–57.

Thussu, D. (2003), 'Live TV and bloodless deaths: War, infotainment and 24/7 news', in D. Thussu and D. Freedman (eds), *War and the Media: Reporting conflict 24/7*. London: Sage, pp. 117–32.

Tilley, C. Y. (1990), *Reading Material Culture: Structuralism, hermeneutics and post-structuralism*. Oxford: Basil Blackwell.

Tsfati, Y., O. Meyers and Y. Peri (2006), 'What is good journalism? Comparing Israeli public and journalists' perspectives', *Journalism*, 7:2, 152–73.

Tulloch, J. (2007), 'Tabloid citizenship: The *Daily Mirror* and the invasions of Egypt (1956) and Iraq (2003)', *Journalism Studies*, 8:1, 42–60.

Tumber, H. (2004), 'Prisoners of news values? Journalists, professionalism and identification in times of war', in S. Allan and B. Zelizer (eds), *Reporting War: Journalism in wartime*. Oxford: Routledge, pp. 190–205.

Tumber, H. (2006), 'The fear of living dangerously: Journalists who report on conflict', *International Relations*, 20:4, 439–51.

Tumber, H. and J. Palmer (2004), *Media at War: The Iraq crisis*. London: Sage.

Tumber, H. and M. Prentoulis (2003), 'Journalists under fire: Subcultures, objectivity and emotional literacy', in D. Thussu and D. Freedman (eds), *War and the Media: Reporting conflict 24/7*. London: Sage, pp. 215–30.

Tumber, H. and F. Webster (2006), *Journalists Under Fire: Information war and journalistic practices*. London: Sage.

Tunstall, J. (1971), *Journalists at Work*. London: Constable.

Tunstall, J. (1996), *Newspaper Power: The new national press in Britain*. Oxford: Clarendon Press.

Van Dijck, J. (2009), 'Users like you? Theorizing agency in user-generated content', *Media, Culture and Society*, 31:1, 41–58.

Van Dijk, T. (1988), *News as Discourse*. Hillsdale, NJ: Lawrence Erlbaum.

Van Dijk, T. (1997), *Discourse as Social Interaction, vol. 1*. London: Sage.

Van Dijk, T. (2009), 'News, discourse and ideology', in K. Wahl-Jorgensen and T. Hanitzsch (eds), *The Handbook of Journalism Studies*. Oxford: Routledge, pp. 191–204.

Van Zoonen, L. (1998), 'The changing gender of journalism', in C. Carter, G. Branston and S. Allan (eds), *News, Gender and Power*. London: Routledge, pp. 33–46.

Vandenberghe, F. (1999), 'The real is relational: An epistemological analysis of Pierre Bourdieu's generative structuralism', *Sociological Theory*, 17:1, 32–67.

Verdès-Leroux, J. (2003), *Deconstructing Pierre Bourdieu: Against sociological terrorism from the Left*. New York: Algora.

Vincent, J. (2004), 'The sociologist and the republic: Pierre Bourdieu and the virtues of social history', *History Workshop Journal*, 58, 129–48.

Voirol, O. (2004), 'Recognizing and ignoring: On the theory of symbolic violence', *Social Science Information* [*Sur les sciences sociales*], 43:3, 403–33.

Wacquant, L. (1996), 'Foreword'. in P. Bourdieu, *The State Nobility: Elite schools in the field of power*. Cambridge: Polity Press, pp. ix–xxii.

Wacquant, L. (2000), 'Durkheim and Bourdieu: The common plinth and its cracks', in B. Fowler (ed.), *Reading Bourdieu on Society and Culture*. Oxford: Blackwell, pp. 105–19.

Wacquant, L. (2004), 'Following Pierre Bourdieu into the field', *Ethnography*, 5:4, 387–414.

Wahl-Jorgensen, K. (2008), 'On the public sphere, deliberation, journalism and dignity: An interview with Seyla Benhabib', *Journalism Studies*, 9:6, 962–70.

Wall, M. (2005), '"Blogs of war": Weblogs as news', *Journalism*, 6:2, 153–72.

Warde, A. (2004), 'Practice and field: Revising Bourdieusian concepts', *CRIC Discussion Papers*, Manchester: CRIC, University of Manchester.

Wasserman, H. and S. Rao (2008), 'The glocalization of journalism ethics', *Journalism*, 9:3, 163–87.

Weaver, D. (1998), *The Global Journalist: News people around the world*. Creskill, NJ: Hampton Press.

Webb, J., T. Schirato and G. Danaher (2002), *Understanding Bourdieu*. London: Sage.

Weber, M. [1922] (1968), *Economy and Society: An outline of interpretive sociology*. New York: Bedminster Press.

Weedon, C. (1987), *Feminist Practice and Post-structuralist Theory*. Oxford: Basil Blackwell.

Weininger, E. and A. Lareau (2003), 'Translating Bourdieu into the American context: The question of social class and family–school relations', *Poetics*, 31: 5–6, 375–402.

Wessler, H. and T. Schultz (2007), 'Can the mass media deliberate? Insights from print media and political talk shows', in R. Butsch (ed.), *Media and Public Spheres*. Basingstoke: Palgrave Macmillan, pp. 15–27.

Wilcken, P. (1995), 'The intellectuals, the media and the Gulf War', *Critique of Anthropology*, 15:1, 37–69.

Wilhelm, A. (2000), *Democracy in the Digital Age*. New York: Routledge.

Williams, S. J. (1986), 'Appraising Goffman', *British Journal of Sociology*, 37:3, 348–69.

Winch, P. (1990), *The Idea of a Social Science and Its Relation to Philosophy*, 2nd ed. London: Routledge.

Wodak, R. (2001), 'The discourse-historical approach', in R. Wodak and M. Meyer (eds), *Methods of Critical Discourse Analysis*. London: Sage, pp. 63–94.

Wright, D. (2005), 'Mediating production and consumption: Cultural capital and "cultural workers"', *British Journal of Sociology*, 56:1, 105–21.

Young, P. and P. Jesser (1997), *The Media and the Military*. Basingstoke: Macmillan.

Ytreberg, E. (2002), 'Erving Goffman as a theorist of the mass media', *Critical Studies in Media Communication*, 19:4, 481–97.

Zamiti, K. (1996), 'Adieu aux armes: Sociologie des sociologues', *Peuples Mediterranéen*, 58–9, accessed from www.peuplesmonde.com/spip .php?article772 (3 January 2005).

Zandberg, E. (2010), 'The right to tell the (right) story: Journalism, authority and memory', *Media Culture and Society*, 32:1, 5–24.

Zelizer, B. (1993), 'Journalists as interpretative communities', *Critical Studies in Mass Communication*, 10:2, 219–37.

Zelizer, B. (2004), 'When war is reduced to a photograph', in S. Allan and B. Zeliger (eds), *Reporting War: Journalism in wartime*. Oxford: Routledge, pp. 115–35.

Zhao, S. and D. Elesh (2008), 'Copresence as "being with": Social contact in online public domains', *Information, Communication and Society*, 11:4, 565–83.

Index

Note: 'n.' after a page number indicates the number of a note on that page

academic field 14, 24, 28–9, 40,
    49n.1, 58, 154, 158–61, 177,
    179n.1, 180n.8
Adorno, Theodor W. 7, 21n.18, 94,
    159
Afghanistan 61, 69, 141–2
agency
  evidence of 68, 90
  viability of 35, 37, 59, 72n.6, 137,
    154, 179n.2
alcohol 90
Allan, Stuart 47, 126, 143, 148
ambivalence 60, 64, 66–7, 80–2, 87,
    112, 135–6, 138, 141
appropriateness 48, 62–4, 67, 110,
    156
Austin, J. L. 6, 41, 53n.39, 62

Bachelard, Gaston 8, 24, 55, 153
Bangladesh 136
bearing witness see witnessing
Benson, Rodney 174
boredom 139
Bosnia 93n.8, 103, 117
broadsheet newspapers 31–2
Butler, Judith 35, 51n.29, 63, 92,
    179n.1

Cameron, Deborah 165
Cassirer, Ernst 7, 72n.2
Chouliaraki, Lilie 111–12, 115

citizenship
  citizen journalism 143, 145,
    147–51
  global 108, 117, 131–3
  and public engagement 127–8,
    133n.7
common sense
  journalistic practice 137
  morality 110
  phenomenology 3, 6, 36–7, 47, 56,
    105
competence 73n.13, 102, 133–9
Conboy, Martin 109
consumption of media 2, 5, 100–2,
    166–8, 121, 123, 125–32
  by citizen journalists 148–9
  by journalists 145–6
Couldry, Nick 12, 63, 166–7
cultural capital 15–16, 21n.23, 26–8,
    43, 50n.11, 65, 79
  negative 33
cynicism 13, 20n.14, 47, 145, 171
  in audiences 121
  in journalists 87–8, 100, 104,
    135–8, 149

Davies, Nick 142
democratisation 2, 17, 47, 161,
    180n.11, 180n.15
Derrida, Jacques 49n.5, 72n.1,
    73n.14, 180n.19

determinism in Bourdieusian theory 14, 20n.10m 35, 39, 42, 72n.7, 128, 134, 154–5, 166
Deuze, Mark 61, 76, 167
disconnection 121, 131–2
disorientation *see* orientation
Distinction 11, 29, 33, 52n.34, 64, 123
dominatedness 14, 26, 75, 98, 101, 126–7, 132
Durkheim, Emile 9, 11, 20n.12, 56, 59

elitism 15–16, 22n.33, 161, 178
  anti-elitism 33, 65, 88–9, 92, 120, 123–5, 166, 169–70
embedding 84–6, 91, 137–40
L'Emprise du journalisme 14–17, 28
esotericisation
  cultural 15–16
  in war reporting 80–2, 99, 168, 180n.16
euphemism 67, 164–5

Falklands War 77, 135
felicity 48, 53n.39, 62–4
Foucault, Michel 3, 7, 35, 39–40, 51n.30, 52n.32, 71, 92, 101, 105, 109, 126–7, 138, 143–4, 163, 171
Fraser, Nancy 115–16, 128–31, 144

Garnham, Nicholas 14, 22n.28, 60, 173
generative structuralism *see* structuralism
Giddens, Anthony 22n.27, 62, 72n.8, 154, 169
Goffman, Erving 4, 6, 19n.2, 37–9, 50n.13, 62, 121, 129
Guardian, the 104, 115–33, 149
Gulf War 135–8, 151n.2, 140

habitus 6, 8–11, 20n.11, 21n.21, 29,

39, 43–9, 51n.25, 51n.28, 52n.33, 52n.35, 52n.36, 73n.13, 174–6
  journalistic 89, 96, 98, 151
  professional 55, 70, 80, 88–9, 96, 98
Hammond, Philip 117–20, 149
Hegel, G. W. F. 7, 19, 34, 118, 127–8, 131, 144, 158
Heidegger, Martin 41–2, 143
Homo Academicus 29, 33, 160
Honneth, Axel 115, 128, 131
humour 64, 67, 84, 89
Husserl, Edmund 4, 6, 19n.5, 34–6, 50n.21, 51n.29
hypocrisy 103–4, 113, 121–2

identity, professional 40, 44–6, 60, 83, 95, 137–8, 141, 145, 155–6, 167–8
Ignatieff, Michael 109, 117
illusio 32, 57, 72n.4, 92, 112
L'Indépendant 50n.18
individualism
  audience 121, 124–5
  cultural 116, 118, 132, 134, 160–1, 170, 178–9
  in war reporting 2, 5–7, 69, 71, 77, 87, 89, 92, 97, 110–11, 147, 156, 171
individuation 41–6, 58–9, 74, 83, 89, 121–4, 140–1, 168, 178
instinct 3, 6, 17, 30–1, 39, 44, 47–8, 63, 69–70, 75, 81, 87–8, 97, 146–50, 163, 171
  moral 105, 110–13
instrumentalism 61, 102, 136, 146
integrity 43, 66, 70, 76–9, 112–13, 120, 136, 139–40, 166
Iraq 122, 125, 136, 148–50
irony 64, 67, 84, 87, 113, 125, 135, 153, 156
irreverence 67, 70, 82, 87–9

Kosovo 69, 136

Laclau, Ernesto 95, 177
legitimacy 10, 16, 22n.29, 33,
    50n.15, 63–5, 81–2, 106,
    114n.6, 153–4, 160–1, 170
Libération 12, 21n.24
liberalism 149, 158, 160, 174–9
Logic of Practice, The 37, 40

Mannheim, Karl 49n.7, 58, 72n.5
Marx, Karl 19n.7, 34, 50n.22, 56
    Marxism 7–9, 21n.18, 34
    neo-Marxism 13–14, 34, 37,
        50n.19, 159
Matheson, Donald 60, 69, 95, 141,
    163–5
Mauss, Marcel 38, 51n.28, 134
McNair, Brian 150
McNay, Lois 51n.29, 130
Merleau-Ponty, Maurice 4, 37–9
moralising 18, 99, 103–8, 117, 120,
    125
Murdoch, Rupert 28–9, 148
mystification 15, 81, 83, 85, 112,
    142, 144–5, 153, 161–70

naivety 84, 84, 139
narcissism
    cultural 117–18, 127, 133n.3,
        178–9
    journalistic 77
neoliberalism 10, 12, 180n.13
new institutionalism 174–5
New York Times, the 79

objectivism 19n.7, 34–5, 40, 44–5,
    50n.19
objectivity, journalistic 22n.30, 31,
    61, 76, 96–7, 155–7
On Television 11–14, 179n.4
opinion polling 23n.36, 106
orientation 67, 88, 92, 100–3,

109–11, 132, 136, 146, 149,
    174–9
    disorientation 132
Outline of a Theory of Practice 37, 40,
    46, 171

Palestine/Israel 122
pooling 68, 76, 86, 135, 137–8
professionalism 48, 61, 69, 95, 105,
    113, 128, 136, 138, 140, 144,
    168–71
Public Connection project 116–18
public relations 140, 143, 153
Putnam, Robert 26, 50n.10, 116

reflexivity 87, 95, 120, 133n.3, 154,
    159, 162–4, 177, 180n.14
relationalism 7, 49n.5, 57
relativism 1, 42, 58–9, 72n.1, 109,
    160
romanticisation
    of journalism 100
    of war reporters 2, 89, 108, 110,
        141, 156
Rushdie, Salman 117

Saussure, Ferdinand de 7, 57, 59,
    62
Schutz, Alfred 35–7
scientific field 17, 161
self-interest 2, 86, 117
selflessness 77–8, 100
Silverstone, Roger 1, 19n.7, 108–9,
    115
Simpson, John 41–4
star reporters 13, 43, 106, 110–11,
    152, 179
structuralism 9, 24, 34, 40, 51n.30,
    62, 163, 177
    generative structuralism 58, 152,
        167
structuration 22n.27, 62, 127, 134,
    141, 151

subjectivism 19, 34–5
symbolic violence 11, 13, 21n.19,
    21n.25, 22n.26, 29, 50n.15,
    129

tabloid newspapers 26, 32–3, 99,
    109, 112, 157
technology 5, 135, 140–7
television journalism 68–9, 79, 85,
    116
terrier, characterisation of journalists
    as 89, 97
Times, The 25, 149
tourism as metaphor 68, 84, 156
Tumber, Howard 101, 137

underdog, characterisation of
    journalists as 60, 89, 140

Vietnam 73n.16, 172

Weber, Max 7–10, 58–9, 81, 88,
    93n.5, 105, 178
witnessing 4, 5, 71, 100–1, 116, 131,
    141–2, 156–7
worldliness 69, 79, 87, 120, 122,
    144, 153

Zelizer, Barbie 115